PUBLIC GARDENS AND
LIVABLE CITIES

PUBLIC GARDENS AND LIVABLE CITIES

Partnerships Connecting People, Plants, and Place

Donald A. Rakow
Meghan Z. Gough
Sharon A. Lee

CORNELL UNIVERSITY PRESS   ITHACA AND LONDON

First published 2020 by Cornell University Press

Library of Congress Cataloging-in-Publication Data

Names: Rakow, Donald Andrew, 1951– author. | Gough, Meghan Z., 1975– author. | Lee, Sharon A., 1944– author.
Title: Public gardens and livable cities : partnerships connecting people, plants, and place / Donald A. Rakow, Meghan Z. Gough, Sharon A. Lee.
Description: Ithaca [New York] : Cornell University Press, 2020. | Includes bibliographical references and index.
Identifiers: LCCN 2020019038 (print) | LCCN 2020019039 (ebook) | ISBN 9781501702594 (paperback) | ISBN 9781501751769 (pdf) | ISBN 9781501751776 (epub)
Subjects: LCSH: Urban gardens—Social aspects—United States. | Urban gardening—Social aspects—United States. | Community development, Urban—United States. | Public spaces—Social aspects—United States.
Classification: LCC SB454.3.S63 R35 2020 (print) | LCC SB454.3.S63 (ebook) | DDC 635.09173/2—dc23
LC record available at https://lccn.loc.gov/2020019038
LC ebook record available at https://lccn.loc.gov/2020019039

We dedicate this book to all those public gardens, community institutions, and individuals striving to make their cities greener, more livable, and healthier environments for the future.

Contents

Foreword

Public gardens matter. In cities and towns across the United States, garden-based organizations of all types are becoming catalysts for community revitalization. A new mandate has emerged: to foster and strengthen connections among the communities that surround them. In tandem with libraries and museums, public gardens are transforming themselves into "third place" community centers, providing common ground for diverse groups of people. At the same time, these organizations are reaching beyond their fences and gates to help build greener, more sustainable neighborhoods, involving themselves in a broad range of community partnerships and renewal projects. These community outreach activities and those taking place at the gardens themselves reveal an entirely new dimension of the mission of public gardens, one that may ultimately prove to be their most relevant and lasting civic contribution of all.

This essential book captures the spirit of these new collaborations, drawing from examples in cities across the United States that involve some of our most admired public gardens.

Traditional Roles

The mission and focus embodied today by American public gardens are an outgrowth of a long and somewhat complex history. While important and influential traditions can also be found in early civilizations in Asia, Africa, Mesoamerica, and elsewhere, gardens in the US have been mostly shaped by European antecedents. Public gardens in Europe evolved in part from the medicinal or physic gardens of the early Renaissance. These early gardens in turn gave rise to the first botanic gardens, which served as cradles of scientific discovery (and sometimes as instruments of economic imperialism, as in the "company gardens" of the colonies). Over time, and in parallel with the creation of the first public parks in the nineteenth century in both Europe and North America, the mission of public gardens—and the size of their audiences—has expanded incrementally, leading directly to the multifaceted institutions we find today.

Contemporary Roles

Most contemporary public gardens in the United States embrace a diverse set of roles that are continuing to evolve in response to changing needs. Urban gardens seem to perform a particularly crucial function, serving as places of natural sanctuary and inspiration for harried urbanites as well as a refuge for plants and wildlife in the face of increasingly fragmented and scarce habitat. Contemporary public gardens also represent places of culture and art, featuring architecture, landscape architecture, planting design, and sculpture, even serving as venues for the performing arts and for changing exhibitions. Some public gardens continue to be centers of excellence in scientific research and have expanded from a traditional focus on plant taxonomy to other areas of research, such as ecology and conservation and even environmental psychology.

Public gardens have a key role in helping to create new generations of environmental stewards and educators, while also fostering environmental literacy throughout their communities. Watching a flower become a seed, and a seed become a plant, is a new miracle for every child who has the opportunity to experience it. Ask anyone working in the public garden field today how they first became interested in plants and nature, and it is likely that every one of them will reference a childhood experience in a natural or naturalistic setting like a garden. The educational experiences and programs offered by contemporary public gardens are not merely important; they can be considered essential, as the survival of our planet may ultimately depend on people learning to care both about and for the natural environment.

Another key aspect of public gardens today is the recent trend in modeling and interpreting environmental sustainability. Many institutions have expanded their remit to become leaders in environmental conservation, highlighting sustainability in their operations and in the construction of new gardens and facilities, with some even helping to reclaim brownfield sites. Plant conservation has become an essential role too. A nationwide network of public gardens—the Center for Plant Conservation—collectively works to help save the most endangered species from extinction, bringing needed research and visibility to the plight of threatened native plants.

Adding to an already broad scope of responsibilities, over the last two decades an entirely new direction for public gardens—community revitalization—has found significant momentum across North America. It is this movement that forms the focus of this book. Public gardens have seized the opportunity to contribute substantively to strengthening the social and ecological fabric of their surrounding communities, in part through taking their programs out into neighborhoods and schools. At the same time, these institutions are reimagining the place of their garden spaces in their communities, becoming even stronger magnets for community interaction by underscoring a fundamental commitment to diversity and inclusion.

This new focus on community revitalization has especially resonated in US cities, where the need for greening projects and citizen engagement on environmental issues is particularly strong. With half of the world's population now living in cities, these pioneering efforts by public gardens are developing program and partnership models that can be replicated in other cities in the United States and, in some cases, anywhere in the world.

The potential for public gardens to serve as agents of community revitalization has been recognized and supported by a broad range of both public and private funders. Through their generous financial support, these community leaders and public agencies have encouraged public gardens to provide their surrounding communities with wide-ranging benefits, including neighborhood safety and beautification projects, STEM education and teacher-training programs in the public schools, initiatives in food security and nutritional awareness, economic empowerment, and environmental protection and sustainability. The social, educational, environmental, and economic reach of North American public gardens has grown substantially over the past several decades and can be expected to continue to increase, especially in strategic partnership with other nonprofit organizations and government agencies.

As with all partnerships, joint programming has sometimes presented public gardens with challenges they had not fully anticipated or were not otherwise prepared to overcome. Similarly, governmental agencies and other types of nonprofit organizations are entering new, uncharted territory by developing collaborations with public garden partners. There is a tangible need for all stakeholders to learn from models of effective partnerships in support of community wellbeing. There is also a need for the operation and outcomes of these partnerships to be formally evaluated, in order to identify and share best practices and thereby inspire even more public gardens to enter into community collaborations.

In an effort to address some of these needs, this book brings together case studies from leading public gardens in urban and suburban areas across the United States, as well as the results of national surveys and interviews with public garden professionals and community leaders. The book aspires to make a significant contribution to the emerging literature on nonprofit collaborations. Staff at public gardens as well as at governmental and nonprofit organizations will find excellent guidance and inspiration to develop productive collaborations for the further advancement of the communities they serve.

Frontiers

Additional frontiers await public gardens as their community commitments develop and mature. Many gardens are working hard to put themselves on the greenest footing possible, so that they can model sustainability in all its forms for their entire community. This is leading to partnerships in street tree steward-ship and urban composting and recycling, to innovations in the management of stormwater, and to projects that showcase efforts to reduce energy consumption and demonstrate new sources of energy, among many other examples.

A particularly exciting leadership opportunity exists in helping to maintain and even re-create places for native plants in cities. Research shows that native birds and insects prefer native plants, and if these native animals are going to persist over time, it will be in part through efforts to maintain and even create habitat for them in proximity to where people live.

Most importantly, public gardens can bear witness to the effects of climate change and share strategies that will help foster resilient communities.

Public gardens matter. Together, we might all make it through the challenges of the present.

Scot Medbury
Executive Director, Quarryhill Botanical Garden
Former President and CEO, Brooklyn Botanic Garden

PUBLIC GARDENS AND LIVABLE CITIES

LIVABLE CITIES AND PUBLIC GARDENS

Over half of the world's population lives in urban areas, a proportion that is expected to increase to two-thirds by 2050. Currently, North America is the most urbanized region in the world, with 82 percent of its population living in urban areas.[1] Our future world will be a largely urban one, as people gradually relocate from rural to urban areas and total population growth increases. This urbanization trend has provoked renewed interest in understanding the relationship between the built environment, the natural environment, and the livability of urban areas.

Cities have long been seen as hubs of knowledge, culture, and innovation, and a number of theories and approaches have been proposed to sustain and build on those traditional perceptions. One theory is that cities spur innovation because of their organizational climate; in other words, cities are dense urban environments with diverse collections of industries that share knowledge and people to create new ideas and solutions.[2]

As urban areas in the United States continue to grow, our demographic makeup is changing and so are the demands on our cities. We are more racially and ethnically diverse than even a decade ago, and older adults represent a growing proportion of the population. Some residents and business owners reveal their livability preferences by voting with their feet, relocating to places that better meet their needs; but for many, relocating is not a viable option.[3] Society is hopeful that cities will adapt and meet changing and diverse preferences, but the question remains: who will lead the effort to make cities more livable, and how?

Livability is a popular concept in public discussions about cities and refers to the extent to which a particular living environment can satisfy its residents' economic, social, and cultural needs, promote their health and well-being, and protect ecological functions. While the characteristics of what residents identify as essential to a livable community will vary from community to community, often they include a sense of safety, good public schools, well-paying jobs, and access to food, parks, and green spaces. For some residents, those characteristics may also include the architecture and street aesthetics, cultural amenities, and walkability.

Livability is distinguished from sustainability mainly by the scale and context of a particular time and place.[4] Sustainability adopts a long view of actions and policies and the ways in which development, according to a report by the World Commission on Environment and Development, "meets the needs of the present without compromising the ability of future generations to meet their own needs."[5] Livability, on the other hand, focuses on current conditions and interventions, incorporating the environmental, economic, and equity priorities on a narrower spatial scale relevant to individual people, neighborhoods, and communities in geographically smaller areas. Efforts to enhance livability are primarily community based and driven by issues of local concern that reflect changing conditions.

A long-standing strategy to enhance the livability of urban areas is to forge connections between people to activate change. These efforts typically adopt a strengths-based approach that, as a starting point, focuses on what is working well, and then builds on the resources, skills, and experience available in a community. Many public gardens excel in identifying community needs and collaborating with partners to address those needs. Such partnerships are the focus of much of this book.

Collaborations are increasing in all community sectors as a strategy to spur innovation to meet challenges in such areas as economic development, education, community capacity building, and environmental sustainability. Through cross-sector partnerships, organizations benefit from shared areas of knowledge, resources, and abilities that no single sector possesses. A municipal government, in response to growing constituent demands coupled with fiscal strains, might forge partnerships with businesses and nonprofit and community organizations to provide more effective remedies to a public problem so that collectively they fulfill functions typically undertaken by a single sector.[6] The prevalence of such partnerships suggests that organizations are increasingly interdependent as they seek out the necessary and complementary resources to support community sustainability initiatives not achievable by a single organization acting alone.[7]

By working across sectors, institutions, and neighborhoods, urban innovators are constructing ways to enhance the ecological, economic, and social life of cities to improve their livability. A couple of decades into the twenty-first century, each sector benefits from increased livability through civic reforms and place-based policies that target underperforming areas, such as "deteriorating downtown business districts and disadvantaged regions."[8] In this cyber age, in which competitive advantage is less dependent on infrastructure to attract and retain businesses and residents, cities are increasingly investing in their livability. *U.S. News and World Report* annually produces an analysis of the most populous metropolitan areas to identify the best places to live.[9] Several factors are considered in its rankings, including job market and affordability, as well as such quality-of-life factors as crime rates, education quality, and satisfaction with the social, physical, and community aspects of daily life.

Community-based interventions known as "placemaking" have been used for decades in the United States to enhance livability by rethinking urban public spaces, a practice informed by listening to and observing the local users of those spaces.[10] Place-based approaches depend on involving residents and capitalizing on the existing assets in communities, such as public transit stops, parks, historic landmarks, and underutilized structures, and their potential to connect people and the public spaces they share. Today, placemaking is increasingly popular with designers, planners, and private organizations such as the Project for Public Spaces that, as a means to reinvent public spaces, advocate supporting grassroots efforts to leverage the physical, cultural, and social identities that define a place.[11] The long-term involvement in and management of these public spaces by residents, or "place-keeping," is a critical component to ensuring the longevity of the environmental, social, or economic assets of the place.[12]

Placemaking, place-keeping, and similar place-based interventions seek to achieve a dual outcome: one that invests in the physical improvements of public spaces and simultaneously invests in the capacity of local residents to initiate ideas, make decisions, and commit to the implementation of improvements to the public spaces in their neighborhoods. In practice, however, the notion can conjure up negative reactions from individuals exposed to placemaking led by those with top-down conceptions of what a place ought to look like, instead of by the unique assets of the local place and its residents.

At the core of livability efforts is a tension between improving the quality of life for current residents and the threat that these interventions may actually expedite the process of gentrification,[13] as well as the displacement of lower-income residents who can no longer afford to live in the neighborhood.[14] For decades researchers have investigated the role of neighborhood revitalization in the displacement of residents and the proliferation of racially patterned neighborhood change, with mixed results.[15] There is general agreement, however, that gentrification has been either an intentional tool or an unintended consequence of revitalization that has targeted neighborhoods with concentrated poverty and people of color.[16] Given this context, community-based interventions aimed at increasing livability in communities must be rooted in social equity and involve the voices, talents, and spirit of those local communities.

Public Gardens as Anchor Institutions

It is clear that partnerships are essential as cities look to leverage their assets to stimulate livable communities. The ingredients for making such places do not exist in one organization, agency, or place within a city, because none has the diversity of resources or capabilities to navigate the complexity of services, innovations, or challenges alone. What cities do have at their disposal is a strong network of civic, cultural, and knowledge assets known as anchor institutions. Examples include universities, libraries, parks, hospitals, and cultural institutions. These nonprofits are rooted to their physical locations and, by definition, have an economic self-interest in helping to ensure that the communities in which they are located are healthy, safe, and generally livable.

Unfortunately, it is the cultural institutions, including museums, performing arts centers, zoos, and public gardens, that are often overlooked as potential partners in initiatives to address community concerns. Public gardens in particular are only briefly recognized as partner anchor institutions in community development literature.[17] Present throughout the United States, these botanical gardens, arboreta, conservatories, display gardens, and historic landscapes are mission-based living museums with professional staff and researchers who maintain collections of plants for display, conservation, and education. Although some see public gardens only as emerald oases that are lovely to visit, their much larger mission is to connect people to plants, which they have long accomplished through outreach initiatives that include education programs, the establishment of school and community gardens, and research into plants best suited to urban environments.

Today, if one looks closely at how cities are implementing livability initiatives such as increased fresh food access, supporting job training in urban horticulture, or using plants to cool areas with high concentrations of impervious surfaces, one will almost always find a public garden at the table. The scientific knowledge and horticultural skills of public gardens can be instrumental for communities trying to restore waterfronts and streams or needing help controlling stormwater or promoting urban ecological restoration.

In his examination of people and nature, E. O. Wilson found that as children's understanding and ability to value natural systems are nurtured, their natural affinity for life, what he terms *biophilia*, is likewise enhanced.[18] Because our experiences with nature vary based on access, education, and opportunity, nature can be meaningful to individuals in different ways, but it can also serve as a common connection across difference.

Like other anchor institutions, public gardens are frequently trusted resources with strong ties to the local community. Given their scientific knowledge, technical expertise, and long-standing presence in many cities, public gardens can use plants as the connectors between disparate groups in a community. Their positive reputations in their communities have contributed to their success in mobilizing local involvement and resident leadership in community-based initiatives.[19] At the heart of community-based initiatives are people who are examples of what David Brooks refers to as the nation's "weavers" of social infrastructure.[20] Weavers are those who talk to neighbors and reach out to strangers to address common issues. Because they are well-known or neutral presences in a community, public gardens can serve as hubs where such weavers can come together to learn, debate, and plan ways to contribute to community livability.

Increasingly, public gardens recognize that they must offer more than a welcome mat at their entrances. To have a real impact on improving the livability of the communities around them, gardens must form partnerships with various local parties, including individuals, representatives from municipalities and nonprofit organizations, and entities such as schools, community centers, and religious institutions.

A thorough grasp of the unique roles public gardens play in communities today is predicated on understanding the complex web of social, political, and economic factors that have driven their evolution and their impact on urban history in the United States. The strong and sometimes conflicting American ideals of land ownership and stewardship, economic prosperity and success, relief for the poor, and the promise of upward social mobility contribute to the cultural fabric in which public gardens have traditionally operated.

The public garden movement in the United States began with the early recognition of botanical gardens as keys to economic development. In the agrarian world of eighteenth-century America, botanical gardens were seen as vital to the economic stability of the emerging democracy. For the country's founders, such institutions were scientific resources where new varieties of plants could be studied and used to improve domestic agriculture, on which the economic health of the nation depended, while the physical health of its citizens was based on identifying and supplying plants with medicinal value. With few laws or treaties governing international trade, botanical gardens were deeply involved in the unencumbered extraction of plant species from foreign lands.

The involvement of botanical gardens in the livability of cities came largely in response to the challenges associated with nineteenth-century urbanization.

Although there was tremendous overall population growth in the US between 1800 and 1900,[21] urban growth proceeded much more rapidly than did the growth of the total population. To put this in perspective, in 1800 the population of the largest US city, New York, was well under one hundred thousand, and by 1900 its population was over three million.

Much of the nineteenth-century economic growth resulted from the Industrial Revolution, which introduced more productive agricultural technologies and steel-frame construction. More efficient agricultural operations reduced the demand for agricultural workers, who flocked to cities seeking work in newly established factories, which served as magnets attracting millions of European immigrants and stimulating the Great Migration of over six million African Americans from the rural South to the industrial North for work.[22]

People desperate to work in cities crowded into high-rise buildings and tenements with poor sanitary conditions. Water contamination due to inadequate or absent sewerage and water treatment resulted in a high incidence of death. The health and environmental concerns of blue-collar workers soon became the concerns of wealthier society members.[23] The fear arose that disease could easily spread and infect the more affluent areas of the city. This worry, coupled with the belief of upper-class, educated men and women that they had an aristocratic duty to assist the disadvantaged, gave rise to a series of reform movements intended to improve sanitation and make the industrial city more aesthetically pleasing.

One response to congested cities in the mid-nineteenth century focused on the creation of parks and open spaces. Rooted deep in the American psyche was a belief that contact with nature and access to open space were inherently uplifting and would have a positive impact on both the health and the moral character of city dwellers. Led by Frederick Law Olmsted, the urban parks movement in the United States emerged with the notion that the provision of urban parkland could provide a much-needed communion with nature and a refuge from the city. When New York City established Central Park in the 1850s, it was like no other public space in the US at that time. Central Park was envisioned as a "green oasis" for persons from diverse walks of life—the rich and poor, old and young, sick and healthy—and set in motion investments in large green spaces in cities throughout the United States.[24] Eventually urban parkland became an expected amenity in major cities.

Reflecting the American impulse toward philanthropy, some of the wealthy so-called robber barons gave back to the country that had treated them so well by investing in cultural and educational institutions such as schools, museums, libraries, and botanical gardens. Much of this was also evidence of another strong dynamic felt by Americans in the nineteenth century: this young nation was still overshadowed by the dominant European culture. By establishing truly American cultural and educational institutions, philanthropists were distinguishing their institutions from dependence on European heritage. Such was the case with the New York Botanical Garden, established in 1891. Socially well connected and wealthy, the Columbia University botanist Nathaniel Lord Britton and his wife, Elizabeth, were inspired by their trip to England's Royal Botanic Gardens, Kew, to promote the creation of a New York botanical garden that would go beyond what green spaces alone could provide. The Brittons wanted a garden that would rival Kew in its structures, plant collections, research efforts, and programs, and thereby serve both as a green oasis for the newly arrived masses of workers and families and as a plant-based scientific institution.[25]

Beautification and civic improvement projects, which included recreational facilities, fountains, and statues, were often combined with investments in landscape design as a means to infuse culture into and improve the aesthetic aspects of urban life. In an effort to increase the cultural clout of the nation's capital city of Washington, DC, and to invest in scientific discovery that rivaled that of Americans' European forebears, Congress chartered the United States Botanic Garden, and in 1850, a greenhouse was built on the National Mall. Like the erection of the US Capitol in 1850 and the Washington Monument in 1888, the botanic garden added to the prestige of the capital.

Urban history tends to emphasize the role of authoritative individuals such as national leaders, visionary architects, or renowned planners in shaping urban growth to support more livable cities. This recounting suggests that cities were seemingly created by a few individuals leaning only on their own vision, skill, and expertise. A less celebrated reform effort during the nineteenth century was grassroots driven.[26] Localized expertise was drawn from volunteers, clubs, and civic organizations focused on efforts to improve the aesthetics, safety, and sanitation in their communities. Those efforts included planting street trees and flowerbeds and building small parks. These grassroots initiatives assumed a shared moral responsibility of all citizens in civic improvement, and a collective effort to focus on small, implementable projects.[27] In the seventy-five years between 1827 and 1902, horticultural societies were created in Philadelphia (Pennsylvania Horticultural Society), Chicago (Chicago Horticultural Society), and New York (Horticultural Society of New York). These societies were formed to connect people with horticulture and to bring them together to create more beautiful, healthy, and sustainable communities. Their roles are as relevant today as they were in the Victorian era.

These early civic improvement efforts provided the bases for mid-twentieth century reforms, such as the Clean Air Act of 1963, the Highway Beautification Act of 1965, the creation of the Environmental Protection Agency in 1970, and the Clean Water Act of 1972. Collectively, these legislative advances further championed the connection between people and nature as an important component of the livability of urban areas.[28]

Demographic changes following World War II included increased birthrates, which led to outmigration from cities into burgeoning suburbs. Coupled with high rates of employment and increased discretionary income, these trends set the stage for an increased interest in gardening, horticultural research, and community beautification. Many new public gardens sprang up in the affluent suburbs of US cities, such as Naples, Florida; Santa Barbara, California; and Richmond, Virginia. In Chicago, for example, the Chicago Horticultural Society established the Chicago Botanic Garden in 1972 in Glencoe, a wealthy, primarily white town north of the city. Its mission is to "cultivate the power of plants to sustain and enrich life," a mission it carries out both on its own site and in communities of need throughout Chicago.[29]

The environmental justice movement, which started in the 1970s, championed initiatives connecting nature and human communities and empowering citizens to protect their quality of life. Increasingly, people looked to the natural environment as a potential amenity with which they might interact.[30] As part of this movement, public gardens switched from being institutions that exploited the natural resources of other countries to ones dedicated to the conservation of individual species, habitats, and regions. The Missouri Botanical Garden, for example, operates the Center for Conservation and Sustainable Development, while the New York Botanical Garden, through its Center for Conservation Strategies, employs over two hundred scientists to work on biodiversity conservation in the US and around the world.

In the twenty-first century, as society has become more aware of the loss of both native plant species and the habitats that support them, public gardens increasingly engage in local plant conservation efforts, without sacrificing their traditional strengths in ornamental display. The five-acre Lurie Garden, which opened in 2004 in the heart of downtown Chicago, uses drifts of native meadow plants to pay homage to Chicago's transformation from flat marshland to innovative urban center; the city's motto is *Urbs in horto* (City in a Garden). The Los Angeles Arboretum is engaged in a multiyear process of dredging the accumulated sediment in Baldwin Lake, restoring the natural flow, and reintroducing native plant and fish species to the lake.[31] The Lady Bird Johnson Wildflower Center is a recognized leader in plant conservation in Texas, working through partnerships on such critical issues as rare plant and invasive species monitoring and research and collecting and banking seeds for conservation and restoration.[32]

Our concept of livability has now expanded to include concerns for sustainable development, smart growth and urban design, and community-identified priorities such as access to fresh and affordable food and urban green space as part of the public realm.[33] What unites these and other efforts is a recognition on the part of public gardens that resources are precious and need to be conserved both directly, through multipronged conservation and sustainability programs, and indirectly, through education programs that make users aware of these issues and the need for individuals to take action.

Cross-Sector Partnerships with Public Gardens

The underlying assertion of this book is that challenges related to improving the livability of communities are more effectively addressed in collaboration or partnership between organizations, and that public gardens are a critical partner for interventions using plants as connectors of people.[34] Partnerships that involve public gardens take many forms, some of which are highlighted in this book, and all of which were created with the intent of providing innovative solutions to economic, social, or environmental problems. Cross-sector partnerships are about transcending the inflexibility of traditional organizational boundaries to achieve a shared vision of the future, and are characterized by collective decision making in which business, government, and civil society actors interact.[35] For organizations that are engaged or may become involved in partnerships, it is important to consider the motivation for partnerships and the various forms they might take.

Like most cross-sector partnerships, collaborative relationships created with public gardens can occur through a variety of configurations and can develop over time. Variations in partnerships are generally viewed as occupying a continuum, characterized in terms of their depth of interaction, integration, and commitment.[36] As illustrated in figure 0.1, when partnership type evolves from *communication* at the left end of the continuum to the potential for *collective action*, the level of time, commitment, and shared decision-making increases.

When organizations communicate, they exchange information. A partnership based on *communication* might include individuals sharing information about a funding opportunity to examine urban greening as a tool for economic development across different networks, sectors, agencies, or jurisdictions. This interaction requires relatively little time and no commitment; if one organization decides not to pursue the funding opportunity, that decision has no significant bearing on either organization. Communication is most effective, however, when clear channels are created across organizations and contacts of particular interest are identified.

As organizations progress to the *cooperation* stage, they exchange information and agree to alter their activities to some degree so as to achieve a common goal. When organizations cooperate, they share resources to help each other succeed,

Communication	Cooperation	Collaboration	Collective Action
Actively exchange information across organizations for mutual benefit.	Share resources and alter activities to help each organization succeed, as needed.	Generate new ideas together and joint decisions to enhance each organization's capacity.	Commitment to integrated planning, data and funding structures targeting long-term impact.

FIGURE 0.1. Continuum of partnership types. This figure is an adaptation of "Collaboration Continuum," in Arthur T. Himmelman, *Collaboration for a Change: Definitions, Decision-Making Models, Roles, and Collaboration Process Guide* (Minneapolis: Himmelman Consulting, 2002), 4.

such as staff, space, volunteers, expertise, and funds. An example of a cooperative relationship is when a public garden and a community school share physical space for classes training neighborhood youth in horticulture techniques. Cooperation requires increased commitment and may include formal partnership agreements or memoranda of understanding stating the objective of the partnership and some level assessment of progress toward a common goal, but the organizations remain independent.

Rather than working independently toward a common goal, *collaborating* organizations exchange information, share resources and decision-making power to address problems, and generate new ideas together. A key difference between cooperation and collaboration is that collaborating partners clearly identify as being committed to working together and acknowledge their interdependence. Outcomes are stronger when the partners work collectively. Collaboration occurs over time as organizations interact formally and informally, negotiating the development of commitments and the implementation of those commitments.[37]

In her seminal work on collaboration, *Collaborating: Finding Common Ground for Multiparty Problems*, Barbara Gray found that cooperation may be an early stage of collaboration, but that collaboration is differentiated as a long-term process through which partners "search for solutions that go beyond their own limited vision of what is possible" and work to implement those solutions together.[38] Collaborating partners commit to sharing the risks, responsibilities, and resources of joint work. In a collaborative relationship, organizations might apply jointly for a funding opportunity and commit to adding a new position or modifying an existing position to accommodate increased investment of time to work on a project. Doing so would create a competitive advantage through their increased capacity from shared resources (e.g., technical, knowledge, human resources) and the ability of cross-sector partnerships to draw on the partners' collective knowledge and expertise to produce innovative outcomes.

Each of the partnership types on the continuum can be appropriate for particular purposes and circumstances. For example, public gardens can find it useful to communicate when they seek to provide information on new or updated programs. In other circumstances, public gardens may invest in more complex cooperating partnerships because they need additional resources or abilities to meet certain goals more effectively, or because they have complementary areas of expertise. The complexity and potential of partnerships build as they move along the continuum, and in most cases the relationships built through communicating and cooperating lay the groundwork of trust that is needed for more complex relationships.

A highly regarded approach to the final stage, collective action, is called collective impact. This is a systematic approach to collaboration that attempts to engage organizations and individuals affected by a given issue with those who can influence that issue. *Collective impact* was introduced as a term in 2011 by John Kania and Mark Kramer and defined as a "commitment of a group of important actors from different sectors to a common agenda for solving a specific social problem" that intentionally works toward large-scale systems change. It is differentiated from other forms of collaboration by five conditions: the organizations involved in collective impact have a common agenda, shared measurement systems, mutually reinforcing activities, continuous communication, and the presence of a backbone organization. This individual or group plays an administrative role in convening and coordinating, facilitating relationships, and ensuring that the initiative stays on track and attracts continued funding.[39]

Scholars and practitioners find that in order for a collective impact initiative to be successful, it must have an influential champion, adequate financial resources, and a collective sense of urgency for change.[40] When fully in place, a collective impact structure allocates resources and support necessary to ensure the continuing commitment of participating organizations long enough to build momentum toward long-term solutions. Collective impact has been endorsed by governmental agencies and foundations, and philanthropic funders have integrated collective impact into calls for proposals.

At the center of collective impact is the aspiration to address inequities related to race, income, and other characteristics that shape complex societal problems, from education to environment to employment. To be truly effective, however, the execution and governance of collective impact initiatives must be designed to address persistent imbalances.[41] Looking at a hypothetical scenario, a collective impact partnership would start by addressing inequities around urban greening within a given community and ensuring that social equity is a priority in the project. Prior to the partners submitting a proposal for funding, they would seek to understand how different groups are affected by the issue and ensure that those most affected help set the common agenda. This form of collaboration would not promise or depend on early wins to maintain partners or support from funders, but would be focused on the long view of a systemic project around inclusive communities.

For any of the partnership stages, it is important for organizations to clearly identify the circumstances for partnering and to consider the desired characteristics of future partners before pursuing a collaboration. Assessing readiness for a partnership is critical because collaboration is not always easy and is not always effective, but it always requires time and varying levels of resources and commitment. Another consideration when selecting partners is power asymmetry. A partnership structure may fail when one organization can impose its will on the others. In these cases, true interdependency between the organizations does not exist, and the less powerful organizations may be ignored or excluded.[42]

Guide to This Book

This book is driven by the thesis that meaningful partnerships between public gardens and other organizations or individuals depend on the development of a common agenda and on making the best use of the resources that each partner brings to the effort.

Each program profiled in a case study involves a partnership between a public garden and organizations or individuals outside the garden. In selecting programs to profile, our primary focus was on the program itself and not on the institutions that originated or operated the program. Next in importance was selecting programs that could be replicated or modified by other gardens. The programs selected are diverse enough so that all public gardens, regardless of location, budget, or size, can see opportunities and unique roles they can play in contributing to the sustainability of the communities in which they are located. The most effective models we found were those that did not necessarily have a history of continual success, but rather showed an evolution that included dealing with obstacles and setbacks. As part of that evolution, we were interested in programs that ensured that all partners benefited from the program and were committed to the goal. Further, we identified ones that built into the planning process and their operations regular evaluations that could be used to modify the program and enabled the program administrators to identify its measurable benefits to the community. Finally, the public gardens and horticultural societies profiled in this book are by no means a complete inventory, but are representative of the programs other horticultural institutions are creating and managing to use to promote the livability of their communities.

No public garden on its own, regardless of its budget and the extent of its networks, can address all of the challenges facing American communities today. Therefore, we have chosen to focus on five areas where partnerships involving public gardens have had a real impact: unsafe and degraded neighborhoods, poor-quality science education, lack of access to fresh and healthy foods, inadequate or nonexistent job training opportunities, and environmental degradation.

This is a text that is meant to be used, not stuck on a shelf. We intend it to be of value to public gardens, any public-sector, private-sector, nonprofit, or civic group, or any resident that seeks to partner with public gardens in their efforts to create more sustainable, livable, and equitable communities. Every chapter includes a series of case studies, each of which examines a different approach to a common community problem in an effort to encourage public gardens and their partners to consider multiple ways to initiate and implement programs. Four central topics are examined in the case studies: livable communities and how they can be achieved, meaningful ways of addressing complex societal challenges, the unique roles of public gardens as community institutions, and the components of truly effective partnerships. In the final chapter, we provide a detailed analysis of strategies for successful partnerships and how they can be evaluated.

Finally, the book is also intended to be used as a reference. In appendix A, we provide a thumbnail profile of each case study garden profiled in the book. Appendix B lists the partners for each program, organized by chapter. Appendix C lists national and international organizations aligned with public gardens.

Partnerships between public gardens and community entities can be messy, time consuming, and in some cases unsuccessful. But they also have the power to effect meaningful changes in the livability of communities that have for too long been underserved.

PROMOTING NEIGHBORHOOD SAFETY AND WELL-BEING

Many cities across the United States are responding to residents' demands for more livable neighborhoods by investing in public spaces that are open and accessible to people, such as sidewalks, parks, and plazas. Placemaking, a strategy mentioned in the introduction, uses public spaces to promote social interaction, stimulate investment in distressed places, rejuvenate structures and streetscapes, and create a safe, well-maintained, and welcoming environment for all users.[1] Placemaking efforts frequently use natural amenities, such as trees and plantings, as tools to attract and engage people in an urban setting. Landscaping and maintenance of public spaces are not just tools to beautify an area; they also promote a sense of safety and reduce crime by signaling that neighbors are actively involved in community spaces.[2] Placemaking increases the perception that there are "eyes on the street,"[3] which acts to deter crime and increase a sense of neighborhood safety.

Placemaking emphasizes the importance and potential of a particular type of community asset: partnerships.[4] Creative interdisciplinary partnerships between residents, local schools and universities, artists, civic leaders, and professionals in fields such as park planning and community and economic development are transforming underutilized public spaces.[5] This chapter examines the approach, process, and outcomes of placemaking partnerships formed with public gardens to promote a sense of safety and well-being at the neighborhood scale. Cases in this chapter emphasize the intentional use of urban greening as a tool to empower residents to actively contribute to positive change, to elevate diverse cultures sharing common spaces, and to capitalize on existing assets in the community to manage vacant land.

The Greening of Brooklyn

In the early twentieth century, New York City was already on its way to becoming the dense cityscape that it is today. The availability of manufacturing jobs and the waves of immigration into the city contributed to its exponential population growth. Innovations in transportation, including bridges, trolley lines, and the first subway line, extended development from Manhattan into the more rural borough of Brooklyn.[6] Brooklyn had always been a diverse borough, attracting residents from cultures with strong ties to gardening. Today, only 54 percent of Brooklyn residents speak English at home as their primary language, followed closely by Spanish, Chinese, Russian, and Yiddish.[7]

Over the past century, Brooklyn has gained over 1 million new residents, many of them immigrants who account for at least 30 percent of the city's population.[8] Brooklyn is now the most populous borough in New York City, with an estimated 2.6 million residents.[9] How does an urban area with such a strong history of concentrated growth and changing demographics sustain a livable community?

Establishing a public garden in the heart of Brooklyn in 1910 was one way to ensure that open and green space was preserved in the face of rapid urban growth. Over its first several decades, Brooklyn Botanic Garden (BBG) invested in the landscape design of its fifty-two-acre site and focused its mission on "the advancement and diffusion of a knowledge and a love of plants" through display gardens, scientific collections, and the first-of-its-kind children's garden.[10] The Children's Garden, which opened in 1914, gave city children from all income groups the opportunity to grow their own food and in the process to learn about the aesthetic, economic, and nutritional value of plants. In a 1922 reflection on the Children's Garden, BBG's curator of elementary education said, "We have tried from the beginning to establish in the minds of the public this fact: That our educational work is not for the poor alone, nor for the rich alone, nor for the middle class, but for all classes and conditions."[11]

The success of the Children's Garden, ostensibly the first "community outreach" effort of the Brooklyn Botanic Garden, and outreach to local public schools helped establish the garden as a community-facing institution.[12] For decades, BBG built relationships with gardeners throughout the region by informally advising community and home gardeners, and for nearly forty years it celebrated the kickoff of the spring gardening season with an annual Making Brooklyn Bloom event.

In the 1980s, Brooklyn was struggling to become a destination for living and working, but the borough—like the rest of New York City—faced the challenges posed by disinvestment, a spiking crime rate, derelict buildings, poor housing conditions, and racial tension, many of which were captured in Spike Lee's 1989 film *Do the Right Thing*. In response to those challenges, New York City adopted a "broken window" approach to policing, which assumes that small crimes and disorder (e.g., graffiti or littering) establish a climate for serious crimes (e.g., robbery or murder).[13] The logic of this now-controversial theory is that if one "window" is broken and not repaired and maintained, it signals that no one cares, and encourages more broken "windows."[14] In practice, this approach resulted in the overpolicing of minority communities, fractured relationships between law enforcement and minorities, distrust among residents, and eventually calls for policing reform.[15]

BBG's GreenBridge

Partly in response to this situation and its negative impact on the borough's quality of life, Brooklyn Botanic Garden in 1993 expanded its outreach efforts and founded an ambitious community horticulture and urban greening program, which it named GreenBridge. The overall goals of GreenBridge were to match BBG's horticultural skills and resources to community-identified needs and to build a network of people and resources dedicated to making Brooklyn a greener, more livable place. Led by Judith Zuk, BBG's president at the time, BBG saw GreenBridge as a commitment to expand access to horticulture and urban greening to the wider community. GreenBridge would use urban greening as the tool to "bridge" cultural differences, and to heal and build new relationships between neighbors working together on neighborhood beautification projects.[16] BBG was poised to use its relationships, reputation, and technical skills to create new connections between the many segments of the Brooklyn community.

GreenBridge operated as a community-based environmental horticulture program promoting urban greening through education, conservation, and creative partnerships.[17] BBG's location between some of the borough's most affluent areas near Prospect Park and some of the poorest neighborhoods enabled it to use horticulture as a common shared value to facilitate community discussions with diverse groups.

BBG recently rebranded its greening efforts under the umbrella of Community Greening, instead of GreenBridge, but the programs remain consistent and include five initiatives, each with a distinct role in promoting urban greening in Brooklyn. The Brooklyn Urban Gardener is an eleven-session train-the-trainer certificate program that instructs participants on basics in urban gardening and community organizing. The Community Garden Alliance is a network of gardeners and provides educational workshops and an annual free plant giveaway as well as social events around sustainable horticulture. The Street Tree Stewards initiative teaches residents to care for street trees. Making Brooklyn Bloom is the long-running annual event to kick off spring planting season, comprising a free daylong program of workshops, speakers, and exhibits about sustainable horticulture. Finally, the Greenest Block in Brooklyn contest promotes sustainable streetscape improvements and community building through annual competitions between blocks and civic groups.

Notably, the Greenest Block in Brooklyn contest was designed in response to a community-identified need. Years before the contest was created, local gardeners started friendly gardening competitions on their blocks. These local home gardeners reached out to BBG for technical advice and eventually requested that someone at the garden act as the judge for their block competitions.[18] Because of its potential to build "bridges" between residents from different backgrounds, the Greenest Block contest is an instructive model of how a public garden can connect people through placemaking.

Building Bridges through Urban Greening Contests

Designed to help Brooklyn residents feel safer and more comfortable by encouraging neighbors to work together to re-green their neighborhoods, the Greenest Block contest promotes and rewards streetscape gardening, tree stewardship, and community-building activities through a friendly, albeit spirited, competition between different blocks or merchant associations. The contest also empowers residents by respecting their neighborhood knowledge and by providing them with the training and resources to implement their ideas for urban greening.

To get the program off the ground, BBG embraced the assets of the borough's diverse cultures and learned how current residents were doing urban greening. "As I traveled around the borough," explained Ellen Kirby, the program's first director, "I saw people living in lower-wealth areas who already knew how to do urban greening and gardening, and I wanted to showcase to others what these neighborhoods could do." After more than twenty growing seasons, Greenest Block can boast that it has influenced greening activities on an estimated 1,600 blocks across the borough and has involved over six hundred thousand Brooklynites in beautification and greening efforts.[19]

The notion of a contest to foster participation and excitement around urban greening is simple, yet an analysis of the nuts and bolts of Greenest Block reveals a strategic and well-orchestrated program. "The block associations in Brooklyn have always been central to the sociopolitical landscape; you can't ignore them," explained Nina Browne, community program manager at BBG.[20] The success of this program is rooted in BBG's decision to use block associations as organizing agents and partners, and in its relationship with influential actors in the Brooklyn area who can serve as contest judges and attract additional support for urban greening initiatives.

ANCHORED BY BLOCK AND CIVIC ASSOCIATIONS

From the start, the contest operated as a partnership with block and merchant associations, facilitated through the Office of the Brooklyn Borough President, which is known for its strong relationship with block associations and has helped cultivate the ascendency of blocks as powerful forces for change.[21] Brooklyn's history of strong block associations stems from common resident concerns such as crime, historic preservation, and unscrupulous landlords.[22] "The key to making the connection between community and horticulture was to first determine the scale at which the community could be focused and organized," reflected Ellen Kirby.[23] Neighborhood blocks were selected as the scale of focus for this initiative because block associations typically possess a level of organizational capacity as well as the potential to build stronger relationships between residents.

As opposed to a competition built around individual front yards, the model for Greenest Block requires that people work together to landscape their block, and it only accepts entries from civic organizations such as official or ad hoc residential block associations, civic groups, or neighborhood organizations. Residential blocks are judged from corner to corner and on both sides of the street,

FIGURE 1.1.   Greening the block in Brooklyn.
Photo by Michelle Gluck.

whereas commercial entries (e.g., merchant associations, development corporations, business improvement districts, or nonprofit business associations) are judged on one side of the street.

In addition to criteria such as variety and suitability of plants, maintenance and total visual effect, and soil stewardship, the contest is able to achieve its goal of building social cohesion in the community by judging the level of citizen participation. Judges look for evidence of community effort in plantings, cooperatively gardened areas on the block, and signage. At least 80 percent of the individuals on the block must participate, which frequently includes more than seventy houses and apartment buildings.[24] Pushing for high levels of participation enables contest organizers to showcase how neighborhood greening can strengthen communities.

A COMMUNITY OF GARDENERS AND NEIGHBORS

For a community-based initiative like Greenest Block to survive, plans must be made to engage a diverse set of stakeholders—the individuals and groups that will champion the initiative and help ensure its future in the face of challenges or economic downturns. One of the ways that BBG builds stakeholders for the Greenest Block contest is through the deliberate involvement of influential judges and the solicitation of support from groups that share common goals. To build long-term support for the contest, the BBG development and communications offices strategically invite journalists, professional horticulturists, donors, trustees, and other VIPs to serve as judges.[25]

The winning block of the coveted Greenest Block in Brooklyn award must pass three levels of judging, with judges spending considerable time visiting and evaluating contestant blocks. In 2018, the contestants represented 160 Brooklyn blocks, encompassing thirty neighborhoods and approximately thirty-two thousand people.[26]

In the first round of judging, the two paid judges spend at least ten to fourteen days reviewing an average of two hundred blocks entered in the competition and scoring each block on the basis of six criteria.[27] Commercial block finalists are identified after this round, and roughly thirty to forty residential blocks are selected to advance to a second round of judging. While the same criteria are used for the second round, special consideration is given to blocks that face special challenges, such as 2014 block contestants from Coney Island still recovering from Hurricane Sandy or blocks with larger numbers of vacant houses or lots. Over the course of three or four days, teams of three volunteer judges each are driven to ten different blocks. Members of the press may follow the judges on their rounds, leading to important press coverage for BBG and the contest. This semifinal round ends with the selection of approximately eight to ten residential finalists.

BBG's president then puts together a small team to review the finalists and select the winners. Prizes are awarded for the greenest storefront, best window box, best community garden streetscape, and other greening efforts, for both residential and commercial blocks. On average, twenty-five awards are given each year, representing first, second, and third place and honorable mention for each category. The total amount for cash prizes is less than $4,000; top winners receive $300 each. According to Nina Browne, "The participation itself is the important thing for this contest, as are the bragging rights of being the Greenest Block in Brooklyn."[28]

Archives of statements from recent commercial and residential winning blocks provide a snapshot of the awardees' commitment and potential:

- 2014 commercial block winner: "We are honored to receive the award of Greenest Commercial Block," said Brigit Pinnell, executive director of the Montague Street Business Improvement District. "We have sought to create an urban oasis where visitors come to shop and linger. This award recognizes . . . planting and maintenance of nearly 50 tree beds along Montague Street. We hope our success will inspire other commercial districts to tap the potential of their tree beds for a greener, more beautiful Brooklyn."[29]

FIGURE 1.2. The winning residential block from the 2013 Greenest Block in Brooklyn contest.
Photo by Alvina Lai. Courtesy of Brooklyn Botanic Garden.

- 2013 residential winner: Sterling Street between Washington and Bedford Avenues was a first-time winner after entering for over ten years. This block is quite large, with sixty to eighty homes, but it achieved nearly 100 percent participation from its residents. Claudia Loftis, chair of the block association gardening committee, commented on the project's impact on the neighborhood: "Every resident on Sterling Street is part of this story: mulching, watering, organizing and fundraising all year round. We built a special community around gardening here—when you saw someone caring for a yard, tree bed or planter, it was frequently a neighbor assisting someone next door or down the block, helping seniors, caring for the communal Children's Garden or maintaining the yard of an abandoned house. . . . We can proudly say we live on the greenest block in Brooklyn!"[30]

Although gentrification can be an unintended impact of urban greening, BBG's Greenest Block contest works to stimulate organized community activism against gentrification. "The contest fulfills a couple of roles in face of gentrification: one is as a catalyst for antigentrification activists. Neighborhood associations are forming to maintain affordable housing and use the contest as a way of getting together to fight it," said Nina Browne.[31] In fact, the contest has helped to establish and revive block associations and inspired the creation of new organizations based on common challenges and interests. The demographic rearrangement associated with gentrification frequently creates a host of challenges and tensions between long-term residents and new residents. Browne finds that on gentrifying blocks, members of different races, ethnicities, and backgrounds are using the contest to get to know one another and to overcome some of their differences.[32] Participating residents have highlighted that the contest creates an opportunity to build bridges between old residents and the flurry of new residents moving into the blocks.[33]

As might be expected, trends to date show a higher level of contest participation in areas of homeownership and where tenants are highly organized, but given the changing neighborhood demographics, the geographic location of block contestants also changes.[34] For example, when the contest started, the Bedford-Stuyvesant neighborhood had the lowest participation, but it now has the highest number of blocks entering the competition. Indeed, a recent survey conducted by BBG found that 70 percent of Greenest Block participants reported that since entering the contest, people on their block spend more time outdoors interacting with their neighbors.[35]

Lessons from BBG's Initiatives

The Greenest Block in Brooklyn contest offers insights into how organizations can partner when they share a common goal. Given BBG's relatively small community outreach staff, maintaining connections with the large number of Brooklyn's block associations must be strategically managed. Brooklyn is divided into eighteen community boards, which are local representative bodies, each consisting of residents who must live, work, or have a specific interest in the community. BBG leverages its partnership with the Office of the Brooklyn Borough President to ensure that among their other responsibilities, the community boards help encourage greening efforts for their districts. This connection broadens the reach of the Greenest Block contest and strengthens partnerships with residents.

In early spring, the Greenest Block contest is advertised in the block association and community board newsletters. To encourage new entries, BBG offers free workshops called "How to Green Your Block" and encourages residents to host a free, interactive walk-and-talk block visit, led by BBG staff, to help brainstorm the block's greening opportunities.

Maintaining partnerships with block associations comes down to cultivating relationships with people doing urban gardening in the borough. "All of our staff are longtime Brooklyn residents, which matters because so much of what we do is about placemaking," said Nina Browne. "We are in relationship all the time, getting to personally know people. Our approach is based in the principles of asset-based community development, which recognizes that the expertise is in the hands of the residents doing this work in their community. Our job is to constantly facilitate peer-to-peer learning . . . to spread this local expertise to others."[36]

Funders are another important partner for Greenest Block. The Brooklyn Community Foundation, a tax-exempt public charity dedicated to strengthening communities, is the contest's founding supporter. Because Greenest Block helps to achieve the company's goal of increasing environmental education and local community sustainability, National Grid New York, an energy company and major contest supporter, sponsors the Leadership in Sustainable Practices Award, which recognizes blocks or community gardens that demonstrate innovative, sustainable horticultural techniques and integrate public education opportunities about the techniques used in their blocks. The 2014 award went to a community garden in Park Slope that serves as a community composting site and hosts educational events about sustainability and gardening for all ages.[37]

The Greenest Block in Brooklyn contest is an excellent example of neighborhood residents coming together to beautify their surroundings, which results in reduced littering, crime, and vandalism. As one participant noted, "Every year more and more people have been getting involved greening our block! We are quite proud of our continued involvement in the Greenest Block contest. Neighbors are inspired by other neighbors and their successes with gardening. It makes our block look beautiful and feel safe."[38]

Learning from and Supporting the Community

The backbone of Greenest Block's success is BBG's partnership with block associations and community stakeholders. The reported impact of the contest on
relationships between residents in Brooklyn is important for urban greening,
but also for community development agendas more generally. Research supports
the finding that social ties, such as those developed in the contest, tend to enable
residents to organize more quickly to address neighborhood concerns related to
crime prevention, beautification, or economic development.[39] In many of the
borough's underserved neighborhoods, where participation in the contest continues to grow, the contest performs a critical role in community building.

While block associations tend to be more common in densely urbanized cities,
civic groups and neighborhood associations are found in most municipalities.
The Greenest Block model presents an opportunity for public gardens, neighborhood associations, and local governments to use urban horticulture as a common interest around which to form new creative partnerships. As the initiating
partner, Brooklyn Botanic Garden took a series of deliberate steps to consider
how the needs of residents in the borough could inform the programming of its
community horticulture programs:

Understand the community context. BBG referenced existing conditions in the
borough to discern the needs of the community and to identify potential common goals between the public garden and other community-based organizations.
It researched secondary community indicator data, considering socioeconomic
variables to understand the changing demographics of residents, housing trends
to understand challenges with vacancies, and crime data to confirm challenges to
the quality of life for residents in Brooklyn.

Spend time in the community. BBG leveraged activities that were already happening informally in the borough and helped to reinforce and formalize them.
BBG staff also looked for existing community assets that could serve as a foundation to initiate relationships between the public garden and the community.
They looked at borough residents' existing interests, hobbies, and skills that could
serve as a starting point for building bridges with the community. After spending
time in borough neighborhoods, they discovered that many new immigrants in
Brooklyn celebrated their cultural heritage through gardening and that horticulture could inspire community relationships.

Partner with existing and trusted organizations. BBG built its community
horticulture program on the strong foundation of established community organizations. Instead of starting another new organization, BBG reinforced the
activities of groups trusted by residents in Brooklyn: neighborhood block and
merchant associations. In partnership with block associations, BBG could build

new relationships with residents and serve as the organizing agent for a community horticulture initiative.

Cultural Identity in Queens

An important part of placemaking is the integration of the social and cultural identities that define a place with those that differentiate it from others. These identities are woven into the sense of a community and provide subtle cues indicating that "you are here." They can often be felt when walking through neighborhoods, observing the ways in which residents care for their surroundings and each other. People tend to feel more comfortable and safe in places where they feel an attachment to their community, where celebrations are held, and where cultures can mix.[40] The foundation for promoting a strong sense of community requires frequent interaction between residents. This interaction, in turn, requires a connection that extends beyond simply occupying the same physical spaces; it should make people feel that they are members of a "group" that shares certain experiences, aspirations, or beliefs.

Promoting this sense of community can be especially challenging in highly diverse communities where social contact between demographic groups may not currently exist.[41] In densely populated areas of our cities, public gardens are initiating and partnering in programs to promote cohesiveness in communities with ethnically diverse populations, as well as those with large immigrant populations. As one of the United States' most popular destinations for new immigrants, and as a place where over 130 primary languages are spoken, Queens is a great laboratory for cultural institutions interested in developing techniques for working effectively with diverse communities.

Queens Botanical Garden (QBG) is located in the heart of Flushing, New York, a bustling, densely populated center in one of the most diverse counties in the United States. QBG evolved from a five-acre "Gardens on Parade" exhibit at the 1939 World's Fair in Queens to a thirty-nine-acre site located across the street from Flushing Meadows Corona Park. The garden has a strong history of being accessible to and integrated into its surrounding community. It was not until 2002 that the garden invested in a secure perimeter fence that could allow development of its entire property as a botanical garden with a controlled environment for plant collections.[42] After fifty years as a free public space open to nearby residents, QBG decided in 2010 to institute an admission fee, causing temporary turmoil within the community, which had viewed the garden as a free public good, similar to libraries, post offices, and public parks, and which had grown to depend on daily use of the space.[43]

The Ambassador Program at Queens Botanical Garden

Strong integration with the community and residents' dependence on the botanical garden's spaces for activities, exercise, meetings, and meditation did not happen accidentally. When Susan Lacerte became QBG's executive director in 1994, she recognized that the diversity of Queens was not reflected in the garden's members. She set a goal to diversify membership, and in 1997 the botanical garden refined its vision to more directly focus on diversity, presenting plants "as unique expressions of cultural traditions,"[44] and it has since worked to embrace and integrate the diverse Queens community into the public garden. With a grant from the New York Community Trust to strengthen connections with underserved communities in Queens, she created the Ambassador Program to explore the needs of different ethnic groups and to identify how the garden could better serve them.

The purpose of the Ambassador Program is to build bridges with nearby residents and include their voices in the garden's programming and physical infrastructure investments. Through an application process, QBG annually recruits a group of twelve to fifteen ambassadors, each of whom represents a different cultural community in Queens. Prospective ambassadors speak the languages of their communities, are active in their affairs, and have demonstrated leadership in their social and professional networks. Ambassadors represent and speak for the public garden and regularly report back on ways it can better serve a particular community.

Although QBG ambassadors act as volunteers, they can reap considerable social, political, and business networking opportunities for themselves in these roles. Ambassadors must attend at least four business, fraternal, religious, or governmental meetings per quarter in their communities, which deepen and expand their professional networks. Additionally, ambassadors receive free QBG membership and are eligible to be appointed to the garden's board of trustees, where they can contribute to decisions and strategic planning for the garden.

Building the foundation for the Ambassador Program required patience and persistence on the part of the garden staff. "The key to the success of the program was reaching deeply into various cultural communities that call Queens 'home,'" Lacerte explained. "We had to resist the temptation to reach out to people we already knew, so we could find people in communities we did not know. We asked elected officials, community board leaders, and others to help identify people who would want to share their communities and their desires with us. When we convened the group, the path did not always go as we had planned, as people had different ways they wanted to share."[45]

Input from the Ambassadors Program enabled the garden to find new ways to use plants and nature as a universal language to connect with the diverse cultures in Queens. Ambassadors worked in their communities to identify ideas for educational programs at the garden, plants that are culturally important to different ethnic groups, and opportunities to incorporate cultural holidays and events into the garden's calendar.

QBG broadened its partnership with the Hindu community and its nearby temple through connections made by an ambassador and, in the process, educated the larger community about the culture and values of the Hindu religion. Members of the temple had approached QBG through an ambassador, inquiring whether the garden would want to be involved in some of its cultural events. As one temple board member said, "Respecting nature is an important part of Hindu religion. The botanical garden offers us the opportunity to make that connection, and we have included the garden as part of the summer camp curriculum that we run. . . . Regardless of religion, everybody loves nature."[46]

Participation and Representation in a Multicultural City

The underrepresentation of minority communities as visitors, staff members, and administrators is a recurring concern for all cultural institutions. In a 1992 report, *Excellence and Equity: Education and the Public Dimension of Museums*, the American Alliance of Museums argued that "museums must become more inclusive places that welcome diverse audiences, but first they should reflect our society's pluralism in every aspect of their operations and programs."[47]

Although New York City is celebrated as one of the world's most multicultural cities, with a world-class cultural sector to match, many residents there do not have ready access to, benefit from, or contribute to this cultural community.[48] In 2015, the city's Department of Cultural Affairs set out to measure the diversity of leaders, board members, staff, and members in city-funded nonprofit cultural organizations. It discovered that in a city where two-thirds of residents identify as nonwhite, nearly 62 percent of the city's cultural workforce is white. More culturally diverse leadership, the department argued, is key to attracting a broader cross-section of visitors.[49]

Not only are socially diverse groups more innovative and effective than homogeneous ones,[50] but they also help cultural institutions connect with minority target audiences that are representative of ongoing demographic changes. Informal educational institutions, such as public gardens, need to create ways in which diverse groups can develop a sense of belonging and identify culturally with the garden, and in so doing promote repeat visits and future memberships. Visitors who are able to engage with the exhibits are more likely to return and feel welcome at the institution.[51]

The impact of this intentional blending of cultures is evident at QBG. As an example, Chinese-speaking members gradually adopted an informal role as "daily ambassadors" at the garden, translating new garden programs, dissuading visitors from picking flowers, and even raising money for special needs. Another compelling example of the garden's celebration of cultural identity is the Queens Botanical Garden tai chi group. Nearly two hundred people, not all of whom are Chinese American, visit the garden each day to practice tai chi. Together, this group participates in competitions under the QBG Tai Chi banner. Their regular presence at the garden has led to informal leadership roles for members of the group. Members had business cards made and elected a president, vice president, secretary, and treasurer. The tai chi group has evolved and now offers tai chi demonstrations and workshops for the public garden and helps with the translation of garden materials. Without being prompted, the group responded to the tree damage and debris that littered QBG following Hurricane Sandy by raising money to help with the cleanup.[52]

While New York City continues to invest in ways to create a fairer and more equitable city by cultivating workforce and audience diversity in the cultural sector, QBG has invested in "reculturing" the public garden itself,[53] by shifting the core values, foci, practices, education, and programs to be more representative of the different cultures in the Queens community. Including different cultural groups in activities that affirm and advance cultural heritage can be instrumental

FIGURE 1.3. The Queens Botanical Garden tai chi group.
Photograph by H. David Stein (https://www.hdstein.com).

in building community and creating place identities, especially when people from different backgrounds come together to learn, discuss, and experience different cultural traditions.[54] "We feel a part of the garden; that is true relationship building," said a Queens resident and representative of the Hindu community.[55]

Learning from the QBG Program

The initiatives of the Queens Botanical Garden to involve the broader Queens community in the garden and its programs offer a range of useful approaches for all public gardens and municipalities that want to integrate the cultural identities and diversity of their communities:

- *Respect diverse viewpoints to build trust.* Whether designing and leading an initiative with community partners or being invited as a partner to implement an existing initiative, Queens Botanical Garden consistently depends on the trust it has built with the community to be successful.
- *Share decision-making power.* The Ambassadors Program may not pay its members, but perhaps more important, it shares power through representation, idea generation, and agenda setting, which is essential for true partnerships.
- *Be flexible and responsive.* QBG has been able to stay nimble with its programming, allowing it to add or tweak initiatives or change the use of garden spaces as opportunities and interests arise.

A Philadelphia Story

When the Quaker William Penn settled the Pennsylvania colony in the seventeenth century, his vision for Philadelphia was that of a "green country town," punctuated by civic parks surrounded by parcels slated for future housing and development.[56] Philadelphia was the first large US city to be laid out on a grid pattern, one that established a strong blueprint for centuries of growth, fueled largely by commerce and trade made possible by the city's central geographic location (then a cornerstone of the colonies). The city's population grew steadily for 250 years, peaking at just over two million in 1950.

Penn could not have predicted the direction of future growth in Philadelphia, however; instead of forming a compact (but uncrowded) settlement pattern, the population began to sprawl outward from the city to the once rural edges. Philadelphia lost half a million residents between 1950 and 1990, while its suburbs gained almost four times that number.[57] The post–World War II suburbanization, coupled with economies shifting away from manufacturing to service sectors, resulted in urban disinvestment, which was felt especially hard in older, once central cities of the Northeast and Midwest that had built their economies on heavy industry.[58] As residents left Philadelphia, many abandoned their homes and property, which quickly fell into disrepair. By 1992, Philadelphia had an inventory of 27,000 abandoned buildings and 15,800 vacant lots.[59] Today there are approximately 40,000 vacant parcels in Philadelphia, 74 percent of which are privately owned.[60]

Philadelphia is typical of other large US cities today, whose percentage of vacant land ranges from about 10 percent (New York City) to 40 percent or beyond in cities such as Phoenix, Fort Worth, and Tallahassee.[61] This dramatic change in settlement patterns challenges cities, as unmanaged vacant land can destabilize neighborhoods, depress property values, and create a downward spiral of abandonment and disinvestment.[62] But the impact of derelict lots goes well beyond reducing property values and burdening local governments with their maintenance costs; vacant and abandoned lots increase crime and reduce the sense of safety in communities, and tend to affect surrounding neighborhoods in similar ways.[63] These negative externalities may also increase vacancies overall by pushing homeowners to leave declining, derelict neighborhoods.[64] This cyclical trend not only strains a city's resources but also creates a compounding obstacle to community revitalization. Due to the costs of maintaining vacant and underutilized properties, cities have a vested interest in promoting land redevelopment or at least ensuring that it is well managed.

For more than half a century, urban scholars have tried to find a solution for vacant land management.[65] Cities today are increasingly adopting formal greening programs as a strategy to correct the negative externalities associated with vacant land and encourage reinvestment. Consistent with Penn's vision for green urban living and its history of greening initiatives, Philadelphia was one of the first cities to explicitly adopt greening at the municipal level.[66] It is estimated that the vacant land in neighborhoods scattered throughout Philadelphia costs each household $8,000 annually in lowered property values. Because vacant land has a blighting effect on nearby properties, some Philadelphia neighborhoods have experienced property value reductions of up to 20 percent.[67]

PHS LandCare Program

For more than two hundred years, the Pennsylvania Horticultural Society (PHS) has played an active role in the development of Philadelphia. Starting in the 1970s,

PHS invested in community greening efforts aimed at revitalizing underused and vacant lots throughout the city. In 1996, the Philadelphia LandCare program was developed through a partnership between PHS and the New Kensington Community Development Corporation. The pilot initiative involved clearing debris from lots, preparing and seeding the lots with grass and trees, and then maintaining care of the lots.

Philadelphia LandCare is now one of the largest vacant land programs in the US, and is a nationally recognized model of vacant land management. The keys to the program's success lie in the strong partnerships it has formed with community-based organizations, universities, and city agencies committed to transforming Philadelphia's vacant lots into neighborhood assets.[68] While greened vacant lots are not the same as public parks, they are similar in their attempt to improve the physical conditions in blighted neighborhoods, and may also have a positive impact on property values by signaling investment.[69]

In the 1990s, PHS commissioned a cost-benefit analysis of the management of vacant land in the city that demonstrated the ineffectiveness and high cost of the city's poorly coordinated cleanup efforts, which lacked a sustained management plan.[70] PHS then worked with Philadelphia's Division of Housing and Community Development (DHCD) to design a role for community development corporations (CDCs) in reducing the impact of vacant land on their neighborhoods.[71] In 1995, PHS and the New Kensington CDC entered into a formal partnership to conduct a test through a DHCD-funded, five-year pilot project.[72] In addition to greening 540 of New Kensington's 1,100 vacant lots, the project refined the PHS process model for vacant land management, recognized the critical role of community-based organizations in these efforts, and identified the administrative actions required of city agencies to ensure the success of the program.[73]

Philadelphia LandCare grew out of the New Kensington neighborhood pilot project. Under annually renewed contracts with DHCD, the LandCare program turns vacant land into neighborhood assets through the landscaping and maintenance of these parcels, which includes removing trash, adding wooden slat fences, and planting to create greened lots that help signal that the properties are cared for, not abandoned. Currently PHS maintains over twelve thousand properties throughout the city. Every year some lots are sold or drop off the society's list, and approximately four hundred lots are added.

The LandCare program involves two primary initiatives—Philadelphia LandCare and Community LandCare. Philadelphia LandCare targets vacant parcels in key areas throughout the city and includes neighborhoods with public safety issues and ones that lack open space and green amenities. In direct consultation with the staff of DHCD, PHS selects targeted neighborhoods and particular sites to be cleaned and greened. PHS and DHCD meet monthly to decide which

FIGURE 1.4 A and **B.** Before-and-after photos of a cleaned and greened Philadelphia lot.
Courtesy of the Pennsylvania Horticultural Society.

lots to clean and to coordinate final selections with Philadelphia's elected officials, community-based organizations, the Planning Commission, and other city
agencies. Collectively, these partners make conscious choices to invest in a neighborhood and advocate for the long-term survival of the LandCare program.

To complete the work, PHS hires city-based landscape contractors who clean
and mow the lots twice per month from April through October. Between fifteen and twenty contractors are selected through a competitive bidding process,
drawing primarily from minority-owned companies and community organizations with landscape maintenance ability. The average cost to clean and green
a property is $1,000–$1,300, depending on size; and bimonthly maintenance,
cleaning, and mowing during the growing season averages $150 per property.[74]

One of the complexities of a vacant land stabilization program is land ownership: most vacant property is not publicly owned. According to Deborah McColloch, the former longtime director of DHCD, in Philadelphia "only ten thousand
of the [more than forty thousand] vacant lots are owned by the city, and this does
not overlap with lots in the LandCare Program."[75] If a selected lot is privately
owned, the landowner is given thirty days to take care of the property; otherwise the City of Philadelphia bills the landowner for the cost of removing the
blight and for ongoing maintenance costs. Failure to pay results in a lien on the
property.[76] DHCD's approach to the public and private ownership challenge is to
recognize that even if it does not own a particular piece of land, the city owns the
problem of unmaintained lots, and therefore needs to respond to unmaintained
privately owned parcels.[77]

Over time, the vacant land management partnership between PHS and
DHCD evolved to include its second component, Community LandCare, which
targets vacant lots that have not yet been cleaned and greened. To do this, PHS
contracts annually with eighteen community organizations to clean and mow
three thousand parcels of vacant land that need to be improved, and to maintain
the already cleaned lots.[78] This community-based model engages and employs
more than one hundred local residents, empowering them with a direct role in
keeping their neighborhoods clean and safe. The Community LandCare organizations are selected by DHCD through an application process every three years.

After considerable lobbying by former Philadelphia mayor Michael Nutter
and years of advocacy from the DHCD, the LandCare program is now part of the
city budget as a line item, which provides it with more stability than its previous
annual funding through discretionary funds. Now recognized as a city service,
LandCare provides needed maintenance and land management in all council districts. The $3 million program now enjoys the support of the City Council,[79] as
well as general support, because it is a low-cost, high-yield program that responds

to residents' call for a solution to the problems of vacant lots, and because of its start as a pilot program in Philadelphia neighborhoods.

The LandCare program is not just intended to clean lots; it also promotes social interaction and increased access to green space in underserved neighborhoods. A 2018 study found that in addition to increasing property values, improving health, and reducing crime, greened lots also provide direct use benefits to neighbors.[80] Nearby residents use the greened lots in Philadelphia for recreational activities, including picnics, barbecues, and children's play, and for community gardens to grow food and flowers. This finding suggests that initiatives similar to the LandCare program could provide equitable access to green space in poorer communities and contribute to creating social cohesion among the residents of those communities.

Integrating Philadelphia's Existing Resources

Every community—regardless of its size or wealth—has assets in the form of people, places, and organizations that can be identified and mobilized for community-based work. There is reason to seek out these local assets and actors; initiatives that integrate a variety of them tend to be more sustainable in supporting social well-being, thriving economies, and healthy ecosystems.[81] Philadelphia is emblematic of the national trend where the power to make more livability is drifting downward from federal and state governments to cities and metropolitan regions, as the collective civic strength of physical, social, and cross-sector knowledge assets are harnessed.[82] Philadelphia is a city with strong institutional assets—a concentration of universities, health care and medical centers, and local organizations that have accrued power and influence in city-level community work.

PHS is a model for identifying and mobilizing existing assets in the Philadelphia area as a foundation of its approach. The society has strategically fostered cross-sector partnerships to convert vacant land to valuable green infrastructure, to utilize ties with the community to empower neighborhood groups to become part of that effort, and to increase the economic value of previously underutilized land.[83] The partnership between Philadelphia university researchers, PHS, and the City of Philadelphia is mutually beneficial: the city provides the university researchers with a convenient and ripe platform on which to conduct experiments and real estate studies; PHS provides the LandCare program to guide interventions; and the research findings help policymakers determine where to most effectively invest limited municipal dollars to improve community conditions.

LandCare's targeted intervention improves the appearance and livability of neighborhoods, and also contributes to various traditional responsibilities and goals of city-level government: public health and safety, strong property values, and sustained investments in the local community. The City of Philadelphia added $500,000 to the LandCare contract in 2016, when it recognized the effectiveness of the LandCare program in supporting these goals. PHS used this funding for a pilot program to incentivize private landscape contractors and Community LandCare organizations to hire formerly incarcerated individuals (see chapter 4 for more detail), and to support the expansion of Philadelphia LandCare.

Many of the impacts of the LandCare program have been documented by researchers from Philadelphia's universities. One series of experiments was led by Charles Branas, professor of epidemiology at the University of Pennsylvania's Perelman School of Medicine. Branas's research demonstrated the impact of vacant land management on the health and safety of nearby residents, specifically that vacant lot greening can reduce violent crime and increase perceptions of safety,[84] and that greened vacant lots are associated with improved health outcomes for neighborhood residents,[85] including increased exercise and decreased stress levels.[86]

Other researchers have demonstrated the economic impact of investments in vacant land stabilization. Research finds that after a vacant lot is greened by Philadelphia LandCare, the values of nearby homes increase by nearly 20 percent.[87] Whereas before the treatment, these same homes were worth 16 percent less than comparable homes, the homes near treated vacant lots now command a premium of 2 to 5 percent. The economic benefits of greening lots accrue with time: when greened lots are maintained, nearby homes continue to appreciate at an additional rate of 0.5 percent every year.[88] Moreover, after the initial benefits of a stabilized lot are realized, each additional cleaned and greened lot adds another 1 percent of value to homes within a quarter mile.[89]

To make a successful partnership between researchers, public gardens and policymakers, Branas emphasizes the importance of forming partnerships around an actual project: "As an example, consider our federal funding from the NIH and the CDC, on which PHS is a primary collaborator. There are also other ways to maintain and grow relationships like this, but there's nothing like a common goal that an actual project with actual tasks and deliverables can provide to bring groups together."[90] The municipality that partners with local researchers also benefits from the credibility of its city becoming a policy leader by introducing intervention models for challenges common in many cities.

Lessons from PHS LandCare

Because Philadelphia LandCare is already a nationally recognized model, PHS regularly conducts training sessions and workshops for cities and community partners from around the country. Session participants come to Philadelphia to see neighborhoods and meet partners integral to the program's success and have PHS staff design a vacant land strategy for their city, including a pilot intervention and a longer-term implementation strategy.

The PHS model offers cities with similar vacant land issues some valuable lessons:

Partner with Community Development Corporations (CDCs). Relationships with local CDCs help PHS develop strong connections and partnerships with residents to help facilitate investment at the neighborhood level. These partnerships allow PHS to pilot program initiatives at a neighborhood level before scaling up to a larger geographic area. Because resident voices are included through the CDCs, there is an increased sense of ownership for the maintenance of cleaned and greened lots.

Capitalize on local universities as partners. Philadelphia, like many cities, is home to multiple institutions of higher education. PHS strategically made connections with researchers whose work informed or could be informed by the epidemic of underutilized and vacant land. The result is a mutually beneficial relationship: PHS efforts are legitimized by rigorous research on the public health and economic development implications of vacant land management, and academic researchers benefit from willing community partners for research interventions.

Work with city agencies to institutionalize program funding. PHS worked in close partnership with city agencies to advocate for the LandCare program to be a permanent line item in the city budget. It was able to use evidence from partner research to make the case that investment in the LandCare program had a positive impact on the entire city and therefore qualified for public support.

The partnerships to promote placemaking in Brooklyn, Queens, and Philadelphia presented in this chapter highlight the importance of local engagement and involvement, the recognition of diversity as an asset to partnerships, and a "long view" assessment of intervention impacts.

Placemaking efforts seem to work well when they enable the involvement of local stakeholders who will have a significant role in the long-term maintenance of placemaking initiatives. While placemaking efforts such as urban greening in Brooklyn and the maintenance of and programming for underutilized lots in Philadelphia influenced the sense of safety and comfort of neighborhoods, the deliberate involvement of residents and other stakeholders worked to create community ownership of the placemaking process. These interventions empowered individuals to make changes to their own front stoops, sidewalks, and blocks.

The action of "doing" horticulture in cities, as one placemaking tool, may contribute to their residents' understanding of the value of plants, but urban greening also builds a bridge across differences. Located in one of the most diverse communities in the United States, Queens Botanical Garden uses plants and beauty as the common language to connect diverse cultures. In Philadelphia, people of all cultures, races, and incomes felt the negative impacts of the city's large-scale vacant land epidemic, which opened the door for a citywide commitment to cleaning and greening.

Finally, what are the long-term implications of placemaking in urban areas? Especially when beautification may be a vehicle for gentrification,[91] programs such as the Greenest Block in Brooklyn need to assess those implications. Research suggests that urban planners, designers, and ecologists should implement "just green enough" strategies to avoid urban greening that leads to gentrification.[92] This strategy focuses on what "green" looks like for existing working-class residents, rather than for the benefit of new residents or development. In many cases, small-scale neighborhood projects are preferred over large-scale civic projects (e.g., parks and waterfronts) that concentrate revitalization resources and tend to stimulate gentrification.[93]

In addition to the type of urban greening project, the residents' engagement in these efforts matters. For example, Philadelphia residents have been able to use the greened lots as playgrounds, picnic areas, and community gardens. Indeed, in some cases residents become more resilient and resist displacement when greening projects are community driven, are shaped by local community concerns, and promote community activism.[94]

IMPROVING THE QUALITY
OF SCIENCE EDUCATION

Underlying the complex problems faced by many urban communities is an undereducated citizenry, the result of underresourced and underperforming school systems. Good job opportunities, overall community safety, and environmental sustainability are much more likely in communities with a citizenry that has been adequately educated and that recognizes the importance of science in today's economy. The US National Academy of Sciences underscores this point: "Individuals increasingly must understand science and technology to thrive . . . and schools accordingly are challenged to provide high-quality science learning experiences to all students."[1]

Science education in US public schools suffers from too little time devoted to the subject, a shortage of trained science teachers, traditional curricula that focus on memorization rather than engaging students, and limited resources for interactive science instruction.[2] In many urban school districts those problems are further compounded by the fact that a higher proportion of their students also suffer from the negative impacts of poverty.

National policies and financial crises have added to the challenges school districts face in trying to provide adequate science instruction. Chief among these policies is the 2002 No Child Left Behind Act, which introduced requirements for the annual testing of students in mathematics and English language arts (ELA) in grades 3–8. The pressure on schools and teachers to have students perform well on the required tests in math and ELA has led to double sessions for these subjects in many elementary schools and almost no time for science.[3] One research study reports that only 19 percent of K–2 classes and 30 percent of classes in grades 3–5 have science instruction on most days of the week, and on the days that science is taught, it is taught for less than twenty minutes in grades K–3 and twenty-four minutes in grades 4–6.[4]

While it is not the only flaw in the way science is taught in urban schools, one that has consistently been the subject of concern has been termed the pedagogy of poverty, whereby instruction in schools with high percentages of low-income students emphasizes the giving of information and directions and the memorization of facts rather than the cultivation of understanding.[5] Compounding the problem, schools with a higher percentage of disadvantaged students who are struggling to perform well on standardized tests devote even less time to science and have a higher percentage of teacher turnover, fewer experienced teachers, and even fewer who are trained to teach science.[6]

Many proposals for improving science education have emerged in the decades since 1958 when Sputnik jolted the United States' sense of its own scientific superiority. But perhaps the most thorough examination of science education and the most workable recommendations for its improvement started with a review, funded by the Carnegie Corporation of New York and the Institute for Advanced Study, of all relevant research on how science and mathematics are learned and how best to prepare all students in those subjects. The resulting report, *The Opportunity Equation*, and two follow-up reports recommended sweeping changes for K–12 science instruction and standards for what students need to do to demonstrate proficiency in each area.

Those changes all revolve around clear evidence that students learn best when encouraged to do authentic science. In other words, students learn to observe, to ask questions, to pose possible answers to those questions, to test those answers, and to draw conclusions that they can then share with one another. As one analysis notes, "Science is not meant to be taught in a vacuum. It provides a critical foundation for understanding the worlds around us. . . . Teaching only the products of scientific work (the facts of science) denies students critical tools of understanding. To get a more complete picture, students also must understand how those facts came to be."[7] This approach to science education is known as inquiry-based instruction. Students engaged in the practice of science are students who actually understand science, and because this type of instruction gives them the opportunity to draw on their own experiences, it also helps to close the gap between the world outside of school and their school experience.[8]

But to achieve effective science education, schools need teachers who are knowledgeable about the practice of science and understand the strategies for inquiry-based instruction.[9] Unfortunately, few elementary and middle school teachers, and not many high school teachers, are likely to have experienced the practice of science themselves. To change their teaching strategies, teachers need professional development programs that engage them with scientists and allow them to experience real-world science. They also need models to show the way to better and more effective teaching strategies.[10]

With the decline in the quality of science education and in the number of trained plant scientists, public gardens have come to recognize their responsibility and role in promoting effective science education in their communities.[11] Many of these science-rich institutions have employed their long experience in providing inquiry-based education programs to initiate partnerships with individual schools, teachers, school districts, and other community institutions, with the aim of revising science curricula and instruction to emphasize scientific concepts and methodologies. Many of these initiatives are focused on the key role of teachers in implementing such curricula and stress teaching the teachers. The resulting programs include not only providing district-approved professional development workshops but also modeling effective teaching strategies and providing teachers with the material they need to guide their students in the practice of science.

As the three case studies that follow will demonstrate, initiatives supporting quality science instruction vary considerably among gardens, but the underlying goals and strategies are consistent: all support students engaged in the actual practice of science and all recognize the importance of empowering teachers. All three institutions have a history of teaching science successfully. To make a difference in their communities, they use that expertise to teach others how science is conducted, how to teach science, and how to counter the pedagogy of poverty that persists in many urban schools. The children involved in the programs described in this chapter are excited about science because of the way it is presented—they are encouraged to observe, to ask questions about what they see, to think of ways to test out possible answers to their questions, and to present their conclusions to their peers.

Supporting Disadvantaged Children in Brooklyn

Located in the heart of New York City's most populous borough, Brooklyn Botanic Garden (BBG) is known for its expertise in plant science. Since 1989, this much-beloved community institution has also honed its K–8 education program into an extremely effective teacher training tool that has influenced science instruction in the classrooms of over three thousand Brooklyn teachers.

The program, known as Project Green Reach (PGR), is the garden's response to the disparity between the science instruction at schools in wealthy neighborhoods, where parent organizations fund extracurricular learning and field trips, and the science programs offered by schools in disadvantaged neighborhoods that do not enjoy such support. PGR's goal is to promote high-quality, inquiry-based plant science instruction for students in grades K–8 in Brooklyn's four hundred Title 1 public and nonpublic elementary and middle schools (i.e., federally designated schools or school districts with a high percentage of students from low-income families). By reaching out to schools in underresourced communities, PGR hopes to foster an understanding of authentic science at an early age and to make the study of science and careers in science options for the children growing up in those communities.

Project Green Reach allows children to observe nature's cycle firsthand, taking part in the cultivation and nurturing of plants and thereby discovering the impact their own efforts can have on the processes of plant growth and development. The teachers have the opportunity to expand their professional skills and share experiences with their peers as they observe and practice inquiry-based teaching strategies.

Each semester, PGR staff and volunteers work with two teachers and their classes at each of twenty schools. Teachers must apply to participate in the program, which costs $200 for the entire semester for two teachers and their classes at each school. That fee covers all components of the program and the resources and materials to support those components, which include two teacher workshops, a ninety-minute in-class lesson, busing to BBG and a sixty-minute guided tour, and a ninety-minute community project visit at the school.

Even with help from the garden's trained volunteers and other garden departments, BBG's educators recognized early on that the two dedicated PGR staff members could not serve all of the Title 1 elementary and middle school classes in Brooklyn. What they could do, however, was to focus on the teachers and train the trainers by using PGR's staff members to model inquiry- and project-based instructional techniques for teachers who, for the most part, had limited backgrounds in science and little training or resources to integrate inquiry-based instruction into their classrooms.[12] Through its semester-long program, PGR staff members educate and support teachers with information and resources and partner with each participating Title 1 school to improve the science instruction available to its students.

Teacher Orientation Workshop

PGR's teacher-centric approach is embedded in the program's structure, starting with an orientation workshop at the garden at which the forty participating teachers are introduced to inquiry-based teaching strategies that emphasize an approach based on student-led projects. PGR staff take the teachers step by step through the program's components, describing how instruction that emphasizes learning by doing fits into each. Because PGR focuses on both elementary and middle school students, the orientation includes strategies appropriate for different age groups (see box 2.1).

BOX 2.1.   Project Green Reach Guidelines

- For grades K–2, the focus is on exploration of the physical world by using the student's five senses. The students then sort and categorize plants based on how they observe them to be similar or different. The teacher serves as a guide to help students develop questions to explore.
- For grades 3–5, the focus is on what science is. Working in teams, students explore the concept of science as a human enterprise, using tools and instruments in their observations. Students develop questions, collect and process data, and look at outside sources for supporting information, with presentations to the whole class at the end of the process.
- For grades 6–8, the focus is on content and building on the students' more sophisticated math and language skills. Because of middle school schedules, students work in teams to investigate different aspects of the same topic and share their findings in presentations. The emphasis here can be on ways to improve their investigations and on broadening each other's understanding of the common ideas.

Courtesy of the Brooklyn Botanic Garden.

During the orientation, teachers experience the practice of science firsthand as they observe and dissect a seed, collect and record questions based on those observations, and brainstorm steps to follow up the questions with an investigation. After choosing one of five curricula topics (Kitchen Botany, Tropical Rainforest, Desert Environment, Bulbs and Flowers, Fruits and Seeds), teachers then pot a plant related to their topic, which they take to their classroom to spark their students' interest and to begin the inquiry process.

PGR in School and in the Garden

A PGR staff member conducts one lesson in each partnering teacher's classroom. A common problem for many elementary teachers is their own inexperience in the most effective ways to teach science. When PGR staff members conduct lessons, the focus is not only on getting students excited about science but also on teaching the teachers how to do inquiry- and project-based science, and on demonstrating how and why that approach is successful. Barbara Kurland, BBG's manager of school programs and partnerships, notes that through the in-school lesson, "teachers have the opportunity to observe best practices of inquiry-based

FIGURE 2.1.   Teachers engaging in a lima bean seed inquiry during Brooklyn Botanic Garden's Project Green Reach teacher orientation workshop.
Photo by Sara Epstein. Courtesy of the Brooklyn Botanic Garden.

science teaching in their own classrooms with their own students in real time. They see the way the students are learning, the 'how' of the method and then the results in terms of their students' responses, including assessment of content knowledge gained, the 'why' it is successful."[13]

The lesson starts with an introduction to the work of a botanist. Throughout the lesson, students are treated as botanists and in that role take the lead in investigating the class plant, during which they speculate on the function of the plant's different parts. Based on that investigation, students design an experiment that addresses at least one of their questions. Finally, students receive plants of their own, which they pot up, care for, and observe for the rest of the semester. The plants are kept in the classroom and serve as the basis for in-class experiments, research, and investigations, all of which the students record.

Before the students visit the garden and after they have experienced the practice of science in their classroom, PGR staff members provide teachers with

FIGURE 2.2.   Student botanist observing a carrot up close during a Kitchen Botany investigation in a Brooklyn public school.
Photo by Kaitlyn Falk Wong. Courtesy of the Brooklyn Botanic Garden.

suggestions and resources for incorporating the garden visit into the classroom experience both before and after the tour. Specially trained BBG staff and volunteers conduct the tour, which includes both a tour of the garden's extensive plant collections and time in one of the education greenhouses, where students can explore plants up close and hands-on. BBG maintains a collection of plants exclusively for schoolchildren to explore during garden visits.

The program concludes at the end of the semester with a teacher-student planting project that allows students to share their botanical and horticultural expertise with the school and the greater community. The planting project is teacher led, but students are involved in its planning and in selecting who will receive the planting. PGR supplies all the plants and planting materials. Projects have ranged from creating plant boxes for the school nurse to planting bulbs at firehouses.

Long-Term Teacher Support

Because changing teaching strategies requires continued support, PGR maintains a website for participating teachers that features resources for projects, suggested ways to encourage students to ask questions, and strategies for guiding students in setting up an experiment. To help teachers better integrate inquiry-based plant science into their lessons, the website includes resources and lesson plans that support the New York State Common Core standards for English language arts and math and the New York City science scope and sequence. For alumni of the program, PGR offers use of the website and full-day professional development programs that provide teachers with resources and materials to support a plant-inquiry unit.

Garden-Based Summer Program

PGR's second component is a three-day-a-week, six-week summer garden-based experience for rising fifth through eighth graders directed by the two PGR staff members with assistance from three summer instructors (usually college students or recent college graduates). Based on their interest in the school-year portion of the program, twelve students are selected each year from those nominated by participating teachers. During their first summer, the students are known as Junior Botanists and focus on ecology (the study of the interrelationships of organisms and their environment) and ethnobotany (the study of how people of a culture and region make use of indigenous plants). Returning students, known as Plant Investigators, undertake intensive experiments with plants and mentor younger students, which helps build their own leadership skills and content mastery. Although the program is very expensive, BBG provides door-to-door bus transportation, which removes an access barrier that many working and newly immigrated families face.

Sonal Bhatt, vice president of education and interpretation, notes that the summer projects often involve growing vegetables, and that "one of the wonderful things about the summer program is that it is culturally diverse and the sharing among participants creates a remarkable setting for sharing food, recipes, and culture around food and cooking."[14]

Midway through the summer program, students go on a three-day, two-night camping trip to Delaware Water Gap, a first-time outdoor experience for many students. According to several of the student participants we interviewed, the camping trip was the highlight of the program because they learned to work together and to depend on each other as they prepared meals, cleaned up, and hiked in the woods. To support the popular summer camping trip, PGR depends on the Youth Opportunities Program of the Appalachian Mountain Club, which offers staff training and reduced fees on camp and cabin sites, and access to canoes, tents, sleeping bags, and other camping gear.

How the Garden-School Partnership Functions

BBG has held contracts with New York City for many years to provide science instruction programs to its schools. Unlike many school districts, the New York

City Department of Education empowers principals with the authority to choose a training option for their staff if they believe it will support the school's learning needs and goals, which are usually discussed with and approved by the school's leadership team. Principals are encouraged to liaise with community partners, which is one of the criteria used to assess school performance.[15]

BBG mails applications to the principals of all eligible schools before the beginning of the school year, but after thirty years, PGR is well known in Brooklyn's elementary and middle schools, and many principals encourage their teachers to apply. Schools provide substitutes so that teachers accepted into the program can attend the orientation workshop and the final evaluation workshop. These workshops are a key element in PGR's efforts to encourage teachers to share and learn from each other's teaching experiences.

At the end of the semester, the principals of schools in the program evaluate its impact on their school and the participating teachers. In recent evaluations, principals noted the significance of the inquiry-based instruction, saying that it made "learning come alive" and helped "generate a higher level of energy and interest for staff and students alike." Because they are well aware that their teachers have difficulty obtaining materials for hands-on science instruction, the principals also recognized the importance of the resources and materials PGR provided. Perhaps most importantly, several principals praised the positive impact of the program on their teachers' scientific knowledge.[16]

PGR's Impact on Teachers and Students

Because the work of science teachers in many schools does not allow the time or the opportunity for collaboration with other teachers,[17] PGR requires participating teachers to attend both the orientation and evaluation workshops. The evaluation workshop at the end of the semester is a special session at which participating teachers evaluate the PGR program's effectiveness, share examples of student experiments and classwork, and explore successful and less successful strategies and lessons.

During the 2015 evaluation workshop, teachers were asked what surprised them the most about the PGR program. The responses were interesting. One teacher was surprised by "how easy it was to implement in the classroom, because it fit right in with our curriculum." Another was surprised by "how much I learned about teaching science through research with my students." Several were surprised by their students' responses to the plants. One said, "Students were motivated to plant and take care of their plants because many students in my class show little motivation in any of their subject areas. This makes me think that including more hands-on activities could motivate my students more and help them enjoy school more."[18]

One teacher was pleased by "how the students came together to learn and worked in groups because they truly put their heart into taking care of the plants. This makes me think that incorporating tasks where the students take the lead is very beneficial." Another teacher noted how engaged her students were during the in-class trip—they were asking so many questions that they made her feel they wanted more science in the curriculum.[19]

Finally, in their written evaluations, teachers noted several improvements in their students' skills, including following up on their own questions through research, developing a scientific investigation, using science vocabulary, understanding the basic needs of a plant, collaborating and communicating with fellow students, and doing math through measuring and graphing.[20]

Based on our interviews with students who participated in both the school year and summer programs and their parents, PGR has made a positive difference in how the students see their future, how they relate to their peers, and how they perform in school. A current ninth grader told us that unlike his experience in previous science classes, which focused only on the surface of an object like a

FIGURE 2.3. Every class participating in Project Green Reach gets a customized tour of the botanic garden, including a greenhouse where they are encouraged to examine the plants up close.
Courtesy of the Brooklyn Botanic Garden.

leaf or a flower, PGR focused on what makes those objects work—the interior. He now wants to be a virologist. Because of the program's emphasis on teamwork, another ninth grader has gone from seeing himself as a loner to deciding that whatever work he does, it must involve dealing with people. A twelfth grader noted how PGR changed the way he thought about the ways one can learn, and he felt he could now take what he learned there and apply it to the world in which he lives. He said that learning was much more than preparing for a test and called it a "preparation for life."[21]

Parents noted in particular their children's enthusiastic response to the program, but also the differences it had made. The parents of Jennifer noted that she had learned a lot about plants and improved her school performance to the point that her teachers took note of the change. Their daughter now wants to be a botanist. Other parents noted the difference made by the camping trip, in particular feeling that their children were more responsible after the trip.[22]

Lessons from Project Green Reach

BBG is a well-established Brooklyn institution with strong support from local political and community leaders. Even with that strength, the garden on its own did not have the resources to improve the quality of science education for all the students in the borough's four hundred Title 1 elementary and middle schools. It chose instead to use its resources to create PGR, a program designed to empower teachers by retraining them to teach science using more effective teaching strategies. As a result, PGR impacts not only the current students of participating teachers but also their future students.

For the many gardens and other community institutions that have public education as part of their mission, PGR offers the following lessons:

For a program to work, it must enjoy a strong institutional commitment. Project Green Reach really became established in 1994 when Judy Zuk, then BBG's president, institutionalized the program by dedicating two full-time, permanent staff positions to it. Zuk then charged the BBG development office with securing funding from foundations and corporations to cover all other costs, including busing students to the garden.

Engage other departments in the program's operations. Because BBG's educators knew they could not carry out such an ambitious program on their own, they involved several garden departments in the program's operations. Trained volunteers lead its very successful garden tours for Title 1 schools and manage the tour's hands-on component using the BBG special school collections. These collections, in turn, are developed and maintained by the horticulture department. The horticulture department also provides the plants and the materials the teachers need to support their hands-on inquiry-based projects.

Focus on programs that support the institution's mission. The garden's mission statement identifies BBG as "an urban botanic garden that connects people to the world of plants. . . . In the Garden, in its community, and well beyond, BBG inspires people of all ages through the conservation, display, and enjoyment of plants; with educational programs that emphasize learning by doing."[23] PGR supports that mission by introducing children to the world of plants, committing resources to the community's schools, and promoting learning through student involvement in the practice of science.

Identify the needs of the program's target audience and strive to meet those needs. To promote effective science instruction, PGR focuses on the needs of the teachers who are being asked to move from teacher-led instruction to student-led investigation. The PGR staff members not only model inquiry-based instruction but provide the materials and the information teachers need to make the change. For students in its summer program, BBG recognizes the difficulties that low-income families would face in transporting their children to the garden for a six-week program, so the garden hires buses to pick up children at their homes and return them each day.

Engaging Students with Their Environment

Named after David Fairchild, a famous American plant explorer, the Fairchild Tropical Botanic Garden (FTBG) in Miami-Dade County, Florida, is an important research institution with major collections of tropical plants. FTBG has always seen education as the driver of its mission to connect people to tropical plants, and the promotion of pre-K through twelfth-grade science education as an integral part of that mission. To that end, FTBG has adopted an approach to improving science education that focuses on engaging all students with their environment based on their individual talents and interests.

In 2002, FTBG educators, working on ways to engage high school students, came up with the idea for an interdisciplinary environmental science competition in which all students could participate no matter where their interests, abilities, or talents might lie. That idea, now known as the Fairchild Challenge, is an annual competition with a multitude of diverse activities designed to involve students in the exploration of the natural world. Its stated goal is to "offer students a clear educational pathway that encourages environmental stewardship, develops leadership in plant science and diversifies the scientific workforce."[24]

The Fairchild Challenge currently reaches roughly 125,000 students each year from 360 public, private, and charter schools. Every year the program staff creates a new theme and menu of challenges for individual students and groups of students. Schools can participate in any number of those challenges, but all run throughout the school year. The best entries from each school are submitted to Fairchild for evaluation by a panel of independent judges. Those entries deemed the overall best are awarded points, and the sixteen top-scoring schools are awarded cash prizes of up to $1,500 to support environmental programs at their schools.

What is unique about the Fairchild Challenge is its appeal to a broad range of students. According to Amy Padolf, the FTBG director of education, a key goal of the Challenge is to open participation to all students and not just those interested in or doing well in science. While all the challenges revolve around issues related to the environment and most particularly the environment of South Florida, they include activities that incorporate the visual arts, theater, music, public speaking, and cooking, as well as the sciences.

A recent Challenge theme, "What's in Your Canoe?," uses as its starting point the sailors who thousands of years ago ventured eastward from Asia to colonize

FIGURE 2.4. Fairchild Challenge activities include the opportunity to learn botanical illustration.
Courtesy of the Fairchild Tropical Botanic Garden.

new lands in sailing canoes laden with food products and plants that would help them forge a new life wherever they found land. Their plants eventually transformed desert islands into bountiful landscapes, and their canoe plants are now found throughout Polynesia. Students are asked to think through which plants they would carry to sustain themselves into the future. (For a detailed list of how that challenge was translated into a broad set of activities, see box 2.2.)

BOX 2.2.   What's in Your Canoe? Fairchild Challenge Activities

- *Design: The Million Orchid Project Mobile Lab.* Students create a design and slogan for the outside of the bus that was retrofitted to enable students to do lab work as part of the Million Orchid project.
- *Environmental Change.* Students choose one plant species, investigate how this species has responded to environmental changes, and document any changes through a five-panel comic strip.
- *Exploring Environmental Sciences.* Students work in small groups alongside environmental experts on research projects in the garden's research labs.
- *Citizen Science: Growing beyond Earth.* In support of NASA's Veg-01 project to see which food plants grow best aboard the International Space Station, students grow plants in their schools, experiment with factors that influence the plants' growth and nutritional value, record their observations, enter the data in an online spreadsheet, and share photos and findings via Twitter.
- *Green Cuisine: Meals for Space Exploration.* Students create food items using plants being developed for growth in space and present their creations at Fairchild's Spring Garden Festival.
- *Botanical Illustrations: Plants from Faraway Places.* Students choose an agriculturally significant nonnative plant used in their everyday life, and through hand-rendered drawing reveal its minute characteristics by highlighting and identifying its parts.
- *Citizen Science: The Million Orchid Project.* Students participate in a research project on propagating and growing endangered native Florida orchids, during which they experiment with factors that influence seedling growth and development.
- *Environmental Debates: Feeding Our Planet.* After researching assigned specific topics related to food security, students compete in the annual Fairchild debates.
- *Research Paper: Growing Food in the Past, Present, and Future.* Students research and write a 1,500-word essay on one of three assigned topics.

Courtesy of the Fairchild Tropical Botanic Garden.

Participating teachers receive benchmarks specific to their class's chosen challenge, but how those benchmarks are achieved is left up to each teacher. Some teachers create an after-school club to work on challenge activities, some make the activities part of classwork, and some work in partnership with other teachers so that multiple classes participate in a single challenge or in multiple challenges.

Expanding the Program through Unique Partnerships

Beyond the annual competition, FTBG has established some unique partnerships that have enabled the Challenge to evolve in interesting ways and have created activities in which students are able to participate in actual scientific research projects. Those partners include universities, a national nonprofit, and a federal agency.

UNIVERSITY RESEARCH ON ORCHIDS AND LIZARDS

Two Challenge activities grew out of graduate student and FTBG research projects connected to an FTBG partnership with Florida International University. Both were citizen science projects driven by volunteers and students. The first, the Million Orchid project, had as its goal the introduction of four different native Florida orchid species into an urban setting as a way to promote biodiversity. As part of the project, middle and high school students tested the impact of a variety of growth factors on native orchid seedlings. The second, Lizards on the Loose, was a middle school activity in which students conducted surveys of the native and nonnative lizards in their schoolyards for a research project led by Florida International University and the University of Rhode Island.

A NATURE CONSERVANCY STUDY OF HEAT ISLANDS

After learning about the Fairchild Challenge citizen science programs, the Nature Conservancy asked Challenge staff to partner in a citizen science project to test the urban tree canopy in Miami and its impact on the heat island effect. Miami is the second-largest heat island in the United States. The conservancy wanted information about the size of the tree canopy and the temperature under and outside the canopy to support its efforts to persuade governments to plant more trees. The FTBG staff challenged elementary school students to collect the data following protocols developed in partnership with the Nature Conservancy. A conservancy intern developed a video to train elementary students to do the work. Fairchild provided participating schools with a thermometer, measuring tape, and a ball of string; the research protocol; and sheets to collect data.

NASA AND GROWING BEYOND EARTH

The Growing beyond Earth project started with a conversation with researchers at Kennedy Space Center. According to Amy Padolf, she and the FTBG director learned about the testing research that NASA was conducting on plant varieties to prepare for long-distance space travel. They offered Fairchild's plant expertise to identify edible plant varieties and the Challenge network of enthusiastic students to conduct all of the replications that the researchers at NASA did not have the space or time to conduct. During 2015, the technical feasibility year, the activity was offered only to high school students. The program is now completely integrated into the Fairchild Challenge and is offered to both middle and high school students as a challenge activity, which means that any school registered for the Fairchild Challenge can participate.

NASA awarded the Challenge a four-year, $1.25 million grant to support the project, in which students test edible plant varieties for growth on the International Space Station. With the NASA funding, the Fairchild Challenge is able to provide all of the necessary materials and training to participating schools. To ensure the consistency of their scientific research, all schools participating in the project receive the same equipment, including a growth chamber, a thermometer/hygrometer, fully developed research protocols, specially designed LED lights, seeds, pots, light timers, and growth medium chosen by the botanists at Fairchild to meet the criteria set forth by NASA.

How the Key Partnership Functions

A key factor in the program's success is the special relationship it has developed with the Miami-Dade County Public Schools, the nation's fourth-largest school district, which stretches over two thousand square miles and serves 345,000 students in 392 schools in rural, suburban, and urban communities. The district's diverse student population is almost 70 percent Hispanic, 22 percent African American or Caribbean American, and 8 percent Caucasian. Almost three-quarters of the students receive free or reduced-cost lunches, and 40 percent of the schools have students who scored a C or below on state-required standardized tests.[25]

Fairchild's partnership with Miami-Dade County Public Schools has been built over many years. It began slowly, with FTBG offering free transportation for field trips to the garden for the district's Title 1 schools. The relationship grew with the inception of the Fairchild Challenge. FTBG staff members engaged the leadership of the district's Division of Math and Science in the design of the original challenges and all of the subsequent challenges to ensure that the projects augment the curriculum, meet the state and national standards, and follow the district's teacher pacing guides. Staff members also work to develop challenges that lend themselves to the regional science fair, which is a major school district priority.[26]

The school district's support of the Challenge has grown over the years, so that the program now plays a larger role in the science instruction of a broad range of students:

- The Challenge is now embedded in the district's entire K–12 curriculum. Initially started as a program to engage high school students in environmental issues, it was so successful that there was a demand for the creation of a middle-school-level set of challenges, which was followed by a demand for an elementary-level set of challenges.
- In 2012, the district initiated a program that established certain requirements for schools with students scoring on average a C or below on standardized testing. The Fairchild Challenge is part of those requirements.
- District schools must apply to be certified as STEM (science, technology, engineering, and math) schools, and one of the requirements is participation in the Challenge.
- The district donated a decommissioned school bus that was transformed by University of Miami School of Architecture students into a mobile research lab of the same caliber as the labs at the garden. The mobile lab travels to middle schools participating in the Million Orchid project to give the students the ability to actively experience the world of research science. The school district pays for the insurance, driver, and fuel.

What Fairchild Contributes to the Challenge

A key factor in the Challenge's continued growth and success is the garden's commitment to the program and its extensive fundraising to ensure that participating schools, teachers, and students have what they need to complete their challenges.

SCHOOLS

FTBG provides all the materials schools will need to participate in the program. To increase students' understanding of and active involvement in certain plant science challenges, participating schools receive a mini botany lab that students can use to conduct very specific plant science experiments. The labs are essentially two shelf racks that include lighting and basic equipment appropriate for the challenge selected by the teachers and the school. To encourage participation, FTBG offers transportation reimbursement to Title 1 schools for Fairchild Challenge events.

SUPPORTING TEACHERS

Each year in August FTBG hosts a Teachers' Information Brunch at the garden, where teachers are introduced to that year's challenges, and in May a Teachers' Celebration Brunch. Because teachers are the partners that make the Challenge work, FTBG staff members work hard to provide them with the materials and information they need to conduct their selected challenge and, in the process, meet district and state subject content requirements. Teachers of core subjects

FIGURE 2.5. Student participants in Fairchild Challenge research activities work with Fairchild's researchers in the garden's laboratories.
Courtesy of the Fairchild Tropical Botanic Garden.

like biology in the Miami-Dade County Public Schools are required to follow a pacing guide to prepare students for the Florida State End of Course examinations. The Fairchild Challenge handbook identifies the state academic standards that each challenge meets, within the description of that challenge's activities, deadlines, and entry requirements. The Fairchild Challenge website includes a Challenges in Depth section, with listings of additional information resources and judging standards for each challenge.

WORKSHOPS FOR PARTICIPATING TEACHERS

Additional workshops are available for teachers who may be unfamiliar with specific research approaches required for some of the challenges. For example, the Challenge offers a workshop designed to familiarize teachers with research protocols and suitable experiments to support the Growing beyond Earth project in partnership with NASA. A similar workshop in support of the Million Orchid project teaches them how to micropropagate the native orchids and how to experiment with factors that may influence their growth and development. Both workshops also provide teachers with the materials they will need to conduct the Challenge activities in their schools.

WORKSHOPS AND PROFESSIONAL DEVELOPMENT FOR NONPARTICIPATING TEACHERS

For teachers who are not participants in the Challenge, Fairchild offers two basic professional development workshops at the garden: one focused on an inquiry-based science curriculum designed to educate students about the relationship between food systems, food choice, and personal health; and one on ethnobotany that explores the connection between culture and plants through hands-on activities.

Teachers who cannot attend the professional development classes at the garden can download course units to use with their classes, including handouts, resources, vocabulary lists, suggested homework activities, labs, and other activities. Available online course units include School Gardens, South Florida Plants and Ecosystems, Ethnobotany, Basic Botany, Plant Adaptations and Conservation, and Tropical Botany.

STUDENT WORKSHOPS

In creating new challenges, Challenge staff members examine the state curriculum, and if they find that a challenge goes beyond material stipulated in that curriculum, they organize a workshop for students. For example, for the Botanical Illustration challenge, students can take a one-day workshop in which they work outdoors with professional artist mentors, learn about local plants, and draw plant life. For the Environmental Debate challenge, the program has partnered with the University of Miami debate team to create a workshop to familiarize students and teachers with the rules of British Parliamentary Debate. For the Growing beyond Earth and Million Orchid projects, students can take a workshop that teaches them how to communicate their research, including conducting a literature search as well as analyzing and visualizing data.

Impact of the Fairchild Challenge

Fairchild Challenge staff members use several tools to track and evaluate the program, including frequent teacher and student surveys, a final survey at the end of the school year, facilitated teacher discussion forums and interviews, direct observation at school sites, and the quality of the student entries. As Padolf notes, in addition to their focus on content, administration, communication, and effectiveness, the evaluations are designed to give the staff feedback on three questions: "What effect do we have on students' environmental awareness, scholarship, and stewardship? How many students, teachers and schools are we reaching, and to what extent? What components of the program are relevant for the teacher and the implementation of the program?"[27]

The student evaluations indicate that 86 percent of the participating high school students can discuss the importance of plants, 85 percent say they know how to help the environment, and 70 percent express an increased willingness to preserve the environment.[28]

Of the teachers surveyed, 99 percent noticed an increase in their students' interest in the environment, 98 percent noted an increase in the students' awareness of environmental issues, and 94 percent reported that their own knowledge of the environment and environmental issues had increased. In response to questions about their reasons for participating in the program, 100 percent of the teachers identified the value of the learning activity, and 94 percent identified the relevance of classroom subject matter to the learning activity and the hands-on nature of student participation. Furthermore, 98 percent intended to participate in the program the following year.[29]

Lessons from the Fairchild Challenge

With its emphasis on reaching all students, the Fairchild Challenge has worked to allow students many avenues through which they can engage with their environment. Few institutions are as robust as the Fairchild Tropical Botanic Garden, which teems with scientists, educators, horticulturists, and professionals, all of whom support the Challenge, but the broad appeal of the program, its cultivation of partners, and its use of the internet to create an information network are strategies that many institutions can emulate. Among the lessons to be learned from the Fairchild experience are the following:

Closely tie the program to the institution's mission. By engaging students in the study and care of plants and the natural world, FTBG educators have created a program closely aligned with the garden's mission, which stresses the importance of increasing a knowledge of plants and gardening.

Find a primary partner with similar goals to give the program a solid base. The Miami-Dade County Public Schools was a natural fit for the Challenge, and involving the district in its early planning and continued development resulted in the program's expansive and growing connection to its primary audience.

Create imaginative programming to achieve your goals. The Challenge works to break down the barriers that exclude students who are not necessarily interested in science by focusing on the roles that plants and science play in every part of their lives.

Explore multiple avenues for the target audience to participate in the program. The goal of the Challenge is to engage all students with their environment. To accomplish that goal, the program's activities are designed to provide entry points that would appeal to students with different interests and talents, including the visual arts, science, writing, working with tools, and cooking, among others.

Explore every opportunity to expand and grow a program. By making their resources available to local universities and government agencies, the Challenge staff and the garden's administration create possibilities for new partnerships and new ways for students to be involved in authentic science.

Chicago's Science Career Continuum

Unlike the training-the-trainers approach of Project Green Reach and the Fairchild Challenge's efforts to involve all students in the natural world, the Science Career Continuum at the Chicago Botanic Garden (CBG) focuses on grooming a relatively small group of promising students for careers in the sciences over a long period of time.

College First, the continuum's initial project, launched in 1994 as a pilot program with the goal of exposing youth, especially African American and Hispanic students who are underrepresented in science fields, to a variety of careers at museums that specialize in STEM fields. Initially the program focused on green industry careers and was structured as a straight internship, with no academic components. Twelve juniors and seniors from three Chicago high schools participated in the program each year.

By 2002, staff members recognized that the junior year in high school was too late for interested students to successfully prepare for undergraduate careers in science, and so they launched Science First to serve as a feeder program for College First. Over time, with input from students, evaluators, and funders, both programs became more focused on science research and college, and a postsecondary component was added. All three form CBG's Science Career Continuum, which works to foster an interest in science as a career among those underrepresented in the field, including women, African Americans, and Hispanics and targets Chicago public school students who have the capacity and the interest to study science, but not the resources or opportunity. The overall goal is to guide participants into college and more specifically into the sciences.

Science First

Depending on the age of the student, Science First is a free, two- or four-week, on-site summer science program for forty middle school and early high school students. The program's intensive, inquiry-based instruction is designed to introduce students to basic ecology and garden resources. In addition to boosting scientific knowledge, the program works to improve students' analytical skills, increase their comfort with science, and help them gain familiarity with careers in the natural sciences.

The garden recruits public school students from all over Chicago, using science teachers as the primary point of contact. Every year, CBG mails a Science First information packet to each science teacher in grades seven through ten. The packet includes applications, fliers, and a cover letter asking the teacher for help in finding science students who might be interested. For schools new to the program, CBG staff members give presentations for parents and students to explain the program's requirements and the importance of treating it as a serious commitment. In the application, students include a recent report card, describe their interest in science and the program, answer questions about school and interests, and, with their parents, sign an agreement to participate.

Competition for the forty slots is stiff. Garden staff members look for applicants with an interest in and the potential to conduct science and a passing grade point average, but most importantly they look for students who demonstrate a commitment and ability to come to the program every day. Priority is given to those from diverse, low-income families with no college background.

Parents and accepted students are invited to the garden for a Saturday orientation before the program begins. In addition to a description of the program and a tour of the garden facilities the students will use, the orientation includes dates for student presentations, a review of the student code of conduct, and an explanation of how absences are handled.

HOW THE PROGRAM WORKS

Because of the garden's distance from Chicago, buses are hired to transport participating students to and from designated bus stops in the city. Many students spend up to four hours in a daily commute, but from their enthusiastic response to the program, most feel it is well worth the time.

A team of CBG staff and middle and high school science teachers directs the sessions. Seventh- and eighth-grade students participate for two weeks, ninth- and tenth-grade students for four weeks. For the ninth- and tenth-grade students, participation in Science First is a paid internship. Students are at the garden from nine o'clock in the morning to three o'clock in the afternoon, five days a week. Daily activities include both classroom observation and investigation guided by the teacher, as well as hands-on science lessons in the field. Students learn about the garden's river, prairie, and woodland habitats, and in the process touch on topics such as genetics, soil ecology, and food webs.

Students use CBG's resources to learn about the practice of science. They improve their observational skills in the display gardens; they interview plant geneticists in the CBG research labs to see what real scientists do; they conduct quadrant studies in the garden's woods and prairie; and they discover the practice of ecology while exploring natural habitats.

With hands-on, nature-based science activities, sixth- and seventh-grade students new to the program are introduced to how science applies to their daily lives, how it is practiced at the Chicago Botanic Garden, and how it is critical to many potential careers. Eighth- and ninth-grade students focus on science inquiry and process and more advanced ecology and botany. They work in groups of three or four on a self-selected research project, which they describe in a public presentation at the end of the session.

Through inquiry-based instruction, students learn the importance of asking questions and seeking possible answers. They also learn that in science there is not necessarily one right answer to questions, and that scientists build on one another's knowledge to identify possible solutions to problems.

College First

The College First component of the Continuum is both a paid high school internship and a college preparation program for twenty eleventh- and twelfth-grade students. It builds on the inquiry-based activities of Science First, whose participants are encouraged to apply.

The seven-week summer portion of the program includes guest speakers, an environmental science practicum, and internship opportunities with staff. Students spend two days each week in group inquiry-based instruction, using CBG resources to learn about nature and science. Two days are spent working one-on-one with a staff member to learn more about specific plant-based career areas

FIGURE 2.6. Chicago Botanic Garden Science First students build hoop houses to create different temperature conditions as part of an experiment researching the impacts of climate change on plants.
Courtesy of the Chicago Botanic Garden.

and to develop job skills and workplace etiquette. Students typically work in the Horticulture Department, the Plant Genetics and Seed Biology Lab, the Seed Bank, the Education Department and Camp CBG, the Butterflies and Blooms Exhibit, Soil Ecology, or Conservation Biology. The students are mentored by garden staff, undergraduate interns, and graduate students from CBG's master's and PhD program in plant biology and conservation offered in collaboration with Northwestern University. The fifth day is dedicated to field trips to other horticultural institutions (such as Garfield Park Conservatory), a university science lab, local natural areas, or places that illustrate career options available in the sciences.

To improve their research and presentation skills, students engage in a research project and present their findings to an audience that includes CBG staff, family and friends, mentors, and community partners. Generally, students research a topic related to their work with their mentor or a garden staff member. Students who successfully complete the seven-week program get three college credits through the City Colleges of Chicago.

The program continues during the school year, with CBG staff mentors meeting monthly with students to help them develop the skills and find the resources to make the transition from high school to college. Those sessions include introductions to science careers, résumé writing, tutoring, and help in navigating the college application process.

Postsecondary Programs

For students who stay with the program, graduate from high school, and enter college, CBG offers several internships and mentoring programs:

- Research Experiences for Undergraduates (REU) internship in plant conservation. The garden and Northwestern University provide REU interns a ten-week summer science-based program under the supervision of a CBG research scientist.
- After they obtain an undergraduate degree, College First graduates can apply for five- and ten-month Conservation Land Management (CLM) internships. CLM interns assist professional staff at the Bureau of Land Management, National Park Service, or US Forest Service. Interns also receive a stipend and expand their résumé and professional connections.
- College First students seeking a graduate degree are eligible for scholarships enabling them to attend the master's or PhD programs the garden offers jointly with Northwestern University.

How the Partnerships Function

CBG recognized early on that its ambitious program to attract urban youth to science careers would require help from other nonprofits and educational institutions. Over the years, the garden has cultivated a network of partnerships that support different aspects of the Science Career Continuum. The partners it seeks must have a mission and programming that align with what Jennifer Schwarz Ballard, CBG's vice president for learning and engagement, calls "the gaps in the garden's expertise or capacity." As she notes, "We developed these partnerships in an effort to provide our students with all the resources they might need, but at the same time, not take away from what the Chicago Botanic Garden does best."[30]

The key long-term partners supporting CBG's Science Career Continuum include

- Northwestern University master's and PhD programs in plant biology and conservation, which support the stepwise mentoring component of the program;
- City Colleges of Chicago's Wilbur Wright College Bridge Program, which provides free college credits to College First graduates;
- Chicago Scholars, a local, nonprofit college support network, which offers summer workshops and sponsors a Scholars College Fair, a First Look Career Conference and Fair, and an Annual Onsite Admissions Forum;
- Chicago Public Schools, which serves as a major recruitment partner; and
- Hive Chicago, another recruitment partner, a network of nonprofits dedicated to connected learning and a venue for member organizations to share opportunities for youth and to pass on those opportunities to other networks.[31]

To maintain these partnerships, Schwarz Ballard says, she and other staff members meet with each partner annually "to confirm their continued participation and discuss any additional needs or partnership opportunities. As the educational context changes, we are always looking for ways to adapt the program to best meet our students' needs, and so may ask collaborators to consider changing or expanding their work with the Garden. We also account for any changes in partner organization operations and consider whether we need to bring in additional support."[32]

The partnership with Northwestern University is the only one with a formal, regularly renewed contract, under which the Chicago Botanic Garden serves as the Botany Department for the university, and its research staff as Northwestern faculty, with classes taught at both Northwestern and the garden.[33]

FIGURE 2.7. Chicago Botanic Garden College First students extract DNA as part of their one-onone mentorship with a garden research scientist.
Courtesy of the Chicago Botanic Garden.

Impact of the Science Career Continuum

Through regular assessments and long-term tracking, program staff members evaluate Science First and College First to determine changes in students' content knowledge, attitudes and interests, and academic success. The evaluation tools include concept mapping, pre- and post-attitude assessments, attendance rates, report cards, staff observation, and mentor feedback. The garden also does long-term tracking of program graduates through an incentivized annual survey.

ASSESSMENT RESULTS

Garden staff members use the regular evaluation process to improve the program for the next year. Based on the results included in its 2008–15 report, the program is achieving its goals:

- Science First participants increased their content knowledge by 18 percent over the course of the four-week program.
- College First students' academic progress was measured by their performance in environmental studies. All students earned college credit in Environmental Studies 101 through the program's partnership with

Wilbur Wright College. Sixteen of them received an A in the course and two received a B.

- In terms of Science First students' attitude toward science, there was a 20 percent increase in positive attitudes toward science over the course of the program, 86 percent believed that they were good at science, and 93 percent agreed that scientists have interesting jobs.
- College First students felt more positive about their ability to have an impact on the environment, and 82 percent indicated that they would consider a science career path.[34]

LONG-TERM TRACKING

Since 2008, 100 percent of College First seniors have graduated from high school, and 94 percent matriculated at a two- or four-year college. Of those, 81 percent have reported earning a postsecondary degree or professional certification by age twenty-five. Of those, 3 percent earned a doctorate, 4 percent earned a master's degree, 64 percent earned a bachelor's degree, 8 percent earned an associate's degree, and 8 percent earned a professional certification.[35] Of those who earned a degree, 65 percent majored in a STEM subject, with 48 percent majoring in science. Schools where College First program graduates have studied include Georgetown University, Northeastern Illinois University, DePaul University, Wright Junior College, the University of Minnesota, Loyola University, Cornell University, Iowa Wesleyan University, Carleton College, and both the Chicago and Urbana-Champaign campuses of the University of Illinois.[36]

INTERVIEWS

Beyond the statistics, the value of the program is revealed in the stories of its graduates and their teachers. One of the College First alumni interviewed for this book, Melissa, is now a graduate student conducting research in horticulture at the University of Illinois, where she received her undergraduate degree. Like all College First students, she was required to do a research project and to present her findings to CBG staff and research scientists, a very intimidating prospect for a high school student. However, as she describes the experience, she "felt like a teacher and relished the idea that she might know something more than others."[37] The experience motivated her to eventually become a professor.

Science First teachers and College First mentors interviewed about their programs noted how important it was for students to have exposure to those working in the sciences and to see a world outside their normal sphere. Terry Moore is a teacher at Fiske Middle School in Chicago's largely African American Woodlawn section, which he describes as a "concrete jungle." According to Moore, exposure

FIGURE 2.8. A College First student presents her summer research to the public at the Chicago Botanic Garden.
Courtesy of the Chicago Botanic Garden.

to the botanic garden "softened" his students. For students who had never been exposed to a peaceful outdoor setting, just being in a garden was therapeutic. The experience helped the students with "goal-setting and thinking longer term." As an educator, Moore tries to keep his students moving forward to break the cycle of poverty and violence. By participating in Science First and going to the botanic garden in a largely affluent suburb outside the city, students who were normally apprehensive about leaving the neighborhood "thought they could go further—maybe to another state, or even another country."[38]

Alumni frequently attribute their desire to pursue science to the Continuum's strong mentorship program. One said, "Before I went to College First I was interested in science, but I never thought I would have the ability to be a scientist. My mentor treated me like a real scientist, not a high school student, and that gave me so much confidence. It really changed what I wanted to do."[39]

Lessons from the Science Career Continuum

The Science Career Continuum is a unique program in many ways, but its creation and evolution offer lessons in partnership development and long-range program management.

Some programs require a long-term strategy to achieve success. The strength of the Science Career Continuum is that it supports plant science education over the long term, starting with programs for middle and high school students and continuing with programs for college and graduate students. At every level, students are aware that they are part of a continuum and are exposed not only to the work of older students but also to that of career scientists.

Cross-department collaborations strengthen the institution and the initiative. The Science Career Continuum works because of the garden's institution-wide commitment to nurturing future plant scientists and leaders in the field. Even at its inception, College First was a cross-departmental collaboration, and over the years, every single department at the Chicago Botanic Garden, from horticulture and grounds to research, communications, and development, has been instrumental in making the program a success. That commitment is evident in the attention the garden staff members pay to the needs of their target audience— urban, underserved, low-income youth from diverse backgrounds. In creating the program, staff members realized that transportation would be a major issue for that audience and a major obstacle to the program's success, so they built into their plan funding for buses to bring the children to the garden. Later they recognized that for these children to go into science careers, they would need to develop the skills and the resources to go to college, so they included college preparatory skills in the instructional plan.

Mentorship adds to the impact of any education program. The emphasis on mentorship is perhaps the greatest strength of the Science Career Continuum. Mentoring is a basic component of the Continuum and involves every CBG department and every student. CBG staff and Northwestern University graduate students mentor college students, who in turn mentor College First participants, who in turn mentor Science First participants. The program provides students with a whole community of support, which results in friendships between summer program instructors, CBG staff, older students, and younger students that help learners with social issues, school issues, and career issues. The program also creates opportunities for interactions between young people from different neighborhoods.

Successful Strategies for Promoting Quality Science Education

Despite differences in their approaches to promoting quality science education, all three of the programs examined in this chapter share certain strategies that are worth noting and emulating. Each program builds on strong institutional support for community outreach. Each networks and makes efficient use of resources to maximize impact. Each draws on the organization's strengths as a scientific institution with expertise in teaching science and particularly inquiry-based instruction that engages students in authentic science; and each promotes the role science plays in everyone's life and the viability of science as a future career.

Building on Institution-Wide Support

Institution-wide support is the bedrock on which all three programs rest. Project Green Reach, the oldest of the programs, depended on outside funding during its early years. Brooklyn Botanic Garden decided that the program was too important to leave to the vagaries of granting agencies and made PGR staff permanent full-time employees. Fairchild Tropical Botanic Garden is a research institution, but its education department recognized that unless children were drawn to careers in science, there would be no future tropical plant scientists. To draw children to those careers, FTBG had to make science instruction more exciting and more open to all children. With its strong education program and commitment to environmental sustainability, the Chicago Botanic Garden recognized that to have future plant scientists, urban children need to be involved in nature, and to do that, the garden needed to bring them from the city into nature.

Maximizing Impact through Partnerships

Jennifer Schwarz Ballard's comments about her program's partnership experience are a good guide for all institutions entering into such arrangements: "Each organization is doing what they do best in partnership for greater impact. In essence that is the point of the partnership—to be efficient about how you use your own staff, focusing on your own area of expertise, and to let others, with other skills, do what they do best."[40]

All three institutions use staff, institutional facilities, and financial support to achieve the maximum impact. Project Green Reach has two full-time staff members and three part-time summer assistants. Each year it supports forty teachers in twenty schools and radically changes the lives of twelve students in its intensive on-site summer program. PGR has done that by

- recognizing the key role teachers play in quality science instruction and the importance of supporting teachers with instructional models;
- offering them the opportunity to practice science and to confer with fellow teachers about what works in the classroom;

- serving as an ongoing source of scientific information; and
- providing wherever possible the basic resources teachers need to help students learn science by doing science.

Fairchild has three full-time staff members who support the participation of 360 schools in the Fairchild Challenge in southeastern Florida. They have done so by creating an exciting program that incorporates the varying talents of children of different ages in the business of science, and by empowering their teachers to structure the program within the school.

Science First/College First chose to focus on an in-depth, long-term program for a small cohort of students over the course of their middle and high school careers. It recruits mentors from throughout the garden to support the students in their scientific investigations, so students experience firsthand the work of professionals in the field. When students move on to college, the program continues that support through continuing contacts with mentors and through summer internships.

Promoting Science and Careers in Science

All three institutions recognize their responsibility in ensuring that children see science as a future career option and that those with an interest in science can pursue that interest. Countering the decline in the number of university botany programs,[41] the Chicago Botanic Garden partnered with Northwestern University to create a graduate program in botany whereby the garden would provide a significant part of the university's botanical research capacity and faculty. Fairchild created a fellowship program for graduate students in tropical plant science and works with the University of Miami and Florida International University to involve them in Challenge projects. Its research department uses high school interns in its labs. Brooklyn Botanic Garden created a Garden Apprentice Program (GAP) open to eighth- through eleventh-grade students who participated in Project Green Reach's summer program. GAP participants assist with Children's Garden programs, work with garden educators and horticulturists, and learn to create education stations.

What Other Institutions Can Do

The programs featured in this chapter are based at large, well-established gardens with strong board and community support. The goals that motivated the creation of these programs, however, are like those of many other public horticultural institutions—connecting people to plants, promoting the value and study of plants, and improving plant science education. To accomplish these goals, the model programs focused on supporting teachers and promoting a method of instruction that works. If gardens want to have an impact on urban communities and to build a broader audience for their institutions, the surest way is through education. Few urban communities have the resources their schools need, and many are open to offers of assistance.

All gardens are engaged in science education in some way, whether by offering tours to school groups, creating children's gardens on their campuses, offering summer camps, or having special weekend programs geared to children. But these programs depend on parents and schools bringing children to the garden and paying for programs and transportation, which are often beyond the resources of many inner-city schools and parents. Taking the onus off urban schools and urban parents does not require the resources of a large garden or paying to transport children to the garden site, but it does require outreach to schools that need help as well as a willingness to take the expertise of garden staff outside the confines of the garden. Programs that work in the garden are often not that hard to replicate in the schoolyard or the school classroom. Aside from the recreational aspects, the curriculum for a summer science camp is not very different from one that would work in a public school. In tailoring garden programs for the classroom, garden educators need to become familiar with state curriculum standards for K–12 science education (generally available on state department of education websites) and recognize that they will have the most impact if they help teachers meet those requirements through effective instruction techniques.

By demonstrating inquiry- and project-based instruction to teachers in urban schools, garden educators can help them be better teachers. As all the case studies in this chapter demonstrate, students who are encouraged to ask questions and are actively involved in exploring possible answers to those questions are better students, more cooperative students, and more interested in school.

ACCESS TO HEALTHY FOOD AND PROMOTING HEALTHY LIVES

What contributes to a healthy community? According to HealthyFamiliesBC, "Healthy eating is the foundation for a healthy life and healthy communities are places where everyone has access to fresh, nutritious and affordable food."[1] Certain principles underlying this report from British Columbia are worth noting: good health is the result of an individual achieving a state of complete physical, mental, and social well-being, and people cannot achieve their full potential unless they are able to control those things that determine their well-being. While these principles place much of the responsibility on the individual, certain assets or resources must be present within the community for individual efforts to succeed. People who feel a part of their community will thrive, and their communities, in turn, will also prosper. But this is a two-way process: individuals need to feel that their local government is aware of and responsive to their needs.

As a society, we expect basic services to be available in every community, but one familiar resource—a full-service supermarket—is frequently absent in low-income urban neighborhoods.[2] The lack of access to the full range of grocery items, and especially fresh fruit and vegetables, is often associated with well-chronicled high rates of obesity, high blood pressure, and diabetes.[3] The complex urban challenge of accessing healthy food is most acute for low-income families of color.[4] In Denver, 49 percent of low-to-moderate-income neighborhoods city-wide lack convenient access to grocery stores, nearly one in six individuals in the city are food insecure, and 53 percent of adults and 31 percent of children are overweight or obese.[5] Twenty-five to thirty million Americans live in urban areas that are more than a mile from a supermarket or large grocery store, and more than half of these people are themselves low-income.[6] The inability of residents to purchase affordable and nutritious foods locally has earned their neighborhoods the label of food deserts, which are defined as "urban neighborhoods and rural towns without ready access to fresh, healthy, and affordable food,"[7] or "urban areas with ten or fewer stores and no stores with more than 20 employees."[8] In addition, in areas where poverty is highest, food prices are often significantly higher and food quality lower when compared to more affluent urban areas.[9]

Without full-service markets, residents in urban neighborhoods have few options. They can shop at local corner stores that offer limited selections of highly processed, energy-rich items;[10] if they don't own a car, they can take a taxi or public transportation to the nearest supermarket, which substantially increases the total cost of weekly shopping;[11] or they can frequent fast-food restaurants with menus that are often filled with fried, high-carbohydrate offerings.[12]

The 2013 *Access to Healthy Food* report makes clear that living closer to healthy food retail outlets is among the factors associated with better eating habits and decreased risk of obesity and diet-related diseases.[13] But the arrival of a supermarket may not by itself change long-standing eating habits. A recent study of the impact of a new supermarket on a low-income, predominantly African American neighborhood in Philadelphia reported that after six months only 27 percent of residents surveyed adopted the new supermarket as their main retail outlet, and only 51 percent shopped there at all. Further, the presence of this full-service market had no statistical effect on the body mass index (BMI) of those surveyed, but did appear to have an impact on individuals' appreciation of having more food types available to them.[14]

What would prevent residents from changing their buying habits from local convenience stores to supermarkets with a wider selection and overall lower prices? One factor might be the established relationships with proprietors of neighborhood stores, especially if those proprietors provided informal store credit to help residents through lean times. Another factor could be a fear that the greater choices in the larger store could lead to impulse buying and higher overall food bills. A final consideration could be a general community resistance to a corporate entity descending on its neighborhood.[15] All three factors proved significant in a large study conducted in Leeds, England, where a full-service supermarket opened in a neighborhood previously labeled a food desert. While the majority of area residents recognized and appreciated the shortened commute to a market, many survey respondents didn't change their unhealthy eating habits, and a high percentage of shoppers were wary of overspending on what they considered luxury items in the new store.[16]

While supermarkets are the most obvious means of improving food access and diets for the urban poor, often they are neither the only solution nor the best one. In some North American cities, municipal officials have recognized that urban agriculture can contribute to more livable and resilient communities.[17] Community gardens are an attractive and increasingly popular alternative means for getting fresh produce to urban consumers.[18]

The current grassroots-driven community gardening movement took shape in the 1970s when residents created community gardens in major metropolitan areas across the country. More recently, this movement has seen a tremendous upsurge. Two million more households reported participating in community gardening in 2013 than in 2008, a 200 percent increase in five years.[19]

But this movement has also faced enormous challenges. Even in seemingly supportive cities like New York, the relationship between community gardeners and the municipality can be negatively affected by zoning restrictions, pressure on established sites from developers, and unsympathetic bureaucrats focused solely on economic returns and an increased tax base.[20] To counter these obstacles, municipally employed urban planners need to embed community gardens into long-term planning efforts and to increase the amount of land permanently assigned to such activities.[21]

Recent studies demonstrate that community gardens can have greater economic impact than may generally be recognized. Domenic Vitiello and Michael Nairn studied community and squatter gardens in Philadelphia in 2008 and found that the value of the produce exceeded $4.9 million, an amount greater than the combined sales of all of Philadelphia's farmers' markets and urban farms.[22] A study of New York City community gardens found that within five years of a community garden's opening, neighborhood property values increased by as much as 9.4 percent and continued to increase over time.[23]

The community gardens that do succeed in resource-deficient urban cores can have a real human impact. In a 2014 study of community gardening in Baltimore, Maryland, most participants reported that they increased the quantity and diversity of vegetables they ate, especially during the growing season. Further, they shared their excess produce with relatives, neighbors, coworkers, church members, and even passersby, thus providing a tremendous multiplier effect to the nutritional impact of their gardens.[24]

A study in Denver, Colorado, examined the variables affecting the consumption of fruits and vegetables, including physical activity, self-rated health, BMI, perceptions of neighborhood aesthetics, neighborhood socioeconomic status, and educational level. Each variable was weighed against whether the survey respondent gardened or not. The researchers found that, regardless of other variables, people who participated in either community or home gardening reported higher levels of fruit and vegetable consumption than nongardeners, and that 56 percent of community gardeners consumed fresh produce at least five times per day.[25] These findings are corroborated by a 2018 study that found that low-income elementary school students who participated in school gardening programs had significantly more in-home availability of vegetables than those in a control (nongardening) group.[26]

When community gardens serve as sites for both food production and community education about food preparation, nutrition, and healthy lifestyles, they can become powerful tools of community development.[27] In our research we found a number of public gardens and their partners that have created programs to ensure that their communities have the assets to promote the health of their residents. What follows are descriptions of four public garden programs that, through various means, have forged meaningful partnerships to improve the health of community residents and of the cities themselves.

Bronx Green-Up

A 2011 report from NEWSONE for Black America identified New York City as one of the nine worst food deserts in the United States and reported that sections of the Bronx had the lowest density of full-service supermarkets of any community in the city.[28] The paucity of food choices is certainly related to the prevalence of poverty in the borough and is a major impediment to the creation of healthy neighborhoods. In 2019, City-Data reported that 61 percent of Bronx residents had family incomes of less than $60,000 and the median household income in the borough was $37,525, compared to $62,909 citywide.[29] While the Bronx may be the most impoverished of New York's five boroughs, growing income inequality is a problem throughout the city. The city comptroller has reported that New York City has proportionately more people in the lowest income brackets than the United States as a whole, fewer people in the middle brackets, and more people at the top.[30]

In response to Bronx residents' concerns about the viability of their neighborhoods, in 1988 the New York Botanical Garden (NYBG) created the Bronx Green-Up (BGU) program to support and organize volunteer efforts aimed at cleaning up garbage-strewn vacant lots in the borough and transforming them into green factories of fresh produce.

As the program's first director, NYBG selected Terry Keller, former director of Green Guerillas, a pioneering New York City community garden organization. With her experience in community gardening, Keller had the knowledge to navigate city agencies and develop strategies to best utilize NYBG's knowledge and horticultural resources to support community efforts.

The program's first major project was to support the efforts of Karen Washington and Jose Lugo to turn a junky, rubble-strewn lot in the Bronx into a

FIGURE 3.1.   Bronx Green-Up participants at a seeding workshop.
Courtesy of New York Botanical Garden.

community garden. Alerted by a community member about their work, Keller
showed up in the BGU van asking whether she and the program could help. From
this initial contact, the Garden of Happiness became the first BGU-supported
community garden. Washington went on to found La Familia Verde, a coalition

of five gardens in the Bronx that has operated a farmers' market for fifteen years, providing much-needed fresh fruit and vegetables to the community. Today the Garden of Happiness is so well established that it views itself as BGU's partner rather than as a recipient of assistance and resources. The garden is often featured on NYBG tours and serves as a site for NYBG workshops.

As it has evolved in the years since being formed, BGU has adopted the mission of providing "horticultural education, training and technical assistance to Bronx residents, community gardeners, urban farmers, local schools and community organizations."[31] The group uses a combination of tools: workshops and certificate programs; technical assistance; site visits; plant material, soil, compost, and mulch for specific projects; partnering with school and youth programs; and special events. BGU provides the technical support and materials needed for community gardens to succeed, but the on-site work of preparing beds, constructing infrastructure, planting, weeding, and harvesting is all done by local residents. In this way, the community gardeners develop a sense of ownership and accomplishment.[32]

In 2018 NYBG sponsored 323 events that reached 4,600 individuals and included thirty-six workshops on various horticultural topics, either at community sites or at NYBG; site visits; technical consultations; and plant deliveries for seventy-one community gardens. Urban gardeners looking to gain additional skills can participate in any of three certificate training options: Pruning (four sessions), Soil Is Alive (three sessions), or Grow More Vegetables (six sessions). To receive a certificate, participants also complete community service hours related to their training, which varies for each class. In addition, those in the Grow More Vegetables class must commit to a group project that passes on something they have learned to others in their community. Recent projects included creating a school garden, providing a seed-starting workshop to an after-school program, and building raised vegetable beds in a church garden. The NYC Compost Project hosted by NYBG and the NYC Department of Sanitation also offers a Master Composter certificate course. This train-the-trainer program has a thirty-hour community service requirement.

How the Partnerships Function

BGU forms strategic partnerships in response to community requests, and staff work to match the needs from a particular request to an organization that can help address that need. As is stated on the program's website, "The program is the visible presence of the Botanical Garden beyond the Garden's gates, inspiring NYC residents to get involved in improving their communities through greening projects."[33] In 2012, for example, BGU partnered with the International Rescue Committee to cobuild New Roots Community Farm, working with hundreds of volunteers over forty workdays. In 2017 it partnered with the Morris Campus (a cluster of four public high schools) and a local organization to build the Morris Campus Educational Farm, creating a production farm with a meditation area from a former underutilized handball court. BGU has also partnered with the Osborne Association's job preparedness program for young people who have been involved with the justice system. By emphasizing civic engagement in its job readiness program, this project is similar to the programs for prison-involved individuals described in chapter 4.

Other notable partnerships with Bronx-based or citywide organizations have included Farm School NYC (to increase urban food production and access), NYC Parks GreenThumb (a citywide community gardening program), NYC Parks TreesCount (a census of city street trees), Butterfly Project NYC (promoting planting and preservation of native plants in urban settings), and the Bronx Land Trust (a collection of sixteen unique community gardens managed by community gardeners). In 2015 a new partnership was formed with the Bronx Hot Sauce project, a collaboration with Chef King Phojanakong, Small Axe Peppers, Grow NYC, and a variety of Bronx community gardens, school gardens, and urban farms. Each spring, the project distributes serrano pepper plants to Bronx community gardeners, who harvest peppers throughout the summer and fall and receive four dollars per pound of harvested peppers.[34]

How It Works

NYBG has faced challenges at times in garnering public-sector support for the program, but has managed to leverage private resources and partnerships to continue its success. That success is predicated on several factors. First, the program gained the quick approval of the NYBG board of trustees because of its grassroots origins and its alignment with the institution's mission as "an advocate for the plant kingdom."[35] Second, although BGU is based in NYBG's horticulture department, it works closely with the children's education department, enabling it to draw on the expertise of both. A third factor is the sheer number of sites and individual lives the program touches. There are more than two hundred community and school gardens throughout the Bronx; of these, BGU works with approximately seventy-five gardens per year. Last, the program is based on sharing knowledge and resources to enable community gardens to succeed and become independent.

FIGURE 3.2. Karen Washington at the Garden of Happiness.
Courtesy of New York Botanical Garden.

Impact of Bronx Green-Up

BGU uses a database to track the number of participants at each workshop, class, and special event, as well as the number of gardens visited and school and youth gardens assisted. For example, in fiscal year 2017, Bronx Green-Up reached 4,184 people. In addition to these metric data, all participants in the certificate programs fill out evaluations regarding new skills gained, knowledge learned, and practices implemented. Bronx Green-Up's Advisory Committee, composed mostly of community gardeners, also provides important feedback to the program.[36] All of these evaluative data have enabled NYBG to rightsize the program to provide just enough assistance to be supportive of individual gardens without making those sites dependent on long-term help.

The current BGU director, Ursula Chanse, has been with the program for more than fifteen years and is inspired by the fact that individuals working in the community gardens, many of whom are volunteers, are dedicated to making their neighborhoods greener, more productive, and healthier. As a native New Yorker who loves green space, she feels that "what's challenging for me being in the city is also what makes my job so rewarding. I see the impact of these spaces every day."[37]

Since BGU's creation, Karen Washington has also seen a major change in how Bronx community members feel about visiting NYBG. What was once perceived as an elite institution for the few now feels like a welcoming green space for all. As she notes, "The Botanical Garden really reaches out to the community, making people feel welcome, not just invited."[38]

But it's the changes in the individuals involved in these gardens that are most significant. In a BGU blog post, a young man shared how his time with Bronx Green-Up had changed his outlook: "As an individual born and raised in the Bronx, I have adapted to buildings, construction, and pollution—the 'City Life.' I used to think that planting a tree in front of your house was the best way of being green. After working for Bronx Green-Up, however, my point of view has changed completely. Donating plants and providing services to local community gardens and schools has opened my eyes to the beauty of the Bronx."[39]

Lessons from Bronx Green-Up

BGU primarily supports existing community gardens by providing both educational and horticultural resources that these sites need to succeed and grow. The BGU approach could be replicated in other large metropolitan areas where a network of community gardens already exists. Using their education programs and horticultural expertise, public gardens can identify resources that community gardens need to reach their full potential and establish programs that provide needed resources at little or no cost.

As NYBG long ago discovered, there can be many challenges to developing such a program:

- Is the community garden led by a trustworthy organization?
- Does the community garden post hours when it is open to the public?
- Does it allow anyone to join, regardless of ethnicity, religion, or residential address?
- Are representatives of local community organizations supportive or obstructive of this program?
- Is the community garden prone to vandalism or theft?
- Are there external funders who will commit to the program for multiple years? What do those funders require?

Green Corps in Cleveland

As a Rust Belt city, Cleveland, Ohio, fares little better than the Bronx. It has one of the highest rates of residential poverty of any urban center in the United States. Based on 2019 data, 33.1 percent of all city residents, and 43.5 percent of children 6–11, live below the poverty threshold.[40] Once one of the largest and wealthiest cities in the US, Cleveland now ranks fifty-third in population, with 379,800 residents in 2019, a 0.5 percent decline from the 2010 census.[41]

In 1996, the Cleveland Botanical Garden (CBG) used a small grant to create the Green Corps program to introduce at-risk youth to organic farming methods and to provide them with opportunities to learn about gardening, nutrition, and environmental issues. Both this program and CGB itself can trace their roots back to the early decades of the twentieth century. A 1916 donation by Eleanor Squires of her collection of 250 horticultural books to the Garden Club of Greater Cleveland formed the basis of what would become the Cleveland Garden Center and, later, the Cleveland Botanical Garden. Throughout the institution's history, it has maintained a strong focus on children's education and community beautification.[42]

In the years since the program's conception, both it and the botanical garden, now a unit of Holden Forests and Gardens, have experienced considerable change. Green Corps has expanded considerably in both numbers and scope and has secured funding from a variety of sources. Under the banner "Growing Youth, Growing Food, Growing Cleveland," the program focuses on helping participants build life skills while also increasing the availability of fresh produce in inner-city areas.

How Green Corps Works

The program is "growing youth" by providing constructive activities to counter the more destructive influences of city life. Students age fourteen to eighteen may participate for up to three years. Total yearly participation averages fifty individuals. The program currently has four learning farms in the neighborhoods of Midtown, Slavic Village, Fairfax, and Buckeye-Woodland, with one part-time and three full-time staff members year-round and four additional full-time seasonal staff from May to October.

To participate, students must submit an application, receive the recommendation of an adult, and be interviewed. Green Corps is more interested in recruiting underperforming youth than straight-A students. Students are paid a minimum wage for each hour of their participation, typically twenty hours per week, and receive half a high school credit for each year of participation. In their first year, participants focus on learning organic gardening methods and developing team-building skills. Year two includes more in-depth curricular choices, such as public speaking and résumé building. In the third year, participants focus on community outreach projects, such as giving simple growing lessons to in-house daycare providers and volunteering at Cleveland MetroParks. Some third-year participants also take community college courses.

The second goal of the program is to increase the availability of fresh, organic produce in underserved neighborhoods. Through their cultivation of a range of vegetables and fruit, the teens improve their own diets and, in many cases, influence what is served in their homes. They harvest thousands of pounds of vegetables and fruit each year to sell at the four farm sites and at local farmers' markets each week. To meet the needs of their clientele, items are priced below market rates and WIC stamps or other alternative forms of payment are accepted. But because of this marketing approach, profits have declined over time, which puts more pressure on identifying external funding sources to sustain the program.

Finally, Green Corps is "growing Cleveland" by transforming vacant lots into thriving, productive garden plots and by bringing back a sense of pride to residents in often neglected neighborhoods. Using provided tools and trucks to haul away trash and compostables, the teens learn how to safely remove both rubble and vegetation from the lots and to prepare them for planting. In the process, the

FIGURE 3.3.   Green Corps youth working at the weekly farmers' market.
Courtesy of Cleveland Botanical Garden.

teens themselves become advocates for their communities, and by meeting and talking with local residents, they help to reduce vandalism, dumping, and other harmful activities.

How the Partnerships Function

To achieve maximum impact, the Green Corps program reaches out beyond its farm sites and into high-visibility venues. Through a partnership with the Cleveland Indians baseball team, in 2017 and 2018 Green Corps teens maintained three raised beds at the team's stadium, Progressive Field, where they grew perennials, herbs, and vegetables; and some additional produce boxes in the players' parking lot were used by the Indians' chef to prepare healthy dishes for the team's players.[43] A second partnership with Professor Mary Gardiner of the Department of Entomology at the Ohio State University has focused on urban agriculture pollinator research, with an emphasis on urban nesting and pollinator services. For this project, the Green Corps teens recorded sightings of pollinators at each of the farm sites.

Through partnerships with organizations such as the Indians and Ohio State Entomology, Green Corps teens learn that the city has much more to offer than the narrow choices that may be available in their neighborhoods.[44]

Cleveland Botanical Garden has reaffirmed the program's importance in its strategic plan, but it is not without challenges. Among the greatest are developing lasting relationships with community organizations, dealing with staff turnover, providing a consistent level of leadership at each of the program's farm sites, and adjusting the program each year based on available funding. While a sense of mutual trust has been built with local groups over time and through achievement, these other challenges are ongoing and need to be addressed each year and at each farm site. Despite these challenges, CBG has continued its commitment to the program.

Impact of Green Corps

In June 2015, a research team from the Mandel School of Applied Social Science at Case Western Reserve University released a *Green Corps Final Evaluation Report* for the years 2009–14. Self-reports from Green Corps participants in 2009 and an evaluation process led by the research team in 2012–14 showed that Green Corps students engaged in healthier eating behaviors; developed greater concern for local environmental stewardship and for global environmental issues; displayed positive personal growth, including increased self-confidence and pride in their new knowledge, skills, and work ethic; improved their ability to communicate with others; and were more successful when working in teams and adapting to often challenging circumstances.[45] The students also contributed to their families' weekly food budget through the produce they brought home, which further enhanced their sense of self-worth and responsibility.

Many participants reported that the enhanced life skills they gained from the program, combined with workshops on résumé writing, interviewing, and the college application process, helped them either to gain acceptance into college or to secure desirable job offers. Several participants expressed an interest in college majors related to what they had learned, including urban planning and botany.

Lessons from Green Corps

Green Corps is an intimate program in which farm counselors work one-on-one with teens who are mostly average students and do not naturally gravitate to leadership roles but who are trying to improve their lives. More than 70 percent of survey respondents in 2014 indicated that Green Corps helped them become more of a leader. As one respondent put it, "I kind of like just thought of it myself, and then they mentioned it to me like, 'Yeah. You're becoming more strong leader-wise and we need you to be like that,' because I realized that I was the only person there with experience."[46]

But to manage and sustain such a program requires highly trained, sensitive, and committed farm managers and counselors. Public gardens attracted to this model must first consider

- the time and expertise required to train staff;
- start-up costs associated with acquiring land for gardens, clearing sites (which often includes toxic cleanups), and building infrastructure (raised beds, fencing, irrigation lines);
- developing trusting relationships with neighbors and community groups;
- components of the training for participating teens (on-site horticulture classes; workshops on interviewing, résumé building, and applying for jobs; sessions on community building, etc.); and
- ways of recognizing and rewarding teens for their efforts.

Growing to Green in Columbus

The Franklin Park Conservatory and Botanical Gardens (FPC) in Columbus, Ohio, initiated the Growing to Green program (GtG) in 2000, with the initial goal of establishing a one-stop shop to support community gardening. The program, as conceived, is a perfect fit for FPC, whose mission calls for "elevating quality of life and connecting the community through educational, cultural and social experiences."[47]

While Columbus, like other Northeast and Midwest cities, struggles with issues of poverty and homelessness, its demographics are less severe than many. Median household income is just above $50,000, and the poverty rate is 26.3 percent. The 2019 population was 879,000, making Columbus the largest city by population in Ohio,[48] and also one of the fastest-growing large cities in the US.[49] The city is approximately 55 percent white, 28 percent African American, and 6 percent Hispanic.[50]

In the years since its inception, GtG has assisted more than 250 gardens throughout the greater Columbus area. The program's longtime coordinator, Bill Dawson, explains that the program works both with groups hoping to start gardens and with already established adult community and youth gardens, as well as with neighborhood beautification groups and public schools. GtG provides the necessary resources to ensure the gardens' success and long-term sustainability.[51]

Given the small GtG staff (Dawson and one intern) and the enormous number of gardens they serve, Dawson has established a network of twelve hub gardens that, according to the program's website, "serve as gardening education centers for their communities and as inspirational resources for anyone interested in community gardening."[52] In addition, Dawson chairs a monthly Community Gardening Steering Committee, including representatives from the city's offices of health, water and sewer, zoning, and recreation and parks, as well as the city council. Together the members of the committee make decisions about how best to support and advocate for community gardening in the city.[53]

School and Youth Gardens

A critical component of GtG is its work with schools and youth groups. According to Dawson, "We serve many community gardens that have students involved long term and seasonally. We serve school gardens and early childhood centers through outreach programming."[54]

Gardening can affect young people socially, intellectually, and nutritionally. The garden is a nonthreatening environment in which cultural differences can be explored, older or more experienced gardeners can assist novices, and children of all backgrounds can celebrate together. Multiple studies have shown that children are more likely to eat vegetables they have grown themselves.[55] This enthusiasm for fresh produce can be infectious and can be shared with other members of the gardener's family.

Much has been written about the value of school gardens. Students learn focus and patience, cooperation, teamwork, and social skills; they gain self-confidence along with new skills and knowledge in food growing; they become more fit and healthy as they spend more time outdoors; they start choosing healthy foods over junk food; and they can develop a sense of ownership and pride in their improved schoolyards.[56] In addition, the garden can be an outdoor classroom for instruction in biology, math, cultural studies, and language arts.

School-based gardens often get started with much fanfare and then fail or fade after a few years. Such gardens face many challenges: continued maintenance over the summer months when classes are not in session; turnover of students, which can lead to a loss of momentum or enthusiasm; loss of a lead teacher, which can result in a dissipated effort; lack of funding for plants and materials; or a change in the school's administration or its priorities. As Dawson points out, the key to success with school gardens is to establish trust and an authentic partnership with the administration and teachers. It is also important to explain how the garden will enhance the mandated curriculum and not be a burdensome add-on.[57]

The school garden at Berwick Alternative Elementary School on the southeast side of Columbus has all the elements necessary to succeed. With the support of the school administration, Keith Jorgensen, an eighth-grade math teacher, started and manages the school's garden. Jorgensen also uses the garden as a study lab to have students solve geometric math problems. GtG helped with its initial development and continues to support its operation. Franklin Park's Women's Board members volunteer their time to help the garden, including building new raised beds and cleaning up border areas around the perimeter. Dawson frequently visits the garden to offer encouragement to the student gardeners and horticultural tips to Jorgensen. On one of Dawson's spring visits, two eighth-grade students were on site; both are enthusiastic members of the Garden Club that Jorgensen organized. Both planned to return to the garden on Wednesday evenings during the summer to water, weed, and harvest.

In contrast to the Berwick school garden, the Highland Youth Garden is a highly developed half-acre site. The garden was created in 2009 in response to the closing of two recreation centers in the Berwick community. Caring local individuals began working with the neighborhood elementary school and youth centers to plan alternative activities for young people, and the idea of a garden program emerged.

The Highland Youth Garden serves multiple schools and youth programs in the Highland neighborhood. Three hundred seventy five children visit and work in the garden during the school year, and two hundred in the summer. It now includes considerable infrastructure: a hoop house, a pergola, an irrigation system, benches, and a perimeter fence. Much of this has been built by individuals from supporting organizations—local Eagle Scouts, Mormon missionaries,

FIGURE 3.4. Reading to schoolchildren at the Highland Youth Garden.
Photo by Bill Dawson. Courtesy of Franklin Park Conservatory and Botanical Gardens.

master gardeners, and Boys and Girls Club members. The garden also recently received a grant from the Battelle Corporation to fund an increase in its paid staffing.

Through its extensive social network, GtG helps the garden identify and reach out to potential users and provides recognition for its achievements. Highland's paid staff member, Jazmyn Benjamin, views the teaching of gardening skills as secondary to providing a safe space for young people to congregate, make cultural connections, and provide for family food security.[58] We visited while Benjamin taught a lesson on basic plant parts to kindergarten and first-grade students, who were engrossed by both the botanical information and the taste of the rhubarb and strawberries Benjamin used as examples.

How the Partnerships Function

From its inception, the GtG program has been supported and enhanced through a partnership with the Scotts Miracle-Gro Company (SMG), which itself has been a presence in central Ohio since 1868. The relationship between the Franklin Park Conservatory and SMG developed gradually as areas of mutual benefit were identified and trust gained. Eventually the GtG youth program became a central locus for that partnership.

In addition to the free products and cash awards that SMG provides to GtG-member gardens, Scotts also underwrites the Scotts Community Gardening Academy, which is administered by the Columbus Foundation and led by

Dawson. Leaders of community or school gardens accepted into the academy receive several days of instruction on organizing and sustaining such gardens, along with a binder of supporting materials. Dawson also leads another Academy workshop on overcoming the challenges faced by community, youth, and school gardens. The workshop focuses on proven approaches learned from GtG's long experience and draws on practical advice from the *Community Gardening Toolkit*, which Dawson and colleagues developed and which emphasizes the need to start small, not overrely on one lead person, choose an appropriate site (soil, solar aspect, security), and build a strong sense of community.[59]

Impact of Growing to Green

According to the 2018 FPC annual report, GtG has helped start, strengthen, or sustain approximately three hundred community or school gardens.[60] To achieve this level of success, GtG has needed support from more than just SMG. Numerous churches, school districts, and civic associations provide sites and volunteer assistance or help with promoting the program. Others that offer resources and opportunities include the City of Columbus, the Franklin County government, local land banks, a tool lending library, the Ohio State University Extension, the Columbus Foundation, the Lowes Corporation, the Greenscapes Landscape Company, and the FPC Women's Board. It is Dawson's responsibility to communicate with all these partners and to ensure that all parties' needs are being met.

The community, school, and youth gardens supported by GtG are enhanced by their participation in the program. Whether by connecting a community or school garden with resources, supplying instructional materials to garden leaders and teachers, identifying volunteers to assist with physical tasks, or simply offering moral support, the small GtG staff has had an outsized impact on the community and youth gardening movement in greater Columbus.

Lessons from Growing to Green

In his twenty-five years working in the program, Bill Dawson has learned a number of important lessons. Chief among these is that a great deal can be achieved with minimal staffing if the right partnerships are formed. In the case of GtG, those are the partnerships with the established hub gardens that serve as information disseminators, and with the Scotts Miracle-Gro Company, which generously donates both materials and funding to the program. But it is also important to recognize the role played by the dedicated leadership of Bill Dawson in the program's growth. Finally, because of its small budget, the program benefits from and requires the full support of the Franklin Park Conservatory and Botanical Gardens to survive.

Sankofa Farm at Bartram's Garden

Created in 1728 by the famed botanist John Bartram, Bartram's Garden is generally recognized as the oldest botanical garden in the United States. Today the garden is a forty-five-acre National Historic Landmark surrounded by one of the most economically depressed neighborhoods in Philadelphia, with a large West African population.

Rather than shielding itself from a local community with many challenges, Bartram's Garden has embraced the cultural richness of its neighbors. While it may seem surprising that such a historic institution would take on such a progressive role, it is actually consistent with the garden's mission "to inspire audiences of all ages to care for the natural world,"[61] and it reflects the character of John Bartram, who trekked thousands of miles to satisfy his curiosity about and passion for the plants of this new country.[62]

Looking both back to the garden's history and toward its future, the board of the John Bartram Association recently approved a Vision 2025 plan, with two of its five identified priorities being Community and Education and Agriculture and Food Sovereignty. Bartram's sees food as the vehicle for building bridges across cultures through crops grown, recipes shared, and dishes tasted.[63]

The garden is acting on these two priorities primarily through the operation of Sankofa Farm on a portion of its property. In recognition of the neighboring community's West African heritage, the farm's name comes from the Akan language and refers to going back and fetching what might have been forgotten, such as the plants of residents' native lands. To develop this African focus for the farm's core purpose, codirectors Chris Bolden-Newsome and Ty Holmberg engaged in many conversations with community gardeners, student interns, and local leaders.

The need for Sankofa Farm could not be greater: of Southwest Philadelphia's 78,140 residents, fully 30 percent live below the poverty line, and 15 percent of residents are first-generation immigrants from Africa, with the largest Liberian immigrant community in the US.[64]

There are three components to Sankofa: a farm involving neighborhood teens, on which fifteen thousand pounds of produce are grown each year; community gardens, with sixty families in the program; and farmers' markets, to distribute low-cost, organic produce at nearby sites. The project has evolved from a sole emphasis on food access to a focus on three themes: being spiritually rooted, intergenerationally connected, and African Diaspora centered.[65]

FIGURE 3.5. Welcome sign at Sankofa Farm.
Courtesy of Bartram's Garden.

FIGURE 3.6. Volunteers working at Sankofa Farm.
Courtesy of Bartram's Garden.

The teen program involves roughly twenty youths and operates both after school during the school year and all day during the summer. The first-year interns know little about farms or farming, so farm managers emphasize a curriculum focused on both gardening and the development of leadership skills, such as finding one's passions and assuming responsibility for one's actions. Returning students focus on operations management, including running the farm stands and serving as program ambassadors. The main objective is to get teens on a college or career path.

Sankofa also operates weekly farmers' markets that offer low-cost, organically grown produce to local residents. The markets fulfill two additional goals of Sankofa: increasing food sovereignty for low-income residents and offering the vegetables from the homelands of West African immigrants.

How the Partnerships Function

When the farm was created in 2011 as the Community Farm and Food Resource Center, there were five partners: Bartram's, the University of Pennsylvania Urban Nutrition Initiative, the Pennsylvania Horticultural Society (PHS) capital fund, the City of Philadelphia, and the Philadelphia Orchard Project. Unfortunately, in 2016 the University of Pennsylvania pulled out due to financial constraints, forcing a reexamination of the importance of the farm. The remaining partners recognized that closing the farm would erode the community trust that had been built after much hard work, and they remain committed to the program. Subsequently, the farm was integrated under Bartram's operational management and renamed Sankofa Community Farm.[66]

Currently, the city leases the land to the John Bartram Association for one dollar per year, and PHS purchases up to eight thousand vegetable transplants from Sankofa for distribution to urban farms and gardens throughout the city. The total annual budget of Sankofa is approximately $245,000, which includes staff leadership, youth stipends, and supplies. Almost 99 percent of these funds are generated through contributions, including grants, corporate sponsorships, and individual donations.

Why Sankofa Works

Sankofa would not have been created if not for the full support of the executive director of Bartram's Garden, Maitreyi Roy, and her board. To increase the total impact of Sankofa, Bartram's has engaged the community in Sankofa's management and now includes a Leadership Circle—made up of African American and migrant residents from nearby apartment blocks—that meets monthly to consider issues and to advise Bartram's on farming and planning goals. Bartram's has also undergone a collaborative planning process with members of the community. As part of this effort, it has actively recruited new board members from the neighborhood and has hired fourteen local students to assist with Bartram's river education program.

Impact of Sankofa

Through feedback from its Leadership Circle and student interns, Sankofa is a model program that engages community members in its development, meets identified community needs, and evolves in response to changing circumstances. The twenty local teens that the farm employs each year have a high school graduation rate of 95 percent, versus 65 percent overall in their high school. Even more impressive, 85 percent of these young people go on to enroll in college. Each year the farm hosts more than 1,500 volunteers, providing those individuals with meaningful activities in a healthy outdoor environment. The garden also harvests more than fifteen thousand pounds of vegetable types preferred by its African clientele, providing a vital link to these individuals' homelands.[67]

The farm and its components are not going to eliminate the difficulties that locals face in terms of assimilation, employment, and declining schools. But it is succeeding in building an authentic, trusted bridge to community members who recognize the garden's role in improving their lives.

Reflecting on the case studies in this chapter, it is clear that moving a community from a failing to a healthy state requires the participation of multiple entities: municipal agencies, social service organizations, community activists, for-profit organizations, and cultural and religious institutions. Each can play a role in making fresh produce more available and more appealing to those living in food deserts. By involving low-income residents in growing their own food, such initiatives will also enable them to feel in control of their diet and not at the mercy of what is available at the corner store. As gardens spring up in previously under-served neighborhoods, communities experience the ripple effects of reduced vandalism, trash, petty crime, and loitering.

Because they are focused on something so fundamental to human culture—growing plants—public gardens can make substantial contributions toward the creation of healthier communities. To be successful in such efforts, however, gardens must identify and respond to the needs of their constituents and regard all individuals and groups, regardless of background, abilities, or economic status, as members of their target audience.

TRAINING AND EMPLOYMENT PROGRAMS

Chronically high rates of poverty among inner-city residents cannot be separated from the associated problems of poor-quality education, high rates of single parenting, and degraded or absent housing. But certainly one of the greatest contributing factors to widespread poverty is the lack of job opportunities and consequently high rates of unemployment. Indeed, research shows that lower poverty rates coincide with decreases in unemployment, and, conversely, rising unemployment pushes poverty rates upward.[1]

Among the obstacles to employment faced by urban residents are those employers who screen out black and other inner-city applicants by not placing employment ads in citywide news media. Some employers often ignore applicants from urban public schools. Others avoid welfare programs or state employment services as referral sources.[2]

While these entrenched forms of institutional discrimination will not be reversed soon, two occupations not traditionally associated with urban centers—agriculture and landscaping—offer inner-city residents new employment opportunities.

Urban agriculture in US cities dates to the colonial era. Boston, Philadelphia, and other East Coast cities reserved commons for the grazing of farm animals, and most private homes included a small orchard and vegetable garden that provided fresh produce for the house and a source of income when there was excess produce. Urban agriculture has thrived and waned in the centuries since, with particularly strong growth during the victory garden movements of the First and Second World Wars.

Metropolitan areas are major markets for fresh produce, but most of that produce either comes from rural farms or is shipped in from other states and countries. Although the common belief is that agriculture and urban development are fundamentally incompatible, since the 1980s cities have seen vacant lots, former warehouses, and even building rooftops become centers for agricultural production.

Several societal trends have coalesced in the past 3–4 decades to drive this burgeoning urban farming movement. One of these is the loss of manufacturing and the associated depopulation of many Rust Belt cities.[3] The population of Detroit, Michigan, for example, dropped from 7.1 million in 1970 to 680,000 in 2010.[4] Accompanying this outmigration was a proliferation of vacant lots. DataDrivenDetroit puts the number of vacant, unimproved lots in the city at 91,000, or 26 percent of all parcels.[5] Estimates vary on the total area covered by vacant lots, with some as high as forty square miles. Even lower estimates put the total at greater than twenty square miles, which is larger than all of Manhattan.[6]

The hopeful sign is that this vacant land has inspired the proliferation of entrepreneurial urban farmers in Detroit, with farms that range from the diminutive two-and-a-half-acre Earthworks Urban Farm to the massive Hartz Farm, which

FIGURE 4.1.   Austin Farm, part of Windy City Harvest.
Courtesy of Chicago Botanic Garden.

grows hardwood trees on three hundred reclaimed acres.[7] As blighted streets and neighborhoods transform into urban farm sites, a concomitant reduction in crime, vandalism, littering, and vacancies has resulted.[8]

It should be noted that urban farms are distinct from community gardens. Urban farms produce food for sale or as a charitable donation to others. In addition to the production of fruits and vegetables, some urban farms involve animal husbandry (chicken farming being particularly popular), apiculture, or floriculture.

A second factor driving the neo-urban farming movement is the desire by many socially conscious individuals to reduce the carbon footprint of the food they purchase by buying locally.[9] According to a 2010 report, an individual's "carbon foodprint" (as contrasted with a carbon footprint) includes all emissions from growing, processing, transporting, and selling food and getting it home and cooked, as well as emissions from discarding or recycling the leftover waste products. On this basis, it is estimated that Americans average a carbon foodprint of over twelve thousand pounds of carbon dioxide equivalent (CO_2e) each year per person, or 21 percent of their total carbon footprint.[10] The closer the food's source is to where it is purchased and consumed, the greater the reduction in the carbon foodprint.

Urban farms are also a good source of employment for previously unemployed or underemployed individuals. Jobs in the growing or processing of fresh produce have an advantage over more technical work, such as plumbing or electrical contracting, in that they require less training and are scalable based on the resources available. An individual can start by farming a single vacant lot or be part of a larger collaborative that farms several acres.

In a study based in New York City, urban farmers described the positive impact of their food production on a number of community factors, including public health through improved food access and nutritional information, environmental education, increased connections between producers and consumers, improved job readiness of neighborhood youth, sense of community through the creation of safe spaces, economic development by providing a model of profitable urban food production, and environment stewardship by converting vacant lots into community green spaces.[11]

To grow food for a profit, urban farmers need adequate training. Public gardens, with their emphases on both horticulture and education, are ideally positioned to provide that training. Many public gardens today feature extensive displays of edible crops and instructions on how best to grow them. One of the most notable is the Heartland Harvest Garden at Powell Gardens in Kingsville, Missouri, "where every tree, shrub, flower and groundcover is part of the story of where our food comes from."[12] Other public gardens also have expertise in variety selection, marketing, and business management, just the skills that start-up urban agriculturists need to learn.

Job Training for Youth

One exemplary program that addresses the needs of would-be city farmers is Windy City Harvest (WCH), the Chicago Botanic Garden's (CBG) continuum of training programs in sustainable urban agriculture. The program can be traced back to the origins of the Chicago Horticultural Society, the parent of CBG, which starting in the 1890s held large horticultural shows to display the best produce and flowers being grown in the region. Windy City Harvest was started in 2002 to address the largely inadequate training that young people received in the installation and programming of school gardens, which resulted in many of those gardens failing, especially over the summers.[13]

In 2003, US senator Richard Durbin, Democrat from Illinois, challenged CBG to create something more meaningful for inner-city youth, and the garden's response was the Youth Farm program to provide job and life skills training as well as horticultural education. With the success of the Youth Farm, a potential funder approached CBG about developing a similar strategy for ex-offenders and difficult-to-employ adults. In 2007, CBG developed Corps, a transitional jobs program, and simultaneously developed the Adult Apprenticeship program to provide a continuum for both Youth Farm and Corps graduates.[14]

WCH now employs over two hundred Chicagoans annually, including low-income people facing barriers to employment based on inadequate education, a criminal justice record, or lack of interview skills. The program operates through four levels or tracks: Youth Farm (underserved teens, college-bound youth, and vocational students), Corps (justice-involved seventeen-to-twenty-one-year-olds and former military), Apprenticeship, and Entrepreneurship and Careers.

WCH Youth Farm Track

The Youth Farm program annually educates and employs eighty to ninety teens from low-income communities at three farm sites in Chicago and one in nearby Lake County. The program provides training in both sustainable urban agriculture and social-emotional learning (SEL) principles. SEL is defined by the Collaborative for Academic, Social, and Emotional Learning as "the process through which children and adults acquire and effectively apply the knowledge, attitudes, and skills necessary to understand and manage emotions, set and achieve positive goals, feel and show empathy for others, establish and maintain positive relationships, and make responsible decisions."[15] The young people in this program graduate with enhanced skills and abilities for coping with life's challenges.

WCH Corps Track

Each year, the Corps program employs thirty to forty justice-involved individuals and veterans in closely mentored, full-time paid transitional jobs and supports them in finding full-time, long-term employment. Participants work at a youth farm from Monday through Thursday, and on Fridays crews participate in Roots of Success and Job Club, which together provide work readiness and literacy skills. The program offers training in developing a résumé and cover letter, preparing for interviews, and searching for jobs. Corps crew members have the opportunity to earn a ServSafe Food Handler's Certificate, a Roots of Success Certificate in Environmental Literacy, or a Certificate of Completion from CBG.

The two highest tracks, Apprenticeship and Entrepreneurship and Careers, address all aspects of establishing a farm, growing crops, and marketing produce. Many participants in these tracks are graduates of the two other Windy City Harvest tracks. An income-based, two-tiered fee structure enables all students to participate in these courses at affordable levels.

WCH Apprenticeship Track

The WCH Apprenticeship track is a nine-month classroom and hands-on certificate course in sustainable urban agriculture. Since 2009, it has been accredited by the Illinois Community College Board in collaboration with the Arturo Velasquez Institute at the Daley College satellite campus of the City Colleges of Chicago. The program provides hands-on horticultural training and teaches job preparedness skills, using a plain-language, team-focused approach to introduce students to production-oriented urban farming systems. All participants must engage in an internship at an existing urban farm, complete program coursework with a grade of C or above, and develop a crop plan for a sustainable farm business. Those who complete these requirements receive an Urban Agriculture Certificate and credits that can be applied to an associate's degree. CBG is hoping to offer an associate's degree in sustainable agriculture in the near future.

In 2012, CBG initiated an incubator program for WCH Apprenticeship graduates, designed to support those interested in starting a small farm business but who need a little extra help along the way. The incubator is home to up to six farm businesses per year.

Overall, the Apprenticeship program has been remarkably successful. Ninety-one percent of program graduates have started their own businesses or are employed within the local food sector. Many of the program's graduates hold positions that require considerable responsibility or entrepreneurial effort, including manager of rooftop gardening, coordinator for the Revolution Brewing Company, manager of edible landscapes for Christy Webber Landscapes, cocreators of Dirt Doll Organics, and manager of Mariposa Gardening & Design. Even the current WCH sales coordinator is an Apprenticeship graduate.[16]

WCH Entrepreneurship and Careers Track

Since 2013, the Entrepreneurship and Careers track has focused on supporting entrepreneurs as they start or manage farms and farm-related businesses. WCH has also added specialty certificates that enrollees in the Entrepreneurship track can obtain: Business and Entrepreneurship for Local Foods, Rooftop Farming, Edible Landscapes, Aquaponics and Vertical Farming Systems, Value Added Products, and Season Extensions. These industry-specific certificates are additional credentials that allow small farm business owners to maximize their earning potential through the recognition of advanced skills.

Each Entrepreneurship class meets five hours per week, for a total of seventy contact hours. Through a combination of classroom work, hands-on experience, and field trips, instruction focuses on applying sustainable urban agriculture techniques to the production of vegetable crops for sale in commercial markets. The last four weeks of the apprenticeship program focus on the business side of farming, and each student develops a crop plan to implement after graduation.

The WCH Entrepreneurship and Careers track has burgeoned because of a partnership with Lawndale Christian Health Center (LCHC), a Chicago-based health services agency that cares for over fifty-five thousand mostly African American and Hispanic patients annually. The partnership builds on each organization's strengths and complementary missions. The Chicago Botanic Garden's mission, "We cultivate the power of plants to sustain and enrich life," recognizes the role of food plants in promoting health and wellness, the therapeutic benefits of gardening, and the tranquility of green landscapes. LCHC's mission to promote wellness and provide quality, affordable health care for Lawndale and neighboring communities encompasses the determinants of health, including physical surroundings and access to healthy food.

The partnership between these two organizations began in 2005, long before the creation of the Entrepreneurship and Careers track. At that time, WCH was searching for a site to expand its North Lawndale Youth Farm to meet the needs of its twenty youth participants and the growing demand for farm-fresh produce at the weekly WCH farm stand. LCHC not only had a site adjacent to its

FIGURE 4.2.   Windy City Harvest apprentice farmer Stacey Kimmons.
Courtesy of Chicago Botanic Garden.

neighborhood health center but also agreed to purchase WCH produce for its café and to host the weekly farm stand.

This collaboration has grown in depth and complexity in the years since, with each partner respecting and benefiting from the resources of the other. WCH has renovated a former LCHC document storage facility located next to the Lawndale Youth Farm and transformed it into the Farm on Ogden, a year-round center offering training to young people and adults in hydroponics and aquaponics (hydroponics integrated with fish culture), assistance to urban farmers hoping to jump-start their careers, and enhanced access to fresh produce in Chicago neighborhoods.

FIGURE 4.3. Shopper at the Farm on Ogden.
Courtesy of Chicago Botanic Garden.

FIGURE 4.4. Exterior of the Farm on Ogden.
Courtesy of Chicago Botanic Garden.

To have the greatest impact on local residents, the partners created Veggie Rx, whose goals are to increase vegetable consumption for SNAP/Link-enrolled individuals with diet-related illnesses and to eliminate or reduce barriers around fruit and vegetable consumption in North Lawndale.

The sheer size of the Farm on Ogden facilitates both WCH instructional programs and the commercialization of produce grown by program participants. A large-scale aquaponics system includes six aquaculture tanks, four interior beds, a production greenhouse measuring 260 by 96 feet, a smaller greenhouse for starting seedlings, and four aquaponics raft beds. The new facilities allow WCH to train up to sixty class members in commercial-scale aquaponics production and offer weekend seminars to hobbyists and small commercial entities interested in aquaponics.

As envisioned by Angela Mason, CBG's associate vice president for urban agriculture / Windy City Harvest, "The Farm on Ogden provides a single space for a seamless progression from WCH introductory programs to the most advanced."[17]

How the Partnerships Function

Even an institution as well established as the Chicago Botanic Garden cannot create a complex program like Windy City Harvest on its own. WCH program components are supported by the Beginning Farmers and Ranchers Development Program of the US Department of Agriculture's National Institute of Food and Agriculture, the Chicago Park District, and the Chicago Partnership for Health Promotion. Commercial clients include Midwest Foods, SAVOR Chicago, Sodexo Food Services, and Eataly Restaurant.

A key to sustaining these partnerships is effective and timely communication. Mason says, "I talk to Lawndale Christian Health Center folks almost daily, other partners I speak to on a monthly or bi-monthly basis."[18] The WCH goal is to be 50 percent self-funded through commercial enterprises and to have the other half come through foundations and grants.

Impact of Windy City Harvest

For those two hundred individuals annually involved with Windy City Harvest, what they learn and experience through the program can truly be life altering. Because of their previous arrest records, poor or incomplete school performance, or lack of work experience, many had very limited employment options before participating in the Windy City Harvest programs. Since the local and organic food movements show no signs of declining, the skills WCH graduates gain are immediately transferable to jobs or self-employment opportunities. In an interview, one graduate detailed his career plans: "In the future, I'm really hoping to have my own incubator and grow produce and sell it within the community. I want to use my Windy City Harvest education to show communities that there is a better way to eat healthy and live healthy."[19]

Additional benefits for graduates include intangibles like an increased sense of self-worth, as well as income to support both themselves and their families. The supportive structure of WCH also allows participants to grapple with the real-life challenges they are experiencing. Eliza Fournier, manager of community gardening at CBG, has said that "for many of our students, the Green Youth Farm is the only place they get to address issues of access to fresh produce, poor nutrition, obesity, and violence."[20]

In considering the total impact of WCH and its four components, it is clear that the program is having a positive impact on communities by providing increased access to fresh produce for urban residents and improved neighborhood appearance and cohesiveness. In addition, programs such as these change residents' overall impression of their local public gardens, from exclusive and nonwelcoming sites to institutions that really care about them and their needs.

But as with other programs, it's important to be realistic. WCH alone cannot solve all the job-related problems of inner-city Chicago. In a city with one of the highest violent crime rates in the US and fractious relations between neighborhood residents and the police force, WCH must be seen as one of many options that need to be provided to a population that in the past has too often been ignored.

Lessons from Windy City Harvest

The urban agriculture movement is not limited to Chicago but can be found in cities across the United States. Many public gardens have the expertise and resources to offer training to would-be urban farmers in essentials like organic farming basics, business planning and bookkeeping, employee management, niche market identification, and season extenders. It isn't necessary to replicate as extensive a program as WCH, but before deciding to create a training program, gardens need to do the following:

Determine the extent of urban farming in their coverage area. An organization that can assist with this research is the American Community Gardening Association (https://communitygarden.org), which, among its many functions, supports and monitors urban farms within a locality.

Identify existing organizations whose activities focus on or include support for urban agriculture. In many urban centers, Cooperative Extension operates urban farming programs.

Explore partnerships. Assess whether to partner with a nonprofit to strengthen an existing program; create a new program in urban farming, either alone or with a community group; or serve in a supporting role of providing expertise but not leadership to already effective programs.

Job Training for Veterans

Finding meaningful work can be a considerable challenge for anyone discharged from the military. The reasons are many and complex. As evidence, in September 2015 the Bureau of Labor Statistics reported that 77 percent of post-9/11 veterans experienced a period of unemployment after leaving the service.[21] Based on 2018 statistics, Iraq/Afghanistan-era veterans in the eighteen-to-twenty-four-year-old range had higher rates of unemployment compared to both their nonmilitary counterparts and veterans who did not serve in these wars.[22] Older veterans, ages thirty-seven to sixty-four, had much higher rates of unemployment, highlighting the need for age-based employment interventions for former military populations.[23]

A report commissioned by Prudential found that 64 percent of surveyed veterans had difficulty transitioning from military to civilian life. In addition, many felt that they had the skills to land competitive jobs, but that their experiences were not respected or understood by potential employers. Finally, three in five expressed concerns about cultural barriers to their gaining meaningful employment.[24] This is consistent with the findings of a 2014 RAND Corporation report that cites the inability of both veterans and employers to match military skills to civilian job requirements.[25]

Our society learned in the post-Vietnam era that returning veterans cannot be ignored, regardless of how one feels about the military campaigns in which they engaged. Veterans of that war have had much higher suicide rates than veterans in general, and suffer from disturbingly high rates of both psychological and physical disabilities. This cohort of veterans often cite a perceived lack of support from family, society, and the Veterans Administration as reasons for their health problems.[26]

As public gardens increasingly turn their attention to audiences in need, more of them are developing programs specifically for veterans. As with the underserved urban residents described in the previous section, public gardens can use their expertise in horticulture, business management, and entrepreneurship to help former military members gain meaningful employment after a period of training.

Chatfield Veterans Farm Program

Research indicates that to reintegrate retired military personnel into society, meaningful employment or training in the first year after their discharge is critical. This is the goal of the Chatfield Veterans Farm program (CVF), a veteran reintegration program sponsored by Denver Botanic Gardens (DBG). Originally developed in 2013 to serve the large postmilitary population in the Denver region, the program has evolved from one with a strictly therapeutic focus to one that encompasses both therapy and vocational training. As such, it is supportive of DBG's mission "to connect people with plants . . . providing delight and enlightenment to everyone."[27]

Through DBG's connections with the Kaiser Permanente Foundation, Josie Hart, the Chatfield Farm program manager, learned about the national Veterans to Farmers (VTF) program, whose mission is to "train veterans in agricultural systems, technologies, and business operations for a fulfilling and sustainable lifestyle."[28] While the two organizations are completely separate, their partnership has provided VTF with needed venues to train and pay veterans to learn urban farming and a well-regarded institution in the Denver region—Denver Botanic Gardens— with which to work. For CVF, the collaboration has provided the means for recruiting participants through an established organization with a national network.

How the Program Works

The CVF program limits participation to ten veterans, all of whom must be ambulatory, given the uneven terrain at Chatfield Farm. Veterans with ambulatory limitations have the option of participating in the VTF greenhouse vegetable program. In 2018, CVF worked with eleven post-9/11 retired military members, most of whom had been recruited through the VTF Facebook page. Ranging in age from twenty-two to sixty, participants received stipends for working on the farm two days a week for twenty-one weeks. Those completing a 315-hour training program receive a certificate from VTF. Both programs have found that stipends are important to motivate participants to take their roles seriously and to limit absences.

Participants work mornings in the Chatfield Community Supported Agriculture (CSA) garden or the market garden where produce is grown for farm stands, and afternoons in the gardens at Chatfield. Participants also work at both the CSA distribution site and one of three farm stands set up near offices of the Denver Department of Social Services, which offer produce at reduced prices to food-stamp-eligible clients.

After its first year, the program was extended from twelve weeks to twenty-one weeks, from spring planting to fall harvest, and hired a program coordinator whose focus is providing quality control of the program's components and

FIGURE 4.5. Participants in the Chatfield Veterans Farm Program.
Courtesy of Denver Botanic Gardens.

finding employment for the program's graduates. Royce Hale graduated from the
Veterans to Farmers program at Chatfield in 2017 and is now a full-time educator
for veterans and other farming students at Chatfield.

Many classes offered through the CVF program take place at the farm and are
taught by Colorado State University extension agents and other area food system
professionals. Because therapy is a necessary component of the reentry process,
Denver Botanic Gardens is also addressing the emotional needs of returning veterans. DBG applied for and received a Rose Foundation Innovate for Good grant
to offer CVF participants a full array of therapeutic offerings, such as horticultural therapy sessions that allow individuals to deal with issues in a nonthreatening environment. DBG also formalized its training in career opportunities and
agricultural business planning and grant writing.

Impact of the Chatfield Veterans Farm

To date, Denver Botanic Gardens has not conducted a thorough CVF program
review, preferring instead to follow the progress of its graduates. From the 2015
cohort, two individuals started their own veterans' training farms, and one has

returned to college to study sustainable agriculture. That individual sees his CVF experience as life changing. "The time spent in the Chatfield Veterans Farm program," he said, "has fundamentally changed the way I look at this nation's food system and has driven me to discover my role in it to create a more sustainable future."[29] He currently cochairs his college's Sustainable Grower's Club.

Anecdotally, the CVF program managers report that their participants have become more conscientious about their food choices, and many have become involved with yoga or mindfulness meditation to assist in their transitions from military to civilian life.

Job Training for the Formerly Incarcerated

While first entering the job market is always difficult, job prospects for formerly incarcerated individuals continue to be dismal. According to the Prison Policy Initiative, the unemployment rate for formerly incarcerated individuals is nearly five times higher than that for the general US population, and substantially higher than in even the worst years of the Great Depression.[30] A report focused on the District of Columbia found that "joblessness among the previously incarcerated is exacerbating overall employment problems and threatening the long-term economic health and security of our neighborhoods."[31]

Another report explored postrelease employment and recidivism among 6,591 ex-offenders released by the Indiana Department of Corrections before, during, and after the economic recession of 2008. The study's authors found that 37 percent of violent offenders, 38.2 percent of nonviolent offenders, 36.3 percent of sex offenders, and 36.9 percent of drug offenders were never employed during the five-year study period. Recidivism rates for this cohort varied from 46 to 54 percent. Most importantly, the study revealed that those offenders with higher levels of education and postrelease employment had a much greater chance of avoiding recidivism, regardless of the individual's conviction category.[32]

Despite the enormity of the problems, public gardens can help former inmates who are in search of meaningful employment. In addition to the Windy City Harvest Corps program that was described previously, two other organizations have been particularly successful in moving postincarceration individuals into training and then employment.

Roots to Re-entry Program

Young people convicted of nonviolent crimes are often incarcerated in county prisons or detention centers for sentences of two years or less. Upon their release, they sometimes find themselves labeled "ex-cons" and face the obstacles that such a label brings, especially in finding employment. Programs aimed at providing job skills, building self-confidence, and keeping young people away from criminal activity have proven very effective at reducing recidivism rates and saving lives.

One such program, Roots to Re-entry (R2R), is the creation of the Philadelphia-based Pennsylvania Horticultural Society (PHS), whose mission is to "connect people with horticulture, and together . . . create beautiful, healthy and sustainable communities." It focuses on teenage males in prison for nonviolent crimes. Started in 2010, R2R grew out of the Horticultural Society's City Harvest program, a hands-on horticulture program that works with inmates in the Alternative and Special Detention division of the Philadelphia prison system.

R2R initially worked with young prisoners in a daily work-release program while they were still incarcerated, but upon release many of them floundered and were rearrested within six months. After much introspection, the program managers realized that there were two major flaws in their model. First, because participating prisoners returned to prison at night and the security of beds and meals, they didn't build the independence they needed to survive outside prison. Second, simply releasing former inmates to the streets without a support network increased the chances that they would return to unsafe activities and the likelihood of rearrest.

To support participants in the most crucial stage of the reentry process, the time directly after release, the current model is a twelve-week program in which

REDUCING RECIDIVISM: FACTORS OF SUCCESS

Links to jobs: PHS learned that just offering a job training program (through the City Harvest program) without a link to a job was not enough.

Support to "show up" for the job: PHS learned that the graduates had many obstacles to overcome to be able to show up consistently for the job.

Responsive to the individual: The Federation of Neighborhood Centers (FNC) learned to extend their learning style support to the employers when employees ran into difficulties at work.

Coordinated case management: Five partners agreed to streamline case management to avoid duplicating efforts.

Compassionate and individualized engagement: FNC learned that building caring relationships with participants prior to release, and continuing them post release, helped to establish support systems and prosocial ties that help them avoid criminal activity.

Magnify importance of physical and mental health to job retention: Partners learned that integrating health care services into a job training program and post-employment supportive services enhanced the importance and relevance of attaining and maintaining good health among the participants.

FIGURE 4.6. Reducing Recidivism: Factors of Success
Courtesy of the Pennsylvania Horticultural Society.

participants are paroled halfway through the training. At that point, they begin an internship with R2R for the remainder of the training. If participants successfully complete both parts, they are eligible for graduation. The new approach has resulted in participants feeling more responsible for their own fate. Recidivism for R2R participants is now 30 percent, versus 65 percent for the general prison population.

HOW THE PROGRAM WORKS

R2R participants receive hands-on training in horticulture, landscape maintenance, greenhouse operations, organic land care, hardscaping, nursery management, carpentry, woodworking, and small engine repair. Under the tutelage of dedicated case workers, they can also attend additional workshops in workforce literacy, health, and job preparedness.

Upon graduation, participants are linked to a network of green industry employers. Much of the success of the program is due to this rapid transition to paid employment. Among the members of the network are KJK Associates, Liberty Tree & Landscape Management, Moon Site Management, the Brickman Group, and the PHS Philadelphia LandCare program.

According to Tim Majoros, former R2R program manager, another important factor in the program's success is that individuals are expected to master new activities on their own, rather than being led along each step in the process. But Majoros also recognizes that the program must provide a nurturing environment in which failure is acceptable and seen as a learning experience. To demonstrate the importance of hard work, Majoros often works on every activity along with the young men. For him, the greatest satisfaction of his position is seeing individuals succeed and develop greater self-confidence in their abilities. He distinguishes between the false confidence or swagger of some inmates and the true self-confidence that many of the R2R graduates gain from learning new skills. He says, "Once I see guys treat themselves right and develop a positive relationship with themselves, I know they're going to be able to cope with whatever hits them."[33]

While some inmates try to use the program to gain an early release, Majoros learned to identify such individuals by their lack of commitment and their efforts to manipulate staff members. Sadly, most of these young men usually drop out of the program and eventually drift back to prison.

On a visit with current enrollees, a program alumnus who serves as a role model spoke about how the program helped to straighten out his life: "There's a light at the end of the tunnel, and this program gives you a push in that direction. But you gotta walk through that tunnel yourself."[34] Upon graduation, this individual was hired by a landscaping firm, where he now works full-time and which values him highly.

FIGURE 4.7. Roots to Re-entry participants work alongside staff members in downtown Philadelphia.
Courtesy of the Pennsylvania Horticultural Society.

HOW THE PARTNERSHIPS FUNCTION

R2R could not exist without the web of partnerships that PHS has formed to support the program. Funding for the program comes from a variety of local landscaping businesses, governmental units in Philadelphia, and private foundations. To coordinate activities and services, these multiple partners have formed a collective known as the Reentry to Workforce (RTW) partnership. From its inception, RTW partners have committed to address outcomes, learn from failures as well as successes, and adapt program elements accordingly.

One RTW partner is the Defender Association of Philadelphia, an independent, nonprofit corporation created in 1934 by a group of Philadelphia lawyers dedicated to providing high-quality legal services for indigent criminal defendants. Byron Cotter, director of the association's Alternative Sentencing Unit, works directly with individuals who have been recommended by the county prison for early release and entry into R2R. Cotter has managed to get each case reviewed by a judge who supports and encourages use of the program. Once participants are enrolled in the program, Cotter encourages them to reach out to him whenever problems develop. While pleased by the accomplishments of R2R, Cotter recognizes that its growth is limited by the number of employers willing to hire its graduates and by some of the participants' lack of a stable home address, which means they cannot be contacted easily.

Another important program partner is Ken Kolodziej, owner of KJK Associates, a Philadelphia-based landscape contracting firm. In 2007, Kolodziej was approached by a PHS staff member who was concerned about the lack of oversight of released inmates. As a result of this meeting, he partnered with PHS in the creation of what would become R2R, and through his involvement he has arranged jobs for many of its graduates.

Kolodziej also created and manages Heritage Farm at the Methodist Youth Home, the largest urban farm in Philadelphia, and has placed several R2R graduates in gardening positions there. One of the graduates, Troy Johnson, now manager of Heritage Farm, was profiled in a 2015 article in the *Philadelphia Inquirer*. in which he states, "You've got to really know you're done with the old lifestyle, done with old habits. That's the only way you're going to overcome."[35] Johnson is grateful for the opportunities R2R provided, and he notes the contrast between his current life and that of former associates who continue to engage in illegal activities and face the criminal justice cycle.[36]

The smooth transition from incarceration to parole would not occur without the involvement of another key partner, the Philadelphia District Attorney's Office. The district attorney can identify which candidates for the program will and will not qualify for work release and parole in the needed time frame. The collaboration between PHS, the prisons, and the District Attorney's Office has allowed qualifying individuals to avoid bureaucratic delays and to build their trust in the judicial system.

In his comments on the partnership with PHS, Louis Giorla, commissioner of the prison, confirmed its value. "They've been a fantastic partner to us," he said. "Working so closely with the courts so they are paroled when they complete the program has created an entire sequence that is seamless, and that's extremely important."[37]

IMPACT OF ROOTS TO RE-ENTRY

By 2015, R2R had trained 144 individuals, of whom 89 graduated from the program and 84 are currently employed. While that is an admirable success rate, Majoros hopes that more program alumni will motivate current enrollees to avoid distractions and learn skills that will help them to reintegrate into society.

Rikers Island GreenHouse Program

The Rikers Island prison complex, located in New York City, is one of the largest correctional institutions in the world, with a daily prison population approaching 10,000 and a staff of 9,000 officers and 1,500 civilians. It consists of ten jails that hold local offenders awaiting trial without bail, those serving sentences of one year or less, and those temporarily placed there pending transfer to another facility.[38] Eight of these facilities house detained individuals, rather than those who have been sentenced.

The Rikers Island GreenHouse program (GHP) was created in 1985 by the Horticultural Society of New York to "break the vicious cycle of recidivism, by most counts as high as 65% in the NYC jail system," according to James Jiler, former director of GHP and the author of *Doing Time in the Garden*.[39] In keeping with the Horticultural Society's mission, the goal of this program is to actively engage participants with plants and nature in order to strengthen their entire being and prepare them for next steps, whether this means returning to the community or starting a prison term. For many of the participants, not only is gardening a novel activity, but spending time in nature is itself a new experience.

HOW THE PROGRAM WORKS

Since its inception, GHP has evolved and grown in response to changing needs. Currently it provides the greatest amount of contact time with individual participants of any social service program on Rikers Island. Each year, horticultural therapists and trained instructors serve over five hundred incarcerated individuals, seven days a week. As expressed in the GHP website, "At five gardens with 160 raised beds, students work together to grow delicious vegetables, useful herbs, and beautiful flowers."[40]

The curriculum involves a mix of garden therapy, science and English literacy, life skill development, and job preparedness. In addition to the horticultural and landscape training, the GHP staff, in partnership with the city's Department of Corrections and Department of Education, instruct detained eighteen-to-twenty-one-year-olds who are working toward their GED diploma in an alternative high school. Participants spend part of each day in the classroom and part working on assigned horticultural tasks. GHP facilities consist of a greenhouse, a classroom, and over two and a half acres of landscaped and productive gardens, designed and built by inmates.

The aim for all participants, whether sentenced or detained, is that they leave the garden feeling better about themselves than when they entered, and that they develop or maintain a sense of hope. This is particularly important for young men facing the possibility of long prison sentences. The program helps students examine their lives, while emphasizing critical thinking and encouraging teamwork and collaboration. The program has reduced recidivism rates by 40 percent and generates up to 417 pounds of organic fruit and vegetables a year.

While the program has a long record of success, it does face challenges that are simply a result of its location in a prison complex. One of these is that the program naturally has no say on release dates. An individual may be participating in a horticultural therapy program, but the therapeutic process is terminated upon release. Also, individuals may be moved between facilities within the Rikers complex, which affects their availability for GHP. Finally, inmates face many distractions while in prison, which can jeopardize their eligibility for the program.

Upon their release from Rikers Island, GHP participants can join the Green-Team, a vocational internship program. GreenTeam interns earn minimum wage, or near it, and continue to develop their horticultural skills while working on municipal landscaping or community improvement projects. But here too, GHP has learned and changed over time. Previously, ex-convicts could begin work with the GreenTeam immediately upon release. Now, individuals with a history of substance abuse (which, sadly, is the majority of them) must actively work on sobriety before enrolling in the program. The GreenTeam also now includes individuals who were not previously incarcerated but may be homeless.

HOW THE PARTNERSHIPS FUNCTION

The program succeeds because of its many partnerships. First and foremost, it depends on the partnership and support of the warden and deputy wardens. According to current GHP director Hilda Krus, "The collaboration with the DOC [Department of Corrections] has been based on open communication, trust and support. We're not coming to work against the DOC, but in close cooperation, and we always strictly respect security regulations. My experience is that the parties involved in general want to improve the situation of the inmate population, and we basically share the same goals."[41]

While the GreenTeam program focuses on horticulture, it also emphasizes life skills. For that work, the program depends on community partners. Five partner organizations work with GreenTeam participants on life skills and job readiness: interviewing for jobs, proper behavior when employed, family relations, avoiding substance abuse, and anger management. These organizations are the Association of Community Employment, Getting Out / Staying Out, the Police Athletic League, Bronx Works, and STRIVE New York. The partners are all social agencies that serve the needs of New York City residents, and 75 percent of Rikers inmates are city residents. Because the partners offer their clients engagements that are not time limited, they provide GreenTeam participants stable, trustworthy support as they transition to life outside prison.[42]

For funding, GHP depends on financial partners, including private donors and foundations as well the New York City Department of Education for the high school program and the Department of Corrections for piloting new efforts. GHP maintains this support by demonstrating its cost effectiveness, in terms of beautification of the grounds, the value of the plants grown in the greenhouses and then distributed to local parks, and reduced recidivism of team members.

Like so many other programs profiled in this book, GHP would never succeed if it were managed by one agency alone. It takes this web of public and not-for-profit organizations, all committed to the same goals, to turn prisoners into contributing members of society. Commenting on the role of the partners, James Jiler observes that "building partnerships with existing non-profits is an essential step in establishing an effective after-care system. It allows a program to extend its boundaries past the wall and fence lines of jail into the communities the students return to."[43]

IMPACT OF THE GREENHOUSE PROGRAM

The number of individuals served by this program is a small fraction of those in the target group. But Hilda Krus contends that the program partners have a greater overall impact by investing heavily in a quality program for a few individuals than they would by reaching out to hundreds of inmates with a superficial effort.

GHP participants fill in entry, intermediate, and exit questionnaires. The entry sheet asks about their experience in horticulture, general work experience, assessment of their strengths in work situations, and what they hope to improve on while in the program, as well as possible fears of nature and plants. The intermediate questionnaire focuses more on what has been accomplished so far, how they feel about the program, and what they want to focus on for their remaining time, as well as what they would hope to see changed. The exit questionnaire asks about their experience in the program, what they learned, what they will take with them, what was most valuable, in which learning situation they felt most comfortable, and what they would suggest to improve the program.

Krus notes that beyond this formal assessment, those individuals who transitioned into the GreenTeam report multiple changes in their lifestyles and habits: "They changed their food habits and now include fresh foods, take their children to the botanical gardens, garden with their families, get laughed about by their friends when they point out plants in the city, go to the farmers market, become members of community gardens, compost their kitchen scraps, go to museums, and decided to go to a substance abuse program because they felt enough self-worth to take care of themselves, or decided to do anger management classes."[44]

Lessons from Veterans and Postincarceration Programs

The programs profiled in this chapter address distinct groups within the overall population: military veterans and incarcerated and postincarcerated individuals. Despite the distinct needs of these targeted groups, the programs share certain attributes:

- They recognize both the qualities and challenges of each individual.
- They keep requirements for participation to a minimum.

- They utilize both internal resources and experts to provide training.
- They provide incentives and rewards to encourage retention in the program.
- They partner with other agencies to provide counseling and effective transitions to the workforce.

The applicability of these efforts to other regions depends somewhat on the demographics of the location. For example, while the nearest prison may be some distance from a public garden, most cities and towns have a sizable veteran population, and it is likely that some proportion of those veterans will have previously served time.

Compared to returning Vietnam-era military members, today's veterans are supported by a wider array of educational and job training programs after leaving service. The GI Bill, for example, now offers the Yellow Ribbons program, which pays tuition and fees for a public college or partial support for a private college. The Transition Assistance Program is a joint effort of the US Departments of Defense, Labor, and Veterans Affairs to inform service members and veterans about the many programs and services available to them, including vocational rehabilitation.[45]

Public gardens cannot replicate the government programs, but they can serve as liaisons between social agencies and those programs, assisting individuals in these special audiences to navigate the best course for each of them. When considering offering services or establishing programs for those who have worn uniforms of one type or another, public gardens can start by asking themselves whether they are doing as much as they can for every audience or are primarily serving their traditional audiences.

Interestingly, the programs profiled in this chapter extend beyond their home base (farm or prison) and reach their broader communities. For Windy City Harvest, that includes the greening of streetscapes and increasing access to fresh produce in each of the neighborhoods in which its thirteen farms are located. In the Chatfield Veterans Farm model, program participants sell produce that they have grown at farm markets in underresourced downtown sites. For both Roots to Reentry and the Rikers Island GreenHouse program, participants transition from their prison-based training to horticulture or landscape internships or supervised job placements in their communities, thus beautifying neighborhoods and green spaces. Beyond providing job training for audiences with special needs, these programs have an impact on their communities by expanding access to healthy foods and establishing neighborhood beautification programs. So while program participants are hopefully setting out to lead more fulfilling lives, their communities overall are becoming safer, more attractive, and healthier.

INITIATIVES TO PROMOTE ECOSYSTEM AND HUMAN HEALTH

Many US cities continue to combat the environmental costs of urbanization, especially the legacies of the Industrial Revolution, which include contaminated waterways, compromised air quality, the siting of hazardous waste facilities near residential areas, and the sustained liability of abandoned industrial properties, known as brownfields.[1] Urbanization is frequently associated with human stressors such as adverse environmental exposures (e.g., water, air, light), social stress (e.g., noise, congestion), and physical threats (e.g., traffic, crime).[2] While every major city experiences some of these adverse effects of urbanization, environmental hazards are overwhelmingly concentrated in low-income communities and communities of color, a correlation that environmental justice scholars have long established.[3] Given that over half the world now lives in urban areas, a number that is projected to increase, cities worldwide are investing in agendas to support the health and well-being of residents across social and racial groups.

Research to better understand the human-environment relationship has expanded over the last century, emphasizing the natural environment as a critical piece of health-promoting efforts. One approach increasingly used by cities is to invest in the green infrastructure of urban areas, or the collection of public and private natural landscapes, corridors, gardens, and other representations of nature, which include street trees, green roofs, and bioswales.[4] Increasing the number of trees in urban areas can help combat the urban heat island effect, which refers to the higher temperatures in urbanized areas, mainly due to the concentration of vehicles and impervious, heat-absorbing surfaces.[5] For example, the shade from tree canopies can have a cooling effect on cities, benefiting the pedestrian walking on city sidewalks and reducing the energy required to air-condition city buildings.[6] Dense vegetation can have multiple impacts on ecological health, such as reducing pollutants from stormwater runoff,[7] filtering fine particulate matter from the air,[8] and dampening city noise pollution by absorbing the sound waves from passing traffic.[9]

While these and other benefits accrue from integrating vegetation into our cityscapes, there is evidence that we benefit from greening in ways that cannot be evaluated through calculations of energy cost savings or particulate matter measurements. For example, studies have found that access or exposure to nature can have positive impacts on mental health,[10] including benefits from both proximity to and active participation in green spaces.[11] There is evidence that exposure to the natural environment has a positive impact on the well-being and development of children,[12] and that it improves the physical health of adults.[13]

Green infrastructure approaches should also engage local residents in the preservation of green landscapes.[14] Capitalizing on the instinctive bond between human beings and other living systems, many cities are finding success in greening their communities by grounding initiatives with a purposeful linkage between humans and the environment. Because they have the knowledge and tools to meaningfully connect people and their environment, public gardens are logical partners for municipalities and community organizations seeking additional resources and assistance to achieve environmental, conservation, and social goals.

This chapter examines four programs where public gardens have contributed their horticultural and ecological expertise to partnerships for the management of public landscapes and to increase public access to nature. In collaboration with other community institutions, the Missouri Botanical Garden, Lewis Ginter Botanical Garden, the UC Davis Arboretum and Public Garden, and Phipps Conservatory and Botanical Gardens have assumed a range of roles, including those of community convener, technical expert, and innovator, as part of initiatives that support the environmental health of their communities.

Urban Conservation in St. Louis

St. Louis is located on the Mississippi River, approximately three hundred miles southwest of Chicago and in close proximity to the Ohio and Missouri Rivers. Because of its favorable location, the city has enjoyed important economic roles throughout its history: as an early trade stop along the rivers, a nineteenth-century center of commerce and trade, and finally as an industrial leader, which continued into the early twentieth century.

As part of the Great Migration, thousands of African Americans moved from the rural South to St. Louis between World War I and World War II, taking advantage of the city's need for industrial workers.[15] In 1900, St. Louis already had more than thirty-five thousand African American residents (over 6 percent of its population), second only to Baltimore.[16] The demographic impact of the Great Migration was unmistakable: the African American population in St. Louis nearly doubled between 1910 and 1940 and created competition for employment as well as living space in the increasingly crowded city.[17]

In response to this influx, segregation and racial isolation increased as whites established new barriers that restricted where African Americans could live.[18] In 1916, St. Louis passed the nation's first referendum to impose racial segregation on housing, a "reform" ordinance that prevented anyone from buying a home in a neighborhood more than 75 percent occupied by another race. Although the US Supreme Court declared racially based housing ordinances unconstitutional the following year, some neighborhoods enacted covenants requiring white property owners to agree not to sell to nonwhites.[19] In the late 1940s, the city's estimated 150,000 African American residents were concentrated into six hundred blocks, "mostly from downtown west to Kingshighway, and from Delmar Boulevard north to St. Louis Avenue," according to an article in the *St. Louis Post-Dispatch*.[20] It was not until 1948 that these covenants were declared illegal by the US Supreme Court's ruling in *Shelley v. Kraemer*, a case that originated in St. Louis.

Despite the Supreme Court decision, segregation persisted through government policies, restrictive covenants, and real estate deeds. St. Louis is now one of the most segregated cities in the United States, a legacy of discriminatory policies and practices that separates whites and blacks in its cities and neighborhoods.[21] The "Delmar Divide," so named by the BBC in a 2012 documentary, highlights the stark racial and economic divisions demarcated by Delmar Boulevard in downtown St. Louis: the neighborhood to the north of Delmar is 98 percent black, with a median household income of $18,000, while the neighborhood to the south is 70 percent white, with a median household income of $50,000.[22]

St. Louis's population peaked at 850,000 in 1950 but has since declined to 320,000. The significant population loss has left the city with an abundance of abandoned areas. However, St. Louis possesses many natural assets, including the Mississippi River, greenways, and an extensive park system. In looking to the future and rebuilding, St. Louis intends to focus on ways to use its vacant and underutilized land as an opportunity to develop a new urban form, one that connects people with nature in ways that will promote economic, social, and health benefits and act to revitalize the city's seventy-nine neighborhoods.

During his last term as mayor of St. Louis, Francis Slay chose sustainability and urban conservation as the guide for redefining the city. In January 2013, the St. Louis Planning Commission adopted the City of St. Louis Sustainability Plan, whose primary objective was "to develop and leverage mutually beneficial opportunities, systems and partnerships" that can use the city's limited resources in efficient and innovative ways to promote a sustainable community for current and future generations.[23] The following month, Slay announced his Sustainability Action Agenda, which outlined priorities for the implementation of the Sustainability Plan. In that agenda, Slay reinforced the need for collaboration between stakeholder groups throughout the city, stating that the Sustainability Plan was "not just city government's plan" and that he hoped "that individuals, community organizations and neighborhoods will both embrace and help implement it."[24]

In July 2013, the City of St. Louis and the Missouri Botanical Garden (MBG) established a cooperative agreement with the Missouri Department of Conservation (MDC) to collectively advance the objectives in the Sustainability Plan, with an emphasis on the mayor's high-priority sustainability implementation items. The partnership focuses on expanding green space, promoting urban resource conservation, and supporting the revitalization of the city's biodiversity and natural resources. The purpose of the cooperative agreement, according to a reference document created by members of the partnership, "is to support the conservation and restoration of natural resources in the City of St. Louis where our organizations have common interests in the social, economic and environmental benefits of quality habitat for people and nature and citizens' understanding of and engagement in natural resource stewardship."[25]

"The timing was right for this partnership to work," explained Deborah Frank, MBG's vice president of sustainability.[26] First, all three organizations had a common interest: urban conservation and ways to improve urban ecoliteracy in St. Louis. Second, MBG already had a strong partnership with the Missouri Department of Conservation, and the MBG director was trying to find ways to better partner with the city. Finally, all three organizations realized they needed each other to achieve their common urban conservation goal. MDC had funding to seed work with the mayor's office and to staff the coordinated effort, but MDC was not authorized to hire. The city was the connection to citizens and urban natural resource management, but lacked the funds to support the initiative. MBG could not finance the initiative, but it had the expertise in urban conservation and biodiversity and was willing to provide advice as needed and to serve as the fiscal agent for the project. Brought together, these organizations had all the resources needed to tackle this effort.

As St. Louis sustainability director Catherine Werner recalled, "The Mayor's Office first reached out to the garden to see if there were financial resources available. When the response was negative but it was clear there was a shared interest, we shifted gears and formalized a valuable role for the garden, handling administrative and contract matters and serving as fiscal agent. I think the garden saw the overlapping interests as a great opportunity and since the Mayor had demonstrated his willingness to lead on sustainability and urban ecology issues in the city, it was a great proving ground for both."[27]

MBG is representative of public gardens that lend their expertise in conservation and plant science to enable implementation of municipal sustainability initiatives. MBG is a respected leader in global botanical research and science education, with expertise in the exploration of science-based approaches to the conservation and sustainable use of plant diversity. It offers similar expertise in education and training at the regional and local levels, utilizing interdisciplinary teams of ecologists and educators to promote connections between city residents and urban nature.

Although the city identified the need and conceived of the urban ecology opportunity, it took the partnership and support of the cooperative agreement to get the effort off the ground. Together, these three entities launched the City of St. Louis Urban Vitality and Ecology (UVE) Initiative, a collaboration designed to better connect people to urban nature while maximizing ecological potential, supporting economic vitality, and fostering social health and well-being. For the first two years of the effort, representatives from the City of St. Louis, MDC, and MBG functioned as the UVE Core Team. Over the next two years, the Core Team expanded to include additional partners that had started providing support for the UVE Initiative outside the MDC cooperative agreement.

How the Partnership Functions

One of the UVE Core Team's first actions in establishing the UVE Initiative was to conduct an inventory and review of their institutions' existing plans and policy documents that might relate to UVE's goals as well as those of prospective partner organizations and city departments. With the financial support of MDC and the supervisory oversight of the city, MBG contracted with a part-time natural resources coordinator, who reviewed the documents to identify goals and issue areas related to connecting people with urban nature. This was an important step toward establishing the framework of the initiative and toward strategically considering additional partners that could invest in the overarching goal while simultaneously achieving their own organizations' goals.

In addition to the City of St. Louis Sustainability Plan and the mayor's Sustainability Action Agenda, eight key plans from the St. Louis region focused on connecting people to nature. These plans included federal-level efforts such as the US Fish and Wildlife Service's Urban Wildlife Refuge Initiative;[28] regional-level guides, including the OneSTL Regional Plan for Sustainable Development;[29] and MBG's BiodiverseCity St. Louis policy guide,[30] as well as local plans including the St. Louis Community Health Improvement Plan.[31]

Communication was important to ensuring that this partnership established connections and served to identify opportunities for collaboration. The Core Team sought input from stakeholders in their monthly meetings. A larger group and various subgroups met quarterly to share information, progress, and outcomes.

As part of the cooperative agreement, the partners mutually agreed to their roles, commitments, and expectations. In its role, the city was to provide day-to-day general guidance for the project and dedicate a significant portion of the St. Louis sustainability director's time to the partnership. MBG served as fiscal agent in the partnership, and also provided on-site technical assistance to the pilot projects, and an in-kind match equal to at least 11 percent of the overall project expenses. MBG contracted with individuals who served as the UVE coordinator (mostly under the direction of the city's sustainability director), who coordinated communication and fundraising, and the UVE planner (housed in the city's Planning and Urban Design Department), who provided support for land use planning, vacancy issues, and policy research. MDC provided technical assistance and dedicated up to $30,000 for project expenses. All three partners agreed to "work together to pursue additional external resources to achieve project goals," as explained by a member of the partnership.

The partners' roles, contracted positions, and functions changed over time: both of the contracted positions for a UVE coordinator and UVE planner moved to the city's Planning Department in preparation for a mayoral administration change, the contracted positions supported by the MDC cooperative agreement moved on to other situations, and there is no longer financial or contractual support for the UVE Initiative. Because of these changes, the UVE collaboration has become a much looser and less structured partnership and tends to function on project-specific bases. The UVE Core Team disbanded in 2017, and the city's urban ecology efforts have largely continued in an informal manner by making use of the connections and resources developed during the initial phase of the UVE Initiative.

An outgrowth of the UVE effort is the Green City Coalition, which works with residents of neighborhoods with high concentrations of vacant properties to transform the lots in an effort to improve neighborhood cohesiveness and health, support job creation, and promote a sense of safety. The coalition includes certain city departments, MBG, and MDC; its focus is on greening vacant land and contributing to the greening of low-income neighborhoods in the city. Similarly, some of the UVE stakeholders are involved in tree-planting and urban biodiversity efforts, which fall more generally within the city's new status as a biophilic city, an initiative discussed in detail later in the chapter.

The Baden Pilot Project

An important initial objective of the UVE Initiative was to develop and implement community-based pilot projects to test engagement approaches, landscape treatment techniques, and policies that might be utilized in subsequent UVE Initiative interventions throughout the city. These pilots were designed to inform the development of a future UVE strategic action plan that would identify high-priority policy modifications and community-based processes, provide strategic prioritization of redevelopment and key natural resource opportunities, and identify actionable items for implementation.

In 2015, the UVE Core Team decided to invest in one pilot project to create, implement, and assess a project intervention. The Baden neighborhood in north St. Louis was selected in part because the city's vacant properties are concentrated in that area. The Metropolitan St. Louis Sewer District (MSD) had targeted properties in Baden for buyout and demolition due to chronic flooding and sewage failures. Starting in 2013, MSD negotiated with property owners to acquire their properties. In the process, MSD demolished more than ninety homes built in the floodplain of a stream and built a small stormwater collection basin in Baden.[32] Even prior to the buyouts that left blocks of homes sitting vacant, the victims of trash dumping and illegal scrapping of metal, residents in Baden felt the decades of disinvestment in their neighborhood that contributed to high crime and poverty rates.

Because sewer basins fill up quickly with water when it rains and increase liability, MSD had never opened one to the public, but the agency was willing to try something different in Baden.[33] As part of the next step, MSD replaced the demolished homes with grassy lots that would manage stormwater and prevent it from rushing into the city's combined sewer system. The plan was to turn multiblock areas in Baden into a stormwater collector and to work with partners to make it an amenity to the surrounding neighborhood.

The Baden Pilot Project was established to redevelop portions of the neighborhood through green infrastructure approaches informed by research and community-based strategies that were both ecologically sound and socially responsible. To do so, the UVE team partnered with researchers and students at Washington University in St. Louis and St. Louis University to assess existing conditions on the site and to plan participatory research projects that would engage local stakeholders.

To successfully involve residents with their environment, the UVE team needed to find a balance between promoting ecology and recognizing the social

FIGURE 5.1. Young people working on a map of community assets.
Photo by MBG staff. Courtesy of the Missouri Botanical Garden.

context and history of Baden residents, many of whom were not familiar with the potential benefits of green space. Some residents questioned whether a greening project would raise or lower property values for the remaining homes.[34] It was clear that the project depended on developing a process that engaged community stakeholders and worked toward outcomes that aligned with their interests.

In 2015, after discussions with community stakeholders and involving the community in the planning process, MBG partnered with a local development corporation to introduce a youth and community garden program in Baden. Five young adults, ages sixteen to twenty-three, were hired to develop and cultivate community gardens. While they learned about ecology, the main emphasis was on character development and youth empowerment.[35] The resulting garden has become a place where young people, families, church members, and seniors can garden and build a sense of community and connection to green spaces. The garden has helped to engage residents, build trust, and demonstrate what is possible through the UVE Initiative.

In discussing the process, Betsy Crites, MBG's youth and community supervisor with the UVE team, emphasized the importance of engagement and involvement with the neighborhood: "At the end of the day, you need to keep the community at the front of your mind. . . . Being present at neighborhood events, community association meetings, and in afterschool programs helps you gain the trust of the community."[36]

Former City of St. Louis alderwoman Dionne Flowers, who represented the Baden neighborhood at the time, said she was optimistic about the possibility of connecting her constituents to green infrastructure; she likened the pilot interventions to creating Baden's "own little botanical garden."[37] While most Baden residents have not been to the Missouri Botanical Garden, this project has allowed MBG to establish relationships with residents with whom they would otherwise not be connected. "For many Baden residents," explained Sheila Voss, the garden's vice president of education, "they now know MBG through our community garden instructors, and associate us with the former vacant lot that is now a thriving community garden."[38]

Although a small project, the youth and community garden has the potential to change how residents in the Baden area interact with their environment. In place of flooding and hazardous sewage overflow, residents have new opportunities to build relationships with nature and each other. One Baden community gardener said, "Seeing our own and other programs in action has shown me that an area can give birth to a sense of community when neighbors are given the opportunity to not just live, but work alongside one other. So much is fostered in these little green spaces: familiarity, trust, cooperation, and mutual respect. I learned that our neighborhood is rich with the knowledge and experience of capable, persevering, good people. I feel the urgency of building a community that taps into that wealth and does not let it go to waste."[39]

The Baden Community Garden project and its gardeners have faced challenges over the years. After three years of holding the lease on the garden property, the Riverview West Florissant Development Corporation decided to step back from its investment and removed its name from the lease. Nelson Curran, the community programs coordinator at MBG, explained that during the summer of 2018, "Missouri Botanical Garden staff, current Baden gardeners, and community leaders involved in the Revitalization of Baden Association (ROBA) worked to find the best way forward for the Baden Community Garden project, in hopes of preserving it as a valuable neighborhood resource. We agreed to take steps toward securing the lease on the garden property under ROBA, and we see

FIGURE 5.2. Baden Community Garden.
Photo by Elizabeth Ward. Courtesy of the Missouri Botanical Garden.

this move as a positive step toward sustaining a healthy, beautiful, vibrant community space for the neighborhood."[40]

A significant element in this transition is that community leaders, as represented by ROBA, value the garden enough to organize and take responsibility

FIGURE 5.3. Young people from Baden learning to mulch pollinator gardens. Photo by MBG staff. Courtesy of the Missouri Botanical Garden.

for the land. The approaches developed in the Baden project will also help shape green space transformations in other underserved St. Louis neighborhoods. Utilizing long-term green infrastructure design strategies such as integrating drainage structures into the built environment, increasing flora and fauna habitats, and building opportunity for active recreation will promote social and environment benefits for residents.

Lessons from the UVE Partnership

At a macro level, the Urban Vitality and Ecology partnership represents a valuable example of what partners can learn through a small, manageable pilot initiative before investing in large-scale interventions. However, perhaps the most important lessons from this case are drawn from the strategic details integrated into the partnership's formation and management:

Identify and align initiatives with common partner goals and priorities. As leaders of the Core Team, the Missouri Botanical Garden, the City of St. Louis, and the Missouri Department of Conservation recognized that although they had each previously aspired to work with the others in some capacity, this time the time was right for their collaboration. This meant that the climate inside their respective organizations (e.g., organizational agenda, resources, political will), as well as the external climate of the St. Louis region (e.g., regional needs, city priorities, political support), was supportive of the partnership. In order to bolster a strong regional support network, these organizations developed a strategic action plan that outlined how the UVE initiative helped to further the goals of numerous regional plans and policy documents.

Recognize the range of unique and complementary resources that partners can bring to a project. Some of the most valuable resources brought to a partnership are not financial. In this case, partners offered access to community networks, expertise in ecological systems, and hands-on horticultural training. Communication and creative thinking helped the UVE partnership realize the most effective types of resources that each organization could commit.

Outline an agreement detailing partner roles, commitments, and expectations. Partnerships can be enormously rewarding, but they can also introduce a level of risk for partner organizations in terms of time, resources, and intended outcomes. To reduce risk and increase confidence in the collaboration, the UVE Initiative was guided by a formal partnership agreement that outlined the roles, commitments, and expectations of each organization. Commitment to a partnership agreement or a memorandum of understanding provides an important anchor of transparency for how a partnership will function.

Beautiful RVA in Richmond

As the capital of Virginia and once the capital of the Confederacy, Richmond is a decidedly southern city. The city's history has played a major role in its social and political fabric and in the patterns of African American settlement within the city.[41] Urban historians recognize the role of politics and power in isolating African Americans living in the urban South and in the eventual collapse of once stable black neighborhoods as more affluent residents moved out from the city to close-in suburbs.[42]

The institutionalization of segregation and exclusion in many cities, including Richmond, is linked to the Home Owners' Loan Corporation (HOLC), a 1930s New Deal agency created to support real estate investments. Through a practice later called "redlining," the HOLC assessed neighborhoods using several factors, assigned a "grade" to each neighborhood, and created a map based on that assessment to guide mortgage-lending practices. Green grade-A neighborhoods were mostly white and more affluent. Red grade-D neighborhoods tended to be less affluent and more diverse and were deemed hazardous for mortgage investors.[43] When a neighborhood was no longer white, it was considered demographically and environmentally "at-risk."[44] The color-coded maps reflected racial lines and effectively withheld capital from African American families and reinforced urban poverty. In Richmond and other southern cities, according to Christopher Silver and John V. Moeser, the African American settlement pattern was a "self-contained, racially-identifiable community separated from the larger white city."[45] To a large extent, the geographic pattern reinforced through redlining persists in Richmond today.[46]

Politics also influenced public art in many southern cities, whose political and civic leaders after the Civil War tended to be former Confederate soldiers. During the late 1800s and early 1900s, monuments honoring the Confederacy on public property solidified this cultural memory. Monument Avenue, one of the most historic and prominent boulevards in Richmond, is lined with statues of three Confederate generals from Virginia (Robert E. Lee, J. E. B. Stuart, and Thomas "Stonewall" Jackson) and the president of the Confederacy (Jefferson Davis).

Public commemoration is what Marita Sturken calls a "form of history making" that influences a community's culture and reflects its agendas.[47] Understanding cultural contexts is important for interventions designed to better connect urban residents to nature. Sociologists, designers, and urban planning scholars note how urban landscapes reflect cultural dynamics in their settlement patterns, access to green spaces, and interactions in those spaces. Cultural memory influences the way people engage in their communities and with each other.[48] For decades, scholars in asset-based community development have suggested that instead of viewing low-income communities as simply a problem that needs to be fixed, we should see the assets in these communities and landscapes, and their potential to inform contemporary design and neighborhood investments in important ways.[49] By recognizing and addressing the connections between people, their neighborhoods, and their landscapes, both ecological and social goals can be met.

An opportunity to simultaneously meet ecological and social goals came in April 2011 when Richmond launched a yearlong sustainability planning process to improve the quality of life for residents and stimulate opportunities for enhanced economic development. The resulting sustainability plan, titled *RVAgreen: A Roadmap to Sustainability*, called for the creation of a citywide beautification program that would "redevelop the urban environment and create a more livable city . . . to help knit the community together."[50] Though this plan clearly called for a program to beautify neighborhoods, corridors, gateways, and public spaces, it also specified that the citywide program be grassroots, collaborative, and complementary to, rather than dependent on, Richmond city infrastructure and fiscal resources. In short, the community would need to initiate the beautification program and find creative ways to support its implementation.

Richmond's new focus on beautification, coupled with growing appeals from residents and members of the urban design, city planning, and public horticulture communities for the city to invest in its public spaces, became a call to action for Lewis Ginter Botanical Garden. Located in Henrico County, Virginia, just outside the city boundaries, Lewis Ginter is representative of public gardens across the United States that are physically disconnected from the urban core but strive to diversify their membership and solidify their relevance to wider target audiences. In the last decade, the botanical garden has put considerable time and resources into examining its commitment to the broader community and its role as a convener, facilitator of dialogue, and collaborating partner.[51]

Inspired by the work of the public garden designer Lynden Miller, who successfully engaged the community around urban greening efforts in New York City, Randee Humphrey, then the education director at Lewis Ginter Botanical Garden, reached out to a small group of designers, planners, and horticulturists to consider how the New York City strategy might work in Richmond. In January 2013, with Lyndon Miller in attendance as a special guest, the group convened a meeting of forty community leaders representing different organizational affiliations. The purpose of the meeting was to provide a platform for these self-proclaimed "allies for a more beautiful RVA" to discuss ways in which cross-sector collaborations could work to improve public spaces in Richmond. In response to the considerable momentum generated from this first meeting, and with support from the allies in the room, Humphrey launched "Beautiful RVA" (short for "Beautiful Richmond, Virginia") as a regional coalition of public and private organizations invested in improving the quality of life in greater Richmond through public horticulture, urban greening, and community-based placemaking initiatives.

The list of individuals and organizations that wanted to be part of the discussion to beautify Richmond's public spaces grew quickly. In order to harness the growing amount of information from the coalition members, Humphrey initiated a biweekly "Ripple Recap" e-mail digest to share newsworthy greening initiatives, calls to action, appeals for volunteer services, and invitations for citizen input on strategic public and private greening projects.[52] To build an "enabling environment" for community-directed urban greening projects, coalition members worked to create the "Community Greening Toolkit," an online repository of resources that citizens can use to help design, budget, and plan beautification projects.[53]

FIGURE 5.4. Beautiful RVA logo.
Courtesy of Lewis Ginter Botanical Garden.

How the Partnership Functions

At its core, Beautiful RVA works to inspire and incubate the potential impact of diverse groups and organizations when focused around a common goal. While small, independent efforts from different sectors contribute to improving community needs, lasting solutions require coordinated efforts that can act to build the capacity for large-scale change. The Beautiful RVA coalition is composed of stakeholders with different yet complementary resources to implement community change.[54] According to Duron Chavis, manager of community engagement at Lewis Ginter, in the Beautiful RVA coalition, "every organization doesn't do the same thing; each organization supports a bigger vision of collective impact by contributing what it does best."[55]

In general, structuring a partnership that will have collective impact requires a well-funded backbone organization to provide overall strategic direction, facilitate dialogue between partners, manage data collection and analysis, handle communications, coordinate community outreach, and mobilize funding.[56] Lewis Ginter Botanical Garden is the backbone of Beautiful RVA. The garden hosts community meetings in its buildings and commits staff to help facilitate a common agenda among stakeholders and locate mutually reinforcing activities between organizations. The garden facilitates continuous communication between Beautiful RVA stakeholders and funded the design and development of a website that acts to advance the collective efforts of Beautiful RVA in strategic ways.[57]

Partnerships with neighborhoods, municipalities, nonprofits, and local universities are critical to securing funding for Beautiful RVA, which is consistent with growing evidence that collaborative approaches significantly influence public policy. Instead of selecting individual grantees, funders are investing in the potential for change brought by larger "systems" of coordinating organizations.[58] The Beautiful RVA coalition uses its members' diverse experience and expertise to its advantage when seeking grants to support its convening, staffing, and communications initiatives. Working together, partners in Beautiful RVA can submit more competitive grant applications that leverage their collective capacities, becoming collaborators instead of competitors for funding.

Ginter Urban Gardeners

A challenge for Beautiful RVA is that its organizations and stakeholders do not represent the racial and ethnic diversity of Richmond. While many of the geographic areas with the greatest need for greening and beautification are in low-income neighborhoods, few of the coalition members live or are located in these areas. To build bridges with urban neighborhoods and residents, Beautiful RVA needed to make a concerted effort to diversify its mission and members.

In 2016, the botanical garden hired Duron Chavis as its first community engagement coordinator. Now serving as manager of community engagement, Chavis is responsible for the garden's outreach and relationship building across a diverse community.[59] He is a native of Richmond and has successfully used community-based urban agriculture to build community relationships and empower local stakeholders as agents for positive neighborhood change. Chief among his tasks is to expand Beautiful RVA to include neighborhood-based urban greening and placemaking initiatives.

The need to diversify cultural institutions is not new, but Lewis Ginter is making major strides in building connections with people of color and low-income residents. Despite the biophilic link between people and nature, Chavis recognizes the complexities of social and environmental sustainability. "Our social ecosystems are just as unsustainable as the ways in which we interact with our environment," he said. "As such, our movement toward cultivating resilient urban landscapes has to be deliberate and intentional in cultivating and maintaining inclusivity. The biggest challenge is to remember that the ecology of our city is affected by the inequity that exists within our social interactions. Healing the land and healing our human-to-human interactions are threads on the same web we are weaving toward a healthy planet."[60] Chavis's goal is to use his community engagement role to help the botanical garden evolve its vision to make the garden a place for all and to extend the garden beyond its walls.

As one of his first endeavors, Chavis implemented Ginter Urban Gardeners, a training program that teaches citizens how to garden, but also how to inspire local change, lead large-scale projects, and coordinate volunteers. This twelve-week program is offered in various Richmond neighborhoods and teaches sustainable

FIGURE 5.5. Beautiful RVA members remediate a stormwater biofilter at Great Shiplock Park along the James River.
Photo by Phuong Tran. Courtesy of Lewis Ginter Botanical Garden.

horticulture, urban greening, and community building. Its goal is to provide citizens with the skills necessary to increase community-supported urban green spaces. Participants are selected through an application process that includes a $150 training fee, which can be waived when it poses a financial barrier for applicants.

The Ginter Urban Gardener program addresses not only sustainable horticulture and how to manage projects and volunteers but also the social history of the community in which the gardeners live. The first Ginter Urban Gardeners cohort intentionally represented a range of races, ages, abilities, and incomes. Part of the goal of this program is understanding difference and diversity, which can make collaboration more difficult.[61] According to Chavis, "The most challenging aspect of Beautiful RVA is consistent with most ecocentric movements toward sustainable cities: the challenge of creating and maintaining inclusivity across lines of race and class. For example, how does Beautiful RVA engage gentrification, affordable housing, and both wealth and health disparities in a way that considers those social factors as part of the urban ecosystem?"[62]

Discussions about segregation and urban renewal and their influence on the relationship residents have with nature are integrated into Ginter Urban Gardener training topics, often with guest speakers who can share local knowledge about Richmond's recent history. Some of the participants are from Jackson Ward, once a nationally recognized center of African American banks, clubs,

FIGURE 5.6.   Ginter Urban Gardeners 2017 cohort.
Photo by Phuong Tran. Courtesy of Lewis Ginter Botanical Garden.

insurance companies, and commercial and social institutions. This neighborhood was redlined in the 1930s because it was home to African Americans, and for similar reasons it was the path for federal urban renewal projects in the late 1950s. The Richmond-Petersburg Turnpike (now part of Interstate 95) bisected Jackson Ward, which was followed by desegregation and white flight that left much of Jackson Ward in the control of absentee landlords and real estate speculators. Today people are moving back to Jackson Ward, including residents who left several decades earlier. Ginter Urban Gardener participants are part of the effort to reclaim and rebuild the fabric of this historic African American neighborhood in a way that is both ecologically and socially responsible.

To enable these efforts, the Ginter Urban Gardener curriculum integrates training, trust building, and working together on greening efforts that recognize the history of the neighborhoods and their residents. In order to support their next steps, graduates of the Ginter Urban Gardener training have the opportunity to submit proposals to have Beautiful RVA fund their urban greening and beautification projects. Budgets from successful grants are used to fund this investment in recent graduates, covering items such as soil, tools, and plant material.

Lessons from Lewis Ginter Botanical Garden

When they are trusted, public gardens have the capacity to bring together diverse stakeholders to discuss common issues related to environmental goals. Lewis Ginter occupies that space as a neutral and trusted partner in the Richmond region. Its leadership role in Beautiful RVA offers approaches that other public gardens might consider as they navigate partnerships to promote nature-friendly environments in urban communities:

Be nimble, open, and ready for new partnerships. Because changing circumstances and new partnerships cannot always be anticipated in advance, organizations need to be flexible enough to embrace new opportunities. When the garden convened the first community discussion with "allies for a more beautiful RVA" around greening public spaces, it could not have predicted the plea it would receive to adopt a leadership role in a new coalition around beautification. The new partnerships that developed through Beautiful RVA happened because interests aligned across sectors and geographies, and the garden knew it could serve in a convening role for these disparate groups.

A diverse organizational staff has a positive impact on efforts to reach diverse audiences. The overarching goal for Ginter Urban Gardeners is to expand the relevance of the botanical garden to underserved neighborhoods in the greater Richmond area, most of which are predominantly African American. To build relationships and trust, the garden staff needs to diversify.

A "backbone organization" can find support for partnership efforts through local grant opportunities. Beautiful RVA adopted a model of achieving small successes that over time build support for additional funding opportunities. For Lewis Ginter, Richmond's Community Foundation grants provided start-up funding for both the Community Greening Toolkit and the Ginter Urban Gardener training program, but now funding is through the garden's operating budget. The garden continuously seeks grants and private philanthropy to offset associated operating expenses.

UC Davis's Learning by Leading

The campus of the University of California, Davis, has many of the environmental problems of a small city, including habitat degradation, food insecurity, and water pollution. It also has a large bureaucracy, making it sometimes difficult to effect change. When Kathleen Socolofsky began her tenure as the executive director of the UC Davis Arboretum in 1998, she had a vision of turning the entire campus into a learning landscape. This vision became a reality in 2008 when the arboretum was reconfigured to include all campus grounds and was renamed the UC Davis Arboretum and Public Garden (UCDAPG). As part of this change, Socolofsky was also named assistant vice chancellor of the university.

Once in this dual position, Socolofsky initiated the campus-wide GATEways project, which envisions the campus landscape as a portal into the university, to welcome visitors and showcase the creative work and spirit of inquiry at UC Davis. GATEways has been transformative, allowing faculty from a wide variety of disciplines to explore ways in which the landscape can contribute to their teaching or research. It has become a catalyst for bringing the combined knowledge of landscape operations and maintenance, habitat restoration, and community engagement to bear on some of the overall environmental issues faced by the campus.

Combining a focus on environmental stewardship with a belief in hands-on, mentor-led education, UCDAPG created the Learning by Leading (LxL) internship program. These leadership internships provide a training ground for students to cocreate, along with UCDAPG staff and academic and community partners, sustainable approaches to local, regional, and global issues. Mentored by experienced staff, more than one hundred promising students each year acquire real-world skills for twenty-first-century careers and become global citizens who inspire ordinary people to accomplish extraordinary change.

One of the key components of LxL is that students are given unusually high positions of leadership and responsibility over what they plan and do. One example is the management of Putah Creek, an iconic symbol for UC Davis. Running for nearly a mile and a half along the southern edge of campus, the waterway serves as a backbone for the arboretum's collections and provides the campus with a recreational and aesthetic amenity and biological resource. Unfortunately the water had become stationary and shallow, and for many years it regularly received an infusion of nutrients from leaves and dust as well as nitrogen- and phosphorus-rich recycled water from campus. This led to a buildup of duckweed and algae, a natural byproduct of what was essentially a stagnant pond.

In the spring of 2017, UCDAPG launched a multiyear project to reduce algae growth and sedimentation in the waterway by increasing water flow, deepening and narrowing the channel, and planting more native wetland vegetation on the banks. A dedicated fundraising effort allowed UCDAPG to launch a new Waterway Stewardship LxL team of students to plant the banks and improve the ecological health of the waterway.

Several ideas that began as LxL student-initiated "Signature Projects" expanded beyond campus and out into the surrounding region. The city of Davis is located in a region with regular droughts and fierce competition for available irrigation water. In 2017 several students from the LxL Sustainable Horticulture team took their experience in designing, constructing, and interpreting sustainable gardens on campus to the City of Davis to share with the public. They applied for and were awarded a grant through UC Davis's TGIF (The Green Initiative Fund) program to partner with a local elementary school to construct a sustainable stormwater/habitat school garden. The goal was to combine UC Davis's strengths in scientific research and community engagement with the elementary school's eagerness to respond to and teach about local environmental issues.

In collaboration with Marguerite Montgomery Elementary School, the interns converted a patch of lawn into a flower garden that provided habitat and food for pollinators; reduced water usage, energy consumption, and maintenance requirements; and replaced water-loving plants with native and climate-adapted species. As part of their outreach effort, the interns created a series of community planting sessions and public workshops designed to engage Davis community residents in building a healthy urban ecosystem, connect them to their landscapes, and educate them on the benefits provided by low-water habitat gardens.

A Native American student at UC Davis wanted to harness the combined knowledge and resources of a large research university to help improve the ecological condition of her tribal lands. She knew that she wanted to help restore the landscape to what it might have been in previous generations, but she didn't know how to begin. When she learned about the LxL Propagation internship, she contacted Taylor Lewis, nursery manager for the arboretum, and enlisted his help in teaching her how to propagate plants that were culturally significant to her tribe. She worked with Lewis over the summer of 2016 at the Arboretum Teaching Nursery to gain the knowledge necessary to grow plants for her tribe, the Paskenta band of Nomaki Indians. "I participated in a joint internship sponsored by the Intertribal Agriculture Council (IAC) and the National Resources Conservation Service [NRCS]," she explained, "but a large part of it included time at the Arboretum Teaching Nursery. NRCS provided the equipment and the greenhouse space for me to grow the plants I was interested in cultivating, but I needed to know more about actual plant propagation techniques. That's where the Arboretum Teaching Nursery came in." She took her newfound knowledge one step further by working with UCDAPG staff to host a group of high school students participating in the IAC's Youth Leadership Summit. With connections to Native American tribes in California, Nevada, Hawaii, and New Mexico, the students learned how to grow culturally important plants for a large-scale environmental restoration project on Maidu land in Plumas County.[63]

How the Partnership Functions

The ultimate success of a university public garden in promoting change and alleviating environmental problems both locally and regionally depends on constituents who bring energy to a cause and are willing to push it forward. LxL is always evolving as a multipronged partnership between UCDAPG, members of the faculty and university administrators, the Department of Grounds and Landscape Management, and the students themselves.

Student interns enrolling in LxL have the opportunity to select from among twelve separate initiatives, but within this structure, new ideas are always sought and considered. More experienced students serve as mentors to incoming interns, and are entrusted with considerable latitude and decision making. UCDAPG staff members provide overall leadership, but as with the Native American student described previously, undergraduates are always encouraged to propose new approaches.

It is unusual for a university public garden director to also serve as a member of the senior administration. But Socolofsky has been able to leverage her vice chancellor position to form alliances with the senior planning and grounds management staff to expedite new initiatives that might otherwise get bogged down in institutional bureaucracy.

Lessons from the UC Davis Arboretum and Public Garden

The LxL program has been so successful that it is now being replicated at several other campuses in the US and Canada. But each college and university is unique, with different programs, natural resources, faculty, and students. So as LxL travels to other institutions, it is vital that each of them adapt the approach to meet their local conditions. But LxL's experience offers a guideline for other schools in several different ways:

Start locally and expand from there. The UC Davis LxL program started as a small initiative, and has only expanded as members of the university administration have embraced it. With the university backing it, LxL could feel confident enough to expand its programs into the city of Davis.

Try out programs first before adopting them widely. As with other examples in this chapter, it was key to UCDAPG to conduct pilot programs to test out partnerships and student-led projects. It can be difficult to make changes in a large bureaucracy, so starting with small initiatives can be less daunting. Successful ones can be used in other, larger projects until they become the norm for getting things done. For example, LxL students first started creating drought-tolerant landscapes in the formal arboretum. Once they proved they could do it well with staff mentorship, the administration felt more confident about allowing them to take on the Putah Creek project on the central campus.

Cocreate with as many partners as you can effectively manage. UCDAPG found that partnering with administrative and academic partners on campus, as well as with nonuniversity community partners, only strengthened the buy-in and ownership of its work. As more people took part in envisioning a project or program, there were more advocates and also more potential funders. And that, in turn, led to more support.

Pittsburgh: A Legacy of Innovation and Philanthropy

Pittsburgh, Pennsylvania, was the US capital of steel production during the late nineteenth and much of the twentieth century. Miles of steel mills and blast furnaces occupied most of the landscape where Pittsburgh's three rivers converged, and for 150 years, coal provided inexpensive fuel used in homes, industry, and river and rail transport. The concentration of mills resulted in such poor air quality that Pittsburgh was notorious for its midday darkness from steel production smoke. Residents living in nearby neighborhoods could not dry laundry outside on most days for fear of coal-stained clothes. Because the smoke from the steel mills meant progress and jobs for residents, the environment, public health, and general quality-of-life concerns were not high priorities.

The deindustrialization of Pittsburgh in the 1980s resulted in huge losses for the city. High-paying factory jobs were gone, and hundreds of thousands of people left the city, seeking opportunities elsewhere. Between 1979 and 1988, the region lost 44 percent of its manufacturing jobs with the collapse of the steel industry, severely affecting the economic and social conditions in working-class mill towns.[64] Campaigns to rebrand Pittsburgh as a "headquarters city" rather than a "steel city" sought to physically and economically reorganize the region around a service-sector economy and emphasize research and development initiatives that leveraged its medical and educational institutions.[65]

Pittsburgh has a strong giving culture. In the nineteenth century, contributions from philanthropists such as Andrew Carnegie, Henry Clay Frick, Henry Heinz, Andrew Mellon, and George Westinghouse introduced community assets such as libraries, museums, hospitals, and universities as a means to improve the city's economic competitiveness and the lives of its residents. And in the second half of the twentieth century, philanthropy was key to enabling the city to survive deindustrialization and played a major role in Pittsburgh's "rebirth" as a city.

Complementing the city's philanthropic tradition were "norms in Pittsburgh to partner on projects," according to Catherine DeLoughry, senior vice president for public affairs at the Allegheny Conference on Community Development.[66] In the post–World War II period when the future of the city was clouded by air pollution, a coalition of civic leaders from business, nonprofits, universities, and government joined to create controls for air and water quality. Incorporated as the Allegheny Conference on Community Development and led by the city's Republican business elite, this coalition organized public- and private-sector partnerships to improve the region's economy and quality of life for much of the second half of the twentieth century.[67] The conference spearheaded environmental cleanup and urban redevelopment agendas and coordinated partnerships that enabled Pittsburgh to survive deindustrialization, diversifying the region's economy from one based on industry to one based on innovation and technology.

In 1991 the conference helped create the Allegheny Regional Asset District to support and finance regional assets such as libraries, parks and recreation, and cultural and civic facilities and programs. The Regional Asset District receives half of the proceeds from the 1 percent Allegheny County sales and use tax; the other half is paid directly to the county and municipal governments by the state treasurer.[68] From 1995 to 2016, the 1 percent county sales tax paid by residents of and visitors to Allegheny County resulted in a $3.4 billion investment in the region. For 2016, the Regional Asset District adopted a $96.9 million budget serving ninety-three regional assets. Approximately 8 percent was allocated to regional facilities, including Phipps Conservatory and Botanical Gardens.[69] The funding of regional assets and the emphasis on innovation and technology has led to some very progressive innovations in the city.

Today, America's "Steel Town" is well on its way to transitioning from reliance on fossil fuels to leadership in renewable energy. Pittsburgh is celebrated as a model postindustrial city, reinvented as a knowledge and technology hub and attracting tech giants like Google and Amazon. While many of the old brick buildings remain stained from the steel mills' thick black smoke, these industrial relics have been repurposed in some areas of the city for new residential development, riverfront recreation, and open space.

Pittsburgh is highly ranked nationally in the number of buildings certified under Leadership in Energy and Environmental Design (LEED), a rating system intended to promote practices in the building and construction industry that are sustainability focused and energy and water efficient, and that promote healthy workplace environments.[70] Two of Pittsburgh's buildings were among the first twelve fully green buildings to be certified in the nation.[71] Civic leaders, investors, and philanthropists continue to support creative and entrepreneurial solutions for improving the quality of life for Pittsburgh residents, but as the city surges from its recent tech boom, some are asking who gets left out,[72] emphasizing the importance of including the broader community in discussions and learning around sustainable innovations.

Turning Cultural Investment into Innovation

Founded in 1893, Phipps Conservatory was a gift to the city of Pittsburgh from the philanthropist Henry W. Phipps, who wanted it to serve as a "source of instruction as well as pleasure for the people."[73] At that time, Phipps focused on importing and showcasing exotic plants from around the world, many of which were introduced that year at the World's Columbian Exposition in Chicago.

After one hundred years under city management, in 1993 Phipps became a privately managed, city-owned nonprofit, and in 1994 Richard Piacentini was hired as the public garden's director. A master planning process for campus expansion was initiated in the late 1990s, focused on improving visitor amenities, expanding revenue-generating opportunities, and replacing dilapidated facilities. However, when the green building industry created its rating protocol in 2000, Phipps decided to pursue LEED certification for its new Welcome Center. With each additional project, Phipps raised the bar, and it began to fully reimagine the campus as an international leader in sustainable architecture and operations.[74] Under the direction of Piacentini, Phipps has been transformed into one of the world's smartest, greenest public gardens. The driving force behind that transformation is a commitment to using innovation as a compelling tool to connect people with nature.

At the forefront of Phipps's efforts to educate audiences about conservation and the environment and to inspire sustainability innovation is its Center for

Sustainable Landscapes (CSL). Unveiled in 2012, the CSL is a 24,350-square-foot education, research, and administration complex designed as a model of human health, ecological health, and sustainability that others can emulate. The CSL is a "net-zero energy" and "net-zero water" building, which means that it generates all its energy with renewable resources and captures and treats all its water on-site. It serves as a demonstration site for those interested in a hands-on, technical understanding of green building certification, and it was the first building to meet four of the highest green certifications: the Living Building Challenge, LEED Platinum, the Four Stars Sustainable SITES Initiative for landscapes, and the WELL Building Platinum project, a designation that only the CSL has received. The CSL building was subsequently joined by a Living Building–certified Nature Lab, and a third facility, the Exhibit Staging Center (ESC). Phipps now has three Living Buildings on its site, each showcasing a different construction type: new (CSL), modular (Nature Lab), and retrofit (ESC). The resulting "living campus" will emerge as the first multifacility living system of its kind in the world.

The CSL's purpose is to inspire a transformation in sustainability thinking outside the public garden, but Phipps also uses it to engage, educate, and benefit its staff. The Facilitated Integrated Design Process that produced the new building's design focused on Phipps's operational needs, the building's functionality,

FIGURE 5.7. The Phipps Center for Sustainable Landscapes.
Photo by Paul G. Wiegman. Courtesy of Phipps Conservatory and Botanical Gardens.

and architectural and engineering systems that could improve employee health and performance. Phipps engaged the community and its staff in bimonthly design charrette workshops with the building design team throughout the two-year design and planning process.[75] This participatory process built considerable internal support from constituents and garden employees, but also provided important education opportunities for garden staff about the innovative green building.

From a Biophilia Network to a Biophilic City

The Center for Sustainable Landscapes instigated a new pioneering era for Phipps and in the process demonstrated the public garden's prowess as a thought leader, innovator, and grassroots organizer. In 2015 Phipps introduced the Phipps Research Institute for Biophilia and Science Engagement, a research initiative designed to inspire others with the concept and principles of biophilia and to examine the connections between human and ecological health, particularly at the intersection of the built and natural environments.

Under Piacentini's leadership, Phipps launched a pilot chapter for a global Biophilia Network in Pittsburgh, which is run through the public garden and is dedicated to strengthening biophilia through education, discussion, and local action. The group meets monthly at the CSL for expert presentations, discussion, and sharing of ideas.

In September 2016, Phipps encouraged Pittsburgh's mayor, Bill Peduto, and city council to take a step beyond the local Biophilia Network and join the Biophilic Cities Project, a global movement that focuses on designing urban environments that incorporate natural features and build abundant opportunities for engagement with nature in urban settings.[76] According to Timothy Beatley, biophilic cities "invest in the social and physical infrastructure that helps bring urbanites to closer connection and understanding of nature, whether through natural history museums, wildlife centers, school-based nature initiatives, or parks and recreation programs and projects, among many others."[77] Signing on as a biophilic city is not simply a formality; it commits the municipality to infrastructure investments that increase urban-nature connections and obligates a city's administration to annually measure progress on a number of environmentally oriented criteria.

The short list of biophilic cities across the globe includes Washington, DC, San Francisco, Milwaukee, Singapore, and Wellington, New Zealand.[78] These share best practices and strategies as they work to pass legislation to implement policies that support a biophilic city and find resources to support new investments. Although the Biophilic Cities Project promotes information sharing across

FIGURE 5.8. Phipps Research Institute for Biophilia and Science Engagement.
Photo by Paul G. Wiegman. Courtesy of Phipps Conservatory and Botanical Gardens.

municipalities with this designation, there is no connection with organizations, sectors, and individuals that might provide local knowledge and financial and political resources, all of which are important for implementation.

During the launch of Pittsburgh as a biophilic city, participants noted that many people were involved in somewhat similar networks (e.g., the Urban Sustainability Directors Network, the Wild Cities Project, and the C40 Cities Climate Leadership Group, among others) involving a wide variety of people interested in a common goal: connecting people to nature. Piacentini felt these disparate but like-minded networks could organize around the local Biophilia Network to capitalize on the strong grassroots energy in Pittsburgh to build advocacy for the biophilia movement, and move the needle faster toward implementation.[79]

The symbiotic relationship between the city and Phipps is founded on a shared goal of environmental leadership. From the perspective of the public garden, it needed to pitch the biophilic cities idea in such a way that it could help the mayor achieve his goals. Specifically, if Pittsburgh agreed to sign on to be a biophilic city, Phipps would support the mayor by helping him carry out his environmental agenda. The financial commitment made by the city to join the Biophilic Cities Project underscores Phipps's role as a trusted adviser to the city.

The relationship between the public garden and elected officials was several years in the making, however. Phipps recognizes that strong partnerships with decision makers are essential to institutionalizing sustainability innovations. As a result, Phipps purposefully links its green building and sustainability innovations with elected officials. Any important openings or exhibits at the garden include presentations by the mayor and other elected officials on the importance of conservation and sustainability. Conversely, because Phipps is a physical asset in the city and a center for sustainability innovation, the mayor and the Allegheny Conference on Community Development use it as a destination for important city guests.

Lessons from Phipps

Public gardens have the expertise that enables them to serve as innovators in their region, introducing new ways of thinking about or interacting with the natural environment. Our review of Phipps reveals subtle yet important approaches that can be used to simultaneously build knowledge and support around innovation:

Hands-on education (in this case around innovation) is the key to gaining buy-in. Phipps adopted this as an inclusive process to gain support from the community and its staff through an integrative team-building design.

Walk your talk. Despite limited experience and available technology to realize his future-oriented vision, Piacentini believed in the idea of green buildings. It was risky, but his passionate belief led Phipps to shift its focus and move in a radically new direction. It also meant that in order to be authentic, the lessons Phipps learned about sustainability in green buildings had to be applied to everything it did, from operations to programs.

Build credibility and your partnerships incrementally. Phipps strategically built its credibility and reputation as a leader and expert in sustainability over a decade.

The initiatives investigated in this chapter demonstrate that efforts to improve a community's environmental conditions must recognize the importance of understanding what the natural environment means *locally* and that a community has more than one story about its relationship to the natural environment. A community's history and the experiences of all its residents influence the perceived relevance of the natural environment, and the ways in which people conceptualize the need for and potential benefits of green space. In the cases of Lewis Ginter Botanical Garden in Richmond and the Missouri Botanical Garden in St. Louis, these environmental initiatives succeeded when they met their respective communities where they were, both physically and experientially.

Despite the different histories and community conditions in Davis, Pittsburgh, Richmond, and St. Louis, a common theme recognized by the public gardens working on environmental initiatives in these cities is the important role of building authentic local stakeholder involvement and support. In all cases, relationships are built with local community stakeholders through deliberate and well-constructed outreach efforts. This can take various forms: while

Phipps adopts a strong role as innovator and demonstration site, Lewis Ginter is a convener and adopts a community-organizing role to activate local change in neighborhoods. The Missouri Botanical Garden serves as local science expert and invests in youth leadership development, which the UC Davis Arboretum and Public Garden also does through the leadership development of its students.

Finally, this chapter reveals an overarching recognition that partners and community stakeholders cannot "buy into" an environmental vision or initiative if they do not understand it. For example, Phipps both dedicates itself to serving as a demonstration of the theory and practice around sustainable architecture and landscapes and *listens* to its staff, members, and community stakeholders to better understand their positions and interests as a means of refining its message and outreach. Creating deliberate opportunities for information sharing and education around the issues builds support and ownership that can be instrumental in implementing an initiative.

STRATEGIES FOR THE DEVELOPMENT OF SUCCESSFUL PARTNERSHIPS

The programs highlighted in this book demonstrate that although small, independent efforts from different sectors contribute to improving community livability, lasting solutions on a larger scale often require coordinated efforts that join the collective strengths of actors from various sectors working toward a common goal. The organizations initiating these programs were able to build and foster partnerships to influence specific livability indicators. In our analysis of these partnerships, we focused on the preconditions and strategic approaches that others might utilize to create or grow partnerships with public gardens. In this chapter, we distill the principal strategies that public gardens and their partner organizations can use to effectively leverage their collective power to create positive community change through the sharing of knowledge and resources. In particular, the chapter focuses on strategies that help public gardens, nonprofits, municipalities, and community organizations identify, select, and cultivate partnerships to create more sustainable, livable, and equitable communities.

An important takeaway from all the programs analyzed in this book is that public gardens offer unique assets and skills that make them attractive partners for initiatives aimed at increasing the livability of urban areas. Municipalities and community organizations partner with cultural nonprofits like public gardens because they recognize that these institutions have positive community reputations and contribute to livable cities. Business and government leaders partner with cultural institutions because they recognize how such organizations aid economic development. Community development groups partner with cultural nonprofits because they see these institutions as a means of promoting the inclusion of all residents in the community's cultural life.

Another takeaway from this research is that, like other anchor institutions, public gardens are increasingly pressured to demonstrate their relevance to the community and their commitment to serving the public good. Through big-vision strategic planning processes, public gardens should clearly identify their unique institutional assets and how those assets can best be utilized to accomplish larger community goals. A component of this self-analysis needs to be an examination of ways in which the garden's scientific knowledge and horticultural resources can be leveraged through partnerships with business, government, and community-based groups, while remaining true to the garden's mission and longer-term vision of itself.

The recommendations and strategies outlined in this chapter draw on the information and experiences gleaned during the course of researching this book. The recommendations are not intended to be exhaustive, but rather to serve as models that public gardens and their partners can adapt based on their specific goals, community context, and assets. While the strategies appear to be sequential, the reader should recognize that building organizational relationships involves missteps, reiterations, and responses to changing circumstances.

Learn about (and from) the Community

When considering a new community-based initiative, it is important to begin by understanding the community. As a starting point, a snapshot of the community can be constructed using secondary data, or data previously collected and publicly available. A common source of secondary data is the US Census Bureau, the federal agency whose primary mission is to conduct the US census every ten years, including counts of the population by age, race, Hispanic origin, and gender. In between the decennial censuses, the Census Bureau conducts a series of surveys to gauge real-time population estimates, which helps states, local governments, and communities plan for needs related to schools, hospitals, infrastructure, and fire or police services. The American Community Survey is an example of an ongoing survey that provides estimates about the economic and social characteristics of the community, such as levels of income, education attainment, migration, housing, language proficiency, and employment. Together, these secondary data points contribute to an understanding of a community in terms of who lives there and how demographics may be shifting, all of which informs possible strengths and needs.

Although secondary data points will capture important elements of the community, the only way to truly understand the community is to talk to and learn from those who know it best—its residents. People in a given community possess knowledge about that community developed over time and based on experience. This knowledge may include information about the community's identity, history, current conditions, and needs that is not contained in data sets but is embedded in local practices, institutions, and relationships. By engaging community members in honest dialogue, representatives from the public garden build a climate of trust that can be indispensable as a program is carried out.

We propose several suggestions for public gardens seeking to establish relationships with their communities. Building on the community assessment of needs and existing resources, public gardens should invest in learning the public history of their community, including its history of social activism, to understand the conditions and power dynamics that have shaped the current environment. Identify existing resident leaders and community-based organizations, commit to learning about and recognizing the efforts they have contributed to building the quality of life in the community. Talk with resident leaders and local organizations to gain perspectives on the needs or desires of the community and to gauge the viability of building a relationship around those goals. In the process, keep in mind that local residents have probably seen more than one well-meaning effort fall on its face and are therefore suspicious of completely new initiatives.

The Pennsylvania Horticultural Society and its municipal partners featured in chapter 1 demonstrate the value and roles of local knowledge and engagement around the concentration of vacant lots in the city of Philadelphia. Although the city was allocating tremendous resources to cleaning vacant lots in the 1990s, this process was not sustainable, and the investments made little improvement to the community conditions. The PHS Philadelphia LandCare program and its partners in the Division of Housing and Community Development (DHCD) began to design a pilot program to test the feasibility of a community-based approach to vacant land management. To establish a community-based program, however, they realized the importance of local knowledge: were neighborhoods concerned with the vacant land, and if so, what efforts were already underway?

PHS and DHCD filled this knowledge and resource gap by establishing a partnership with the New Kensington Community Development Corporation, which had a shared interest in converting vacant land to green space. The New Kensington CDC possessed assets important to a community-based effort, including information about resident priorities and firsthand knowledge about the impacts of residents' diminished neighborhood pride, sense of safety, and maintenance of property in their neighborhood. Together these partners created a plan to clean and maintain the lots more efficiently, one that actively involved community volunteers. They submitted the plan to the city, and the result is a very successful LandCare program that is now a line item in the city budget.

An examination of the ways in which a new initiative can have the greatest impact needs to include an exploration of opportunities to better support marginalized or otherwise overlooked portions of the community. Denver Botanic Gardens, for example, identified young military veterans as an underserved community based on data showing high rates of unemployment among this group. As described in chapter 4, DBG partnered with the Kaiser Permanente Foundation and a Denver-based Veterans to Farmers program to design the Chatfield Veterans Farm program, focused on helping to facilitate veterans' transition back into the labor force.[1] While the overall goal of the program is to connect military veterans with careers in small-scale farming, the program administrators recognize that many members of their clientele struggle with mental health and social issues. They therefore utilize an approach that "engages the mind, body and soul in a holistic approach to sustainable living." During twenty-one weeks of training, participants learn various horticultural and business techniques and build their self-confidence and sense of identity as entrepreneurs.[2] Many graduates have gained employment with area farms, or in other agriculturally related businesses.

Identify Community Assets

Community-based initiatives should emerge from a strengths-based approach that is first informed by the existing assets. Assets include the skills, talents, and abilities of individual people, the public places and spaces within the community, and the local institutions that can be leveraged to strengthen the community. Adopting an asset-based approach to partnership development increases the likelihood of locally appropriate and relevant initiatives that can be carried out and replicated by other local organizations and residents. It also empowers community members and gives them shared ownership of the project.

The success of Brooklyn Botanic Garden's urban greening efforts described in chapter 1 is grounded in the recognition of local assets. BBG staff saw the residents and businesses of individual blocks in the borough as important partners in the beautification of Brooklyn's neighborhoods. The BBG staff walked through the neighborhoods, talked with residents, and realized that many of them already had a knack for growing plants, mainly in window boxes, and that their knowledge and technique could benefit a broader greening initiative. BBG shared this preliminary research and the idea of using horticulture and urban greening as a tool to improve the quality of life in parts of the borough with local elected officials, whose job it was to advocate for residents. These officials helped to link BBG with their networks of community leaders and neighborhood residents around this common goal. The result has been the long-standing and extremely successful Greenest Block in Brooklyn contest, much of the success of which is attributed to the strong foundation of research and relationship building that BBG invested in from the outset.

Building local leadership can be challenging, especially in low-income or underserved areas where residents are often more focused on day-to-day survival. Nevertheless, potential leaders are present in every neighborhood, waiting to be nurtured. Creative partnerships involving public gardens invest in community organizing and leadership development as part of their strategy. Such efforts go beyond mobilizing community *support* for the partnership's goal and work to organize community *capacity* by cultivating leaders and enabling them to be change agents. The public garden may not be the organization best positioned to provide leadership training, especially if one of its partners is community based and has leadership development as its primary focus.

When Karen Washington moved to the Bronx, New York, in 1988, she had already been a community activist for a number of years. Community outreach staff members from the New York Botanical Garden recognized Karen's talents and passion and recruited her to help develop the nascent Bronx Green-Up program, described in detail in chapter 3, dedicated to assisting Bronx residents with growing their own food. Since that early collaboration, Karen has become a nationally recognized expert in urban farming, forming the community garden coalition La Familia Verde, helping to launch City Farms Market, and cofounding Black Urban Growers. In 2014, she was awarded the James Beard Leadership award for her advocacy and vision. Karen Washington's trajectory in community-based leadership exemplifies the potential of vision, dedication, and partnerships to build individual capacity.

A community asset can also be a physical structure or place, such as a school, hospital, church, library, or recreation center, or a public place that already belongs to the community, such as a park. When a well-used community asset is removed, it can be quite disruptive to a community, especially its young people. This was the case in the lower-income Berwick neighborhood of Columbus, Ohio, when two local recreation centers closed in 2009 due to lack of funding. While individuals like Karen Washington have been motivated by the presence of food deserts in their neighborhoods, this was a case of a recreation desert, and the community response was the creation of the Highland Youth Garden. Under the auspices of the Growing to Green program of the Franklin Park Conservatory, introduced in chapter 3, and fourteen other sponsors including the City of Columbus, a nearly half-acre garden was developed that now serves young people as a safe, supportive space for after-school and summer activities. The garden serves 375 students from Highland elementary schools and the Educational Academy for Boys and Girls during the school year and as many as 200 young people each week during the summer.[3]

Inventory and Assess Internal Strengths

Understanding the conditions inside your organization is critical to understanding how it might contribute to the livability of a community. What are the organization's strengths, and what is it known for? In what ways is the organizational mission being met or unmet? What resources and capacities are available to further realize elements of the mission? For public gardens, one likely strength or asset is the garden's knowledge about plants and plant science. Building on this credibility, public gardens in recent years have directed their scientific resources toward environmental issues that range from mitigating climate change to stemming the loss of plant biodiversity to improving the air or water quality in their communities.

As detailed in chapter 3, the NYC Compost Project is an example of a partnership built around the assets of public gardens: plant expertise and ability to teach and train the public. To fulfill a city goal of reducing the amount of waste going to landfills while simultaneously helping to rebuild the city's soils, the New York City Department of Sanitation partnered with several public gardens in the city to educate the public on how to produce and use compost in an urban setting. In the Bronx, the Compost Project works with the New York Botanical Garden to offer the Master Composter certification program, in which enrollees learn all aspects of community composting over eight Thursday evenings. All of the information shared through these classes and other Compost Project materials is scientifically backed and factual. Working on projects like this has the added benefit of enabling gardeners to make the connection between sustainability and individual health.[4]

Another strength of public gardens is their expertise is developing scientifically based education programs. The Fairchild Challenge, as described in chapter 2, is a hugely successful program of the Fairchild Tropical Botanic Garden designed for middle and high school students to engage in citizen science projects. Since 2015, NASA has partnered with Fairchild to work with scientists from NASA in testing edible plant varieties to determine which could be grown on the International Space Station. Over the past four years, over fifty thousand students and their teachers have been testing factors that may influence plant growth, flavor, and nutrition. NASA will use students' data to determine which plants are selected for further testing and will be potentially grown in space.[5]

Public gardens also have the ability to reach far beyond their physical footprint to influence regional sustainability. When the environmental initiative is located away from the city, however, the garden needs to establish a connection to its urban visitors and audience. The Chicago Botanic Garden does this in its work with the Illinois Department of Natural Resources researching soil health and its role in prairie and woodland species restoration. The garden's communication office promotes the relevance of the research with public statements about how restored habitats contribute to improved water and air quality for Chicago area residents. This level of public outreach requires a high degree of coordination between scientists, educators, and interpreters within the garden, and between garden staff and community and regional partners, to make sure that the messaging is both coherent and consistent.[6]

The people power of public gardens rests largely on the commitment of huge numbers of volunteers. At Cheyenne Botanic Gardens, in Cheyenne, Wyoming, for example, 90 percent of all labor is contributed by volunteers, and that volunteer workforce comprises seniors, youth at risk, individuals with physical or intellectual disabilities, and those in transitional housing. Volunteer tasks are matched to the aptitude of the individual, and no one is turned away based on their abilities. Often the fate of meetings between disparate groups is based not just on who is invited and involved, but on where the meeting is held. Another strength of public gardens is that their physical spaces are often viewed as neutral territory by representatives of community groups. This is the case for the diverse members of Beautiful RVA, who meet regularly at Lewis Ginter Botanical Garden around a table where all viewpoints are respected.

A final asset that public gardens contribute to collaborations with community groups is their experience in seeking external support, including technical expertise in grant writing and solicitation of private gifts. While the Growing to Green program featured in chapter 3 has partnered with hundreds of public schools and youth groups in the greater Columbus area, its parent organization, the Franklin Park Conservatory and Botanical Gardens, has a strong track record of applying for and receiving government and corporate grants that support the program. The Scotts Miracle-Gro Company has been especially supportive, and this is a relationship that Franklin Park continues to nurture by featuring the company's logo in many of their outreach materials and by publicly recognizing the corporate support. The relationship is mutually beneficial, since Scotts is associated with the positive image that Franklin Park enjoys in the region.

Build Institution-Wide Support

Efforts to promote the livability and health of communities quickly lead to discussions about the resources appropriate to support these initiatives and how collaborative action might build the institutional capacity to deliver such improvements. A new community-based initiative cannot be conceived of and carried out by a single staff member, or even a single department. To be successful, the entire organization—administration, senior staff, and board—must believe that the project supports the garden's mission and priorities.

In most cases, senior staff members will serve as the advocates for the initiative, convincing board or staff members that the effort is worthwhile and appropriate. To do so, advocates must do their homework, starting with researching the experiences of other public gardens or communities with similar initiatives. Identifying governmental or philanthropic grants that could support the proposed effort can go a long way toward building institutional support. Finally, advocates should review the institution's most recent strategic plans and annual reports to identify ways in which the proposed initiative could build on existing efforts.

Inherent in a commitment to partner on an initiative is a pledge to provide the resources necessary to sustain the effort. As illustrated in chapter 5, when Lewis Ginter Botanical Garden began convening discussions about its role in launching Beautiful RVA and the Ginter Urban Gardeners program, it was with the support of its board and staff, who recognized that these efforts furthered the garden's mission of "connecting people to plants to improve communities."[7] This required laying the groundwork for discussions with board members: sharing information on community needs, linking proposed initiatives with the organization's mission, and providing evidence that there was both the demand and the external funding opportunities to sustain this investment over a longer-term period.[8]

Social equity initiatives are ones that break down barriers to opportunity for underserved populations. Members of the garden's key constituencies may question why a horticulturally based organization would get involved with social equity issues. Brian Vogt, CEO of Denver Botanic Gardens, has heard several arguments along these lines. When garden members and supporters say that working on diversity and inclusion is going to be hard, he responds that every step forward is progress. When they express the concern that such a focus will hurt fundraising, he counters that since his garden adopted its diversity and inclusion agenda it has seen a huge increase in overall support. Behind his efforts to expand the garden's audiences is his belief that the key is meeting people where they are, appreciating all that they bring to the table, and developing programming based on real needs.[9]

The gardens with the strongest track records in getting organization-wide support involve as many departments as possible in the initiative's creation and development. The Chicago Botanic Garden's Science Career Continuum, highlighted in chapter 2, involves every department in some aspect of the mentoring and operations of the program. Because for many of the students the program extends from middle school through college, it means that the close bonds established between staff and students reinforce the likelihood of student success.

Apply an Equity Lens to All Initiatives

Social change goals frequently intersect with community development agendas, so it is important for partners to deepen their collective understanding about equity and its role as a key contributor to the issues being addressed. When place-making efforts seek to bring data-driven solutions to diverse and low-income communities, it is important to apply an equity lens to examine the ways in which residents of those communities are involved in the process and to anticipate how efforts might lead to unintended consequences for residents.

Negative outcomes of interventions such as urban greening must be considered early. For example, recent media reports have focused on the "Tale of Two Brooklyns"—the contrast between some neighborhoods that have seen a dramatic increase in wealth and other neighborhoods that still struggle with the legacy of decades of poverty and neglect.[10] Brooklyn is not unlike many other urban centers in the United States that strive to create vibrant, safe urban neighborhoods without also creating a wave of gentrification.[11] After decades of fleeing to the suburbs, middle- and upper-income populations are returning to downtown neighborhoods and in the process are changing the urban landscape and the affordability of housing.[12] Gentrification is a gradual process in which upper- or middle-income families displace low-income residents, mostly people of color, who can no longer afford the higher rents or property taxes that result when neighborhoods are upgraded.

As a result, many mayors and urban planners are working with community leaders to find innovative solutions to make neighborhoods safer, healthier, and more aesthetically attractive while simultaneously keeping cities affordable for all income levels. Sometimes urban greening and beautification initiatives lead to what is known as "green gentrification" or "environmental gentrification,"[13] whereby greening initiatives intended to make older and lower-income areas more livable instead stimulate gentrification and the displacement of the residents those same strategies were designed to serve.

In forming partnerships whose intentions are to improve the lives of community members, public gardens must strive to avoid contributing to such gentrification efforts. One way to do this is to conduct an internal diversity and inclusion audit. Brooklyn Botanic Garden has created a rubric called TARP, which stands for "team, audience, representation, and programming." In all of its education and community-outreach initiatives, BBG considers how it presents itself to the public and how it meaningfully and authentically reflects the needs of each audience. As stated by Sonal Bhatt, vice president for education and interpretation, success is predicated on bringing about a culture change at the garden and on building empathy and understanding of one another.[14]

Another approach is to collaborate on projects that clean and green degraded lots and blocks in ways that positively affect neighborhood stability while avoiding social upheavals. The previously mentioned PHS LandCare program, in partnership with the City of Philadelphia, is an excellent example of this "just green enough" strategy.

It can also be difficult to anticipate how neighborhood greening efforts might affect long-term residents. A recent report by the Federal Reserve Bank of Philadelphia that studied large cities across the US found that the amount of displacement of original residents attributable to gentrification is relatively small. In addition, the researchers found that many low-income residents remained in their neighborhoods and benefited from the changing characteristics of the community.[15]

We should note that it is not just large public gardens with huge budgets that are able to adopt social equity approaches. The relatively small Bellevue Botanical Garden in the state of Washington has worked with the City of Bellevue's Diversity Advantage Team to examine ways in which the garden can attract new demographic groups to its site, and how it can effectively reach out to members of these groups. The administrators and staff of the garden recognize that such an approach requires intentional relationship building with a broad group of people within the community. But they are committed to making continual progress over a long period.[16]

Locate Complementary Partners

A key finding of our research is that gardens must be selective about the programs in which they invest and the organizations with which they collaborate.

With constant pressures on budget, staffing, and facilities, most US public gardens and horticultural societies recognize that they simply cannot pursue every programmatic opportunity. Rather, each institution must carefully triangulate the community-identified needs, the specific resources and abilities the organization can contribute, and other partners with common agendas that might provide complementary skills and resources.

Potential partners, including corporations, governments, community groups, and local citizens, will have differing objectives, but locating where those objectives intersect is key to establishing a workable cross-sector initiative. In the case of organizations with formal structures, a useful source for locating intersecting missions or goals is their strategic plans. Before they initiated formal discussions with one another, the organizations that eventually formed the Urban Vitality and Ecology (UVE) Initiative in St. Louis spent time reviewing the missions, policy documents, and strategic plans of the other organizations. As detailed in chapter 5, these partners used a process that helped them to identify "urban conservation" as the common goal that could be supported by each individual organization.[17]

A resource profile of local organizations is a useful tool that can help to identify organizations with the assets to support an initiative. Such profiles extend well beyond the financial assets that might be brought to a partnership. Some of the most useful assets include technical knowledge around a particular task, expertise in a topic area or facilitation process, or human capital in the form of a strong volunteer base.

Ideally, each partner organization occupies a different place within a collaborative partnership, offering unique resources that are mutually beneficial to the partner organizations. Entities should know their own and their partners' capabilities and how these different resources contribute to the partnership's ability to achieve the desired outcome. Returning to the UVE example, one partner (the Missouri Department of Conservation) had funding, another partner (the City of St. Louis) had established relationships with the local communities, and a third (the Missouri Botanical Garden) had the expertise in urban conservation and could provide technical assistance on the ground. However, if an institution fails to own and then communicate its strengths and capabilities to the community at large, it may limit its opportunities for collaboration with other organizations.

In addition to identifying potential partners, public gardens and horticultural societies can further enhance initiatives by enlisting subject-matter experts as resources or consultants. When the PHS LandCare program needed research on the impact of improved lots on neighborhood crime, the staff enlisted Charles Branas, then a professor of epidemiology at the University of Pennsylvania's Perelman School of Medicine, to conduct a study. Similarly, the GreenHouse program of the New York Horticultural Society depends on the Rikers Island warden and deputy wardens' expertise on the behavior of incarcerated youth, even though they are not formal members of the partnership.

Use Small, Incremental Efforts to Inform Large-Scale Changes

Most of the programs or initiatives highlighted in this book began as opportunities to be tested or ideas worthy of modest funding. Over time, partners modify or refine approaches to better address the community-identified needs, or to more effectively utilize the skills and resources of partners. In short, there is an incremental nature to partnerships and the ways in which partners manage their collaborative efforts.

Community partnerships supported by large external grants may be under pressure to quickly mount substantial efforts to share with their funders, but it is far better for the partners to agree on small initial steps that can be used to assess the effectiveness of chosen approaches. A pilot testing of a new initiative, for example, provides useful information on such important questions as whether the program is being promoted effectively with members of the target audience, whether the goals of the initiative are being supported by the actions taken, and whether the pedagogy associated with the project is clearly communicated to all involved.

Starting with discrete initial efforts also allows for early-stage course corrections. Perhaps the venue where the program is being offered is one that participants have difficulty accessing, or the time when it is offered may be problematic for those holding full-time jobs. Correcting these logistical shortcomings before a large-scale effort is launched can ensure that it will be successful. Small, early efforts also provide opportunities to celebrate successes, building confidence and trust in community partners.

Be Nimble and Responsive

Community resilience, according to the RAND Corporation, is "a measure of the sustained ability of a community to utilize available resources to respond to, withstand, and recover from adverse situations."[18] Partnerships between public gardens and community groups can help neighborhoods and entire cities respond to and recover from natural and human-made disasters. Immediately after the 9/11 attacks, Judy Zuk, then the president of Brooklyn Botanic Garden,

decided to provide free entry to the gardens for all. News of this conciliatory ges-
ture was spread by community groups throughout the borough and city, and for
weeks afterward, BBG was filled with individuals seeking solace from the awful
events and their aftermath.

Being nimble means acting both in a reactive manner, as BBG did post-9/11,
and proactively, especially in those locations most susceptible to natural disasters.
By developing recovery plans *before* a disaster hits, the garden can determine how
it will best meet its internal needs and what resources it might be able to direct
to its neighbors. Montgomery Botanical Center in Coral Gables, Florida, lies just
inland from the Atlantic Ocean. Given the frequency and severity of Atlantic
storms, along with rising sea levels, Montgomery recently conducted a rigorous
analysis in which it estimated that the ocean will continue to rise nine millimeters per year over a hundred-year span. Therefore, it is expected to rise nine
hundred millimeters, or just under three feet, in the next century. Based on this
calculation, the center determined that during this period, forty-three acres, or
one-third of its site, would be flooded. Fortunately, only 8 percent of its current
collections are planted in this low-lying area, sparing the rest of its accessions.[19]

In 2009, when the emerald ash borer was devastating tens of thousands of
ash trees in the greater Worcester, Massachusetts, area, members of the state
legislature responded by creating the Worcester Tree Initiative (WTI). After a
number of years of successfully planting a diversity of replacement trees and
educating citizens on their proper care, WTI has evolved into a program managed by Tower Hill Botanic Garden in nearby Boylston, Massachusetts. This new
partnership provides WTI with the organizational and grant-writing skills of the
garden, allowing it to more effectively achieve its goals to address pest infestation
in coming years.[20]

Public gardens also need to be nimble in responding to new municipal initiatives. When then New York City mayor Michael Bloomberg announced the
Million Tree Initiative in 2007, BBG quickly offered its expertise in species selection to aid this massive effort. Similarly, the University of Washington Botanic
Gardens is supporting the city of Seattle's Trees for Neighborhoods program,
which is one component of Seattle's reLeaf Program. The goal of this program is
to make it easy and fun to plant trees by providing proper planting instruction
and by bypassing the daunting permitting process for property owners. As of
2016, residents had planted approximately 5,300 trees.[21]

It is possible for a public garden to survive without reaching beyond the garden's gates or developing community partnerships, continuing to appeal to traditional (and homogeneous) audiences. But as public gardens consider their
mission statements or broader strategic plans, they must contend with questions

of relevance and broader impact. Will the public garden assume the role of a mere anchor institution physically rooted to a community, or will it commit to an anchor *mission* that consciously applies the garden's place-based power and knowledge assets to make neighborhoods safer, improve access to healthy foods, or contribute to quality science education?

All public gardens have the potential to play a part in improving the livability of the neighborhoods, cities, or regions in which they are located. The strategies outlined in this chapter can be used by public gardens to assess their readiness for partnerships, to lay the groundwork for partnerships, or to further enhance an existing partnership. The strategies are likewise valuable for residents, community organizations, local governments, or other institutions that might benefit from partnering with a public garden. Partnerships that harness the collective assets and placed-based power of the partners can have an impact on persistent socioeconomic challenges that are too complex for a single organization to address. Finally, partnerships between neighborhoods and anchor institutions such as the public garden create tangible benefits for anchor institutions. Stabilizing or strengthening communities and building the capacity of residents and local organizations to effect positive change in their neighborhoods results in more attractive places to live, work, and do business.

A LOOK AT THE FUTURE
OF PUBLIC GARDENS

The American Public Gardens Association (APGA), which represents public gardens across North America, envisions "a world where public gardens are indispensable."[1] But what will it take for public gardens to be viewed by an increasingly diverse population as indispensable in their lives?

One way is for gardens to expand their public image through partnerships with other organizations designed to promote the livability of their communities. In the previous chapter, we identified strategies for gardens to form successful partnerships, but to be a viable partner in the future, a public garden must make internal and external changes that will enable it to be more proactive in dealing with major issues. This chapter is about how a garden transitions itself to being partner-ready in the future and how it can have a positive impact on emerging environmental, demographic, and social trends.

The scientific community generally recognizes that we have entered a new epoch, the Anthropocene, which is characterized by the overwhelming global evidence of human interference in all natural systems. Activities including farming, logging, poaching, fishing, and mining are altering the natural world at a rate unprecedented in human history.[2] In early 2019, the United Nations Intergovernmental Science-Policy Platform on Biodiversity and Ecosystem Services released a 1,500-page report that concluded that as many as one million plant and animal species are at risk of extinction, posing a dire threat to ecosystems that people all over the world depend on for their survival. In most major land habitats, from the savannas of Africa to the rain forests of South America, the average abundance of native plant and animal life has fallen by 20 percent or more over the past century.[3]

The APGA defines public gardens as institutions that maintain "collections of plants for the purposes of public education and enjoyment, in addition to research, conservation, and higher learning."[4] To respond to and positively influence the trends of this new epoch, public gardens must move beyond these traditional roles and examine ways in which they can improve conditions for all living organisms, including humans. In a reshaping of the biblical story of Noah's Ark, the public gardens of the future will be celebrated as the leading institutions in the worldwide effort to preserve precious species.

Gardens can best lead the way by establishing and demonstrating effective biodiversity conservation strategies in the midst of rapidly changing natural landscapes. One strategy is to preserve locally, regionally, or globally endangered species in their native habitats, which is known as *in situ* conservation. The New York Botanical Garden, for example, is committed to such work in Amazonia, Southeast Asia, the Caribbean, and the South Pacific islands. In Myanmar, scientists are studying the largest remaining tract of primary forest in Southeast Asia, and in Cuba they are identifying the most critically endangered native species to inform conservation policies.[5]

A second strategy is for public gardens to establish *ex situ* seed banks or gene banks at their sites that will preserve the genetic identities of species threatened or extirpated in the wild. *Ex situ* conservation, as defined by the Convention on Biological Diversity, is "the conservation of the components of biological diversity outside their natural habitats."[6] Goal 8 of the Global Strategy for Plant Conservation calls for "at least 75% of threatened plant species in *ex situ* collections, preferably in the country of origin, and at least 20% available for recovery and restoration programs by 2020."[7] This lofty goal must be a target for public garden conservation programs in future years.

Rather than cloistering their research programs in anonymous buildings, gardens should develop research centers in public areas with large viewing windows that enable visitors to see science in action. This is the approach of the Chicago Botanic Garden at its Daniel F. and Ada L. Rice Plant Conservation Science Center, where each year over 1.1 million visitors and schoolchildren have the opportunity to view over two hundred plant scientists, land managers, students, and interns whose research is critical to fulfilling the garden's conservation mission.[8]

Coupled with the loss of biodiversity, climate change is the existential threat to life on this planet, and the time has long since passed when its existence was up for debate. Weather patterns are changing, sea levels are rising, droughts and rain events are becoming more extreme, and greenhouse gas emissions are now at their highest levels in recorded history. Public gardens need to use every opportunity provided by their educational programs, interpretative materials, and public messaging to help the general public understand the causes and results of global climate change and the actions they can take as individuals and in their communities to mitigate its effects and, where mitigation is not possible, adapt to change.

Examples of effective interpretive material already exist, including exhibits such as the Climate Change Garden at Cornell Botanic Gardens, which depicts how rising temperatures will affect many of the common vegetables we grow.[9] Brooklyn Botanic Garden has adopted a different approach: through a series of ponds and weirs, the garden's stormwater management system reduces the impact of heavy storm flow while bio-remediating the contained water. BBG interprets this system for visitors so they can better understand the wise management of rainfall in this era of increasing storm intensity.[10]

Public gardens also need to be paragons of sustainable behavior, whether through LEED-certified buildings, SITES-approved landscapes, the use of solar panels and windmills, reduction or elimination of pesticides, or the use of electric vehicles. Some public gardens are already at the forefront of sustainable practices, as exemplified by the Center for Sustainable Landscapes at the Phipps Conservatory and Botanical Gardens, which generates all of its own energy and treats all storm and sanitary water captured on-site. In managing both collections and buildings, public gardens must demonstrate ways of living well with less exploitation of nonrenewable resources.[11]

Since the 1990s, the world has experienced unprecedented urban growth. In 2015, close to four billion people—54 percent of the world's population—lived in cities, and that number is projected to increase to five billion people by 2030.[12] Not only are our cities becoming more crowded, but they are also becoming more diverse in terms of race, ethnicity, spiritual beliefs, sexual orientation, and ability. The latest UN Sustainable Development Goals reports that "rapid urbanization has brought enormous challenges, including growing numbers of slum dwellers, increased air pollution, inadequate basic services and infrastructure, and unplanned urban sprawl, which also make cities more vulnerable to disasters."[13]

The public garden of the future will need to partner with architects, urban planners, and progressive corporations to produce a new generation of green buildings and urban gardens, so that cities will become centers of clean air and renewable energy and provide all their residents with easy access to nature. Rutherford H. Platt and the other contributors to *The Humane Metropolis: People and Nature in the 21st-Century City* call for a future humane metropolis, one that is greener, safer, and healthier, more people friendly, and more socially equitable.[14] To help create such livable future cities, public gardens need to study and model cross-sector initiatives like St. Louis's Urban Vitality and Ecology Initiative and explore innovative collaborations in which each partner contributes one piece of a larger project.

To become indispensable in people's lives, public gardens must also welcome and celebrate people from all backgrounds and socioeconomic levels. A public garden's staff and visitors should be as diverse and distinct as its plant collections. To ensure that no individual or family feels excluded, gardens need to demonstrate their respect for and desire to collaborate with representatives of different ethnicities in developing programs, collections, and exhibits. The indigenous peoples of North America have been essential partners in public projects at the Arizona-Sonora Desert Museum, Vallarta Botanical Gardens, and Matthaei Botanical Gardens of the University of Michigan, each of which has explored the unique contributions of First Nations people to our collective culture.[15] The Japanese Cherry Blossom Festival (Sakura Matsuri) at the Brooklyn Botanic Garden and Chinese Culture Days at the Missouri Botanical Garden are other examples of authentic celebrations of ancient cultures.

Inclusive public gardens also integrate therapeutic approaches into their programming for those with physical limitations and those with mental or psychological conditions. The horticultural therapy programs at the small Tucson Botanical Garden and large Chicago Botanic Garden are models of how audiences with special needs can be served.[16]

Compounding the enormous environmental, biological, and social challenges is an increasing societal prejudice against science.[17] Public gardens have both an opportunity and obligation to counter this antiscience bias by sharing objective knowledge with their audiences and by engaging young people in the pursuit of science. To convince a younger generation of the impact that science and the natural world have on their lives, gardens of the future need to work with schools and other community organizations to develop programs that introduce children to plants and animals starting at a young age.

An excellent example of such a program is the Fiddleheads Urban Forest Preschool associated with the University of Washington Botanic Gardens. In keeping with the school's motto that childhood is a journey, not a destination, counselors at the school guide the young children in nature exploration and play in a forested setting, regardless of the weather.[18] Children with a solid sense of what nature is and the laws by which it operates are more likely as adults to be skeptical about unsupported scientific claims and to make thoughtful decisions about how they live their lives on a fragile planet.[19]

The Atlanta Botanical Garden has created an excellent venue for engaging adults in learning about science. Once a month on Thursdays during the growing season, it offers free Science Cafés to visitors, featuring local and national speakers on a variety of scientific topics, from pollinator behavior to the ecology of bog pitcher plants. Each of the presenters is a recognized expert in the field, so participants are assured that the information being shared is accurate.

While the programs outlined in this and previous chapters are exemplary models, many fall short in one critical area—evaluation. Public gardens and their partners typically collect data about the number of program participants and their demographics, but often fail to progress beyond that point. Evaluation is key to producing programs that efficiently use a garden's and a partnership's resources to produce successful and effective outcomes. Among the types of evaluation most useful to future gardens is formative assessment, which draws on feedback from participants to refine a program in its early stages before progressing to a major initiative launch. Also critical are summative evaluations, which assess the behavioral or intellectual impact of the program on participants. Finally, gardens need to conduct longitudinal studies that examine the program's lasting effect two to five years after its completion.

Moving forward, public gardens and their community partners will need to engage in comprehensive program evaluations for a number of reasons. First, they are often required by external funders, and failing to conduct evaluations can jeopardize current or future support. Also, such evaluations can identify possible future collaborations or better operational structures for each of the partners. Because of the critical nature of the issues these programs are intended to address, a thorough assessment can also inform future efforts by pointing out the approaches that had the greatest impact and those that were lacking and why.

The advancements we have recommended here are varied and complex, but achievable regardless of the institution's size. Those public gardens that will be most successful will be ones that develop well-conceived, inclusive, and stepwise plans for physical development, educational programming, interpretive strategies, and fiscal solvency. It is also critical that they remain flexible, open to change, and courageous. This requires diligence, awareness of consumer and environmental trends, a commitment to risk, and flexibility.

Armed with these traits, public gardens will indeed become indispensable to their communities, and will be among the leaders that have the resources and strategies capable of addressing emerging issues to strengthen the livability and sustainability of those communities.

PUBLIC GARDENS FEATURED IN CASE STUDIES

Bartram's Garden

Location:	Philadelphia, PA
Year established:	1728
Acreage:	45 acres
Mission:	To protect and enhance the landmark Bartram's Garden and House; advance the Bartram legacy of discovery, gardening, and art; and inspire audiences of all ages to care for the natural world.
Annual budget:	$3.2 million
Type:	501(c)(3) in cooperation with Philadelphia Parks and Recreation

Brooklyn Botanic Garden

Location:	Brooklyn, NY
Year established:	1897
Acreage:	52 acres
Mission:	To connect people to the world of plants, fostering delight and curiosity while inspiring an appreciation and sense of stewardship of the environment.
Annual budget:	$20.1 million
Type:	501(c)(3) on land owned by the City of New York

Chicago Botanic Garden

Location: Chicago, IL
Year established: 1972
Acreage: 385 acres
Mission: To cultivate the power of plants to sustain and enrich life.
Annual budget: $37,457,000
Type: 501(c)(3), under authority of Chicago Horticultural
                     Society

Cleveland Botanical Garden

Location: Cleveland, OH
Year established: 1930
Acreage: 10 acres
Mission: To advance and inspire a deeper understanding of plants
                     to enhance life.
Annual budget: $3 million
Type: 501(c)(3), as a division of Holden Forests & Gardens

Denver Botanic Gardens

Location: Denver, CO
Year established: 1930
Acreage: 23 acres
Mission: To connect people with plants, especially plants from the
                     Rocky Mountain region and similar regions around
                     the world, providing delight and enlightenment to
                     everyone.
Annual budget: $20.9 million
Type: 501(c)(3)

Fairchild Tropical Botanic Garden

Location: Coral Gables, FL
Year established: 1938
Acreage: 83 acres

Mission: Dedicated to exploring, explaining, and conserving the
                  world of tropical plants.

Annual budget: $7.7 million

Type: 501(c)(3)

Franklin Park Conservatory and Botanical Gardens

Location: Columbus, OH

Year established: 1895

Acreage: 88 acres

Mission: Inspired by horticulture, Franklin Park Conservatory and
                   Botanical Gardens elevates quality of life and connects
                   the community through educational, cultural, and
                   social experiences.

Annual budget: $11.1 million

Type: 501(c)(3)

Horticultural Society of New York

Location: New York, NY

Year established: 1900 (incorporated 1902)

Mission: To sustain the vital connection between people and
                   plants.

Annual budget: $3 million

Type: 501(c)(3)

Lewis Ginter Botanical Garden

Location: Richmond, VA

Year established: 1984

Acreage: 50 acres

Mission: Connects people through plants to improve
                   communities.

Annual budget: $7 million

Type: 501(c)(3)

Missouri Botanical Garden

Location:	St. Louis, MO
Year established:	1859
Acreage:	79 acres
Mission:	To discover and share knowledge about plants and their environment in order to preserve and enrich life.
Annual budget:	$38.6 million
Type:	501(c)(3)

New York Botanical Garden

Location:	Bronx, NY
Year established:	1891
Acreage:	250 acres
Mission:	The New York Botanical Garden is an advocate for the plant kingdom. The garden pursues its mission through its role as a museum of living plant collections arranged in gardens and landscapes across its National Historic Landmark site.
Annual budget:	$65.2 million
Type:	501(c)(3) on land owned by the City of New York

Pennsylvania Horticultural Society

Location:	Philadelphia, PA
Year established:	1827
Mission:	To connect people with horticulture, and together to create beautiful, healthy, and sustainable communities.
Annual budget:	$28.1 million
Type:	501(c)(3)

Phipps Conservatory and Botanical Gardens

Location:	Pittsburgh, PA
Year established:	1893
Acreage:	15 acres

Mission:	To inspire and educate all with the beauty and importance of plants; to advance sustainability and promote human and environmental well-being through action and research; and to celebrate the garden's historic glasshouse.
Annual budget:	$15.3 million
Type:	501(c)(3), but owned by the City of Pittsburgh

Queens Botanical Garden

Location:	Queens, NY
Year established:	1946
Acreage:	39 acres
Mission:	An urban oasis where people, plants, and cultures are celebrated through inspiring gardens, innovative educational programs, and real-world applications of environmental stewardship.
Annual budget:	$4.3 million
Type:	501(c)(3), on land owned by the City of New York

CASE STUDY GARDEN INITIATIVES AND PARTNERING ORGANIZATIONS

Chapter 1

Brooklyn Botanic Garden
Greenest Block in Brooklyn
    Office of the Brooklyn Borough President
    National Grid New York

Queens Botanical Garden
Ambassador Program
    New York Community Trust
    Queens Botanical Garden tai chi group

Pennsylvania Horticultural Society
Philadelphia LandCare program
    City of Philadelphia Division of Housing and Community Development
    New Kensington Community Development Corporation
    University of Pennsylvania's Perelman School of Medicine

Chapter 2

Brooklyn Botanic Garden
Project Green Reach
    New York City Department of Education
    Youth Opportunities Program of the Appalachian Mountain Club

Fairchild Tropical Botanic Garden
Fairchild Challenge
  Miami-Dade County Public Schools
  Florida International University
  University of Miami
  Nature Conservancy
  NASA

Chicago Botanic Garden
Science First / College First
  Chicago Public Schools
  Northwestern University
  US Bureau of Land Management
  National Park Service
  US Forest Service

Chapter 3

New York Botanical Garden
Bronx Green-Up
  La Familia Verde / Garden of Happiness
  Osborne Association
  Farm School NYC
  NYC Parks Project Green Thumb
  Butterfly Project NYC
  Bronx Land Trust
  Bronx Hot Sauce project
  Grow NYC

Cleveland Botanical Garden
Green Corps
  Mandel School of Applied Social Science at Case Western Reserve University
  Cleveland MetroParks
  Cleveland Indians
  Department of Entomology, Ohio State University

Franklin Park Conservatory and Botanical Gardens
Growing to Green
  Scotts Miracle-Gro Company
  Columbus Foundation

Berwick Alternative Elementary School
Franklin Park Women's Board
Battelle Corporation

Bartram's Garden
Sankofa Farm
Pennsylvania Horticultural Society
City of Philadelphia
Philadelphia Orchard Project

Chapter 4

Denver Botanic Gardens—Chatfield Farm
Chatfield Veterans Farm Program
Kaiser Permanente Foundation
Veterans to Farmers
Denver Department of Social Services
Rose Foundation

Pennsylvania Horticultural Society
Roots to Re-entry
KJK Associates
Liberty Tree & Landscape Management
Moon Site Management
Brickman Group
Reentry to Workforce partnership
Defender Association of Philadelphia
Philadelphia District Attorney's Office
Philadelphia Department of Prisons

Horticultural Society of New York
GreenHouse program
Association of Community Employment
Getting Out/Staying Out
Police Athletic League
Bronx Works
STRIVE New York
New York City Department of Education
New York City Department of Corrections

Chapter 5

Missouri Botanical Garden
Urban Vitality and Ecology Initiative
   City of St. Louis Department of Planning and Urban Design
   Missouri Department of Conservation
   Metropolitan St. Louis Sewer District
   Washington University in St. Louis
   St. Louis University

Lewis Ginter Botanical Garden
Beautiful RVA
   City of Richmond

Phipps Conservatory and Botanical Gardens
   City of Pittsburgh
   Biophilic Cities project

NATIONAL AND INTERNATIONAL ORGANIZATIONS ALIGNED WITH PUBLIC GARDENS

American Alliance of Museums

Website: http://aam-us.org/
Mission: To champion museums and nurture excellence in partnership
with its members and allies.

American Association for the Advancement of Science

Website: https://www.aaas.org
Mission: Seeks to "advance science, engineering, and innovation
throughout the world for the benefit of all people."

American Community Gardening Association

Website: https://communitygarden.org/
Mission: To build community by increasing and enhancing community
gardening and greening across the United States and Canada.

American Horticultural Society

Website: http://ahsgardening.org/

Mission: To open the eyes of all Americans to the vital connection
between people and plants, to inspire all Americans to become
responsible caretakers of the Earth, to celebrate America's
diversity through the art and science of horticulture, and
to lead this effort by sharing the society's unique national
resources with all Americans.

American Horticultural Therapy Association

Website: https://www.ahta.org

Mission: To promote and advance the profession of horticultural therapy
as a therapeutic intervention and rehabilitative modality.

American Public Gardens Association

Website: https://publicgardens.org/

Mission: Serves public gardens and advances them as leaders, advocates,
and innovators.

American Society for Horticultural Science

Website: http://www.ashs.org/

Mission: Committed to promoting and encouraging national and
international interest in scientific research and education in all
branches of horticulture.

Association of Science and Technology Centers

Website: https://www.astc.org

Mission: Committed to advancing public understanding of science and
contributing to the development of a scientifically literate
society.

Association of Zoos and Aquariums

Website: https://www.aza.org/
Mission: Dedicated to the advancement of zoos and aquariums in the
              areas of conservation, education, science, and recreation.

Botanic Gardens Conservation International

Website: http://www.bgci.org/
Mission: Aims to collect, conserve, characterize, and cultivate samples
              from all of the world's plants as an insurance policy against
              their extinction in the wild and as a source of plant material
              for human innovation, adaptation, and resilience.

Center for Plant Conservation

Website: https://saveplants.org/
Mission: Dedicated to saving rare plant species from extinction.

Garden Club of America

Website: https://www.gcamerica.org/
Mission: To stimulate the knowledge and love of gardening; to share the
              advantages of association by means of educational meetings,
              conferences, correspondence, and publications; and to restore,
              improve, and protect the quality of the environment through
              educational programs and action in the fields of conservation
              and civic improvement.

Garden Conservancy

Website: https://www.gardenconservancy.org/
Mission: To save and share outstanding American gardens for the
              education and inspiration of the public.

National Garden Clubs

Website: http://www.gardenclub.org

Mission: Provides education, resources, and national networking opportunities for its members to promote the love of gardening, floral design, and civic and environmental responsibility.

National Trust for Historic Preservation

Website: https://savingplaces.org/

Mission: Protects significant places representing our diverse cultural experience by taking direct action and inspiring broad public support.

North American Association for Environmental Education

Website: https://www.naaee.org

Mission: To bring the brightest minds together to accelerate environmental literacy and civic engagement through the power of education.

Acknowledgments

We want to take this opportunity to thank the many public garden professionals, municipal employees, and nonprofit administrators who contributed information and photographs to this project in hopes of furthering more collaborations between community institutions that enhance the livability of our cities. We also want to thank Jennifer Schwarz Ballard, vice president for learning and engagement at the Chicago Botanic Garden, for giving the entire final manuscript a careful review, and Ruth Babylon for reviewing the early chapters.

Finally, like many authors before us, we want to acknowledge the important role our families have played in bringing this book to publication. Our special thanks to Sue F. V. Rakow, Philip Lebowitz, and Chris, Anna, and Lily Gough for their patience, help, and support throughout the development of the book.

Notes

INTRODUCTION

1. United Nations Department of Economic and Social Affairs, *2018 Revision of World Urbanization Prospects*, May 16, 2018, https://www.un.org/development/desa/publications/2018-revision-of-world-urbanization-prospects.html.

2. Jane Jacobs, *The Economy of Cities* (New York: Random House, 1969). See also Richard Florida, Patrick Adler, and Charlotta Mellander, "The City as Innovation Machine," *Regional Studies* 51, no. 1 (2017): 86–96.

3. Mark Ferguson, Kamar Ali, M. Rose Olfert, and Mark Partridge, "Voting with Their Feet: Jobs versus Amenities," *Growth and Change* 38, no. 1 (2007): 77–110.

4. Meghan Z. Gough, "Reconciling Livability and Sustainability: Conceptual and Practical Implications for Planning," *Journal of Planning Education and Research* 35, no. 2 (2015): 145–60.

5. World Commission on Environment and Development (WCED), *Our Common Future* (Oxford: Oxford University Press, 1987), 37.

6. Donald F. Kettl, "The Job of Government: Interweaving Public Functions and Private Hands," *Public Administration Review* 75, no. 2 (2015): 219–29.

7. John M. Bryson, Barbara C. Crosby, and Melissa Middleton Stone, "Designing and Implementing Cross-sector Collaborations: Needed and Challenging," *Public Administration Review* 75, no. 5 (2015): 647–63.

8. David Neumark and Helen Simpson, "Place-Based Policies" (NBER Working Paper No. 20049, August 2014), 1

9. "2019 Best Places to Live," *U.S. News and World Report*, accessed June 1, 2019, https://realestate.usnews.com/places.

10. See examples from the 1960s New York City placemaking efforts informed by observations led by Jane Jacobs, William H. Whyte, and others.

11. Project for Public Spaces, "What If We Built Our Cities around Places?," November 1, 2004, https://www.pps.org/reference/greatcitiesinitiative.

12. Nicola Dempsey and Mel Burton, "Defining Place-Keeping: The Long-Term Management of Public Spaces," *Urban Forestry & Urban Greening* 11, no. 1 (2012): 11–20.

13. The term *gentrification* was first introduced into urban scholarship in 1964 by Ruth Glass, who characterized it as a rapid process in which "all or most of the original working-class occupiers are displaced and the whole social character of the district is changed." Ruth L. Glass, *London: Aspects of Change* (London: MacGibbon and Kee, 1964), xviii.

14. Ruth Fincher, Maree Pardy, and Kate Shaw, "Place-Making or Place-Masking? The Everyday Political Economy of 'Making Place,'" *Planning Theory & Practice* 17, no. 4 (2016): 516–36.

15. Stacey Sutton, "Gentrification and the Increasing Significance of Racial Transition in New York City, 1970–2010," *Urban Affairs Review* 56, no. 1 (2018): 65–95.

16. Miriam Zuk, Ariel H. Bierbaum, Karen Chapple, Karolina Gorska, and Anastasia Loukaitou-Sideris, "Gentrification, Displacement, and the Role of Public Investment," *Journal of Planning Literature* 33, no. 1 (2018): 31–44.

17. Meghan Z. Gough and John Accordino, "Public Gardens as Sustainable Community Development Partners: Motivations, Perceived Benefits, and Challenges," *Urban Affairs Review* 49, no. 6 (2013): 851–87.

18. Edward O. Wilson, *Biophilia* (Cambridge, MA: Harvard University Press, 1992), 79.

19. Gough and Accordino, "Public Gardens," 851–87.

20. David Brooks, "A Nation of Weavers: The Social Renaissance Is Happening from the Ground Up," *New York Times*, February 19, 2019, https://www.nytimes.com/2019/02/18/opinion/culture-compassion.html.

21. During this period, the total population in the US increased from five million to seventy-six million.

22. Isabel Wilkerson, *The Warmth of Other Suns: The Epic Story of America's Great Migration* (New York: Vintage Books, 2011).

23. Jon A. Peterson, "The Impact of Sanitary Reform upon American Urban Planning, 1840–1890," *Journal of Social History* 13, no. 1 (1979): 83–103, http://www.jstor.org/stable/3786777.

24. Roy Rosenzweig and Elizabeth Blackmar, *The Park and the People: A History of Central Park* (Ithaca, NY: Cornell University Press, 1992).

25. Peter Mickulas, *Britton's Botanical Empire: The New York Botanical Garden and American Botany, 1888–1929* (New York: New York Botanical Garden Press, 2007).

26. B. Szczygiel, "'City Beautiful' Revisited," *Journal of Urban History* 29, no. 2 (2003): 107–32.

27. Szczygiel, "'City Beautiful' Revisited," 107–32.

28. Richard L. Andrews, *Managing the Environment, Managing Ourselves: A History of American Environmental Policy*, 3rd ed. (New Haven, CT: Yale University Press, 2006).

29. Richard Lighty, "A History of the North American Public Garden," *Public Garden* 11, no. 1 (1996): 8–11.

30. Robert D. Bullard, *Dumping in Dixie: Race, Class, and Environmental Quality* (Boulder, CO: Westview, 1990); Rachel Carson, *Silent Spring* (Boston: Houghton Mifflin Harcourt, 2002); Robert Gottlieb, *Forcing the Spring: The Transformation of the American Environmental Movement* (Washington, DC: Island, 2005).

31. "Save Baldwin Lake," Los Angeles County Botanic Garden and Arboretum, November 20, 2019, http://www.arboretum.org/save-baldwin-lake/.

32. Lady Bird Johnson Wildflower Center, June 5, 2018, https://www.wildflower.org/our-work/plant-conservation.

33. Kameshwari Pothukuchi, "Five Decades of Community Food Planning in Detroit: City and Grassroots, Growth and Equity," *Journal of Planning Education and Research* 35, no. 4 (2015): 419–34; William Peterman, *Neighborhood Planning and Community-Based Development: The Potential and Limits of Grassroots Action*, Cities and Planning (Thousand Oaks, CA: Sage, 2000).

34. This book uses the term *collaboration* interchangeably with *partnership* because of the prevalence and overlapping use of these terms in practice and in the literature.

35. Barbara Gray, "The Process of Partnership Construction: Anticipating Obstacles and Enhancing the Likelihood of Successful Partnerships for Sustainable Development," in *Partnerships, Governance and Sustainable Development: Reflections on Theory and Practice*, ed. Pieter Glasbergen, Frank Bierman, and Arthur P. J. Moi (Northampton, MA: Edward Elgar, 2007), 27–41.

36. Ann Marie Thomson and James L. Perry, "Collaboration Processes: Inside the Black Box," *Public Administration Review* 66 (2006): 20–32.

37. Helen Sullivan and Chris Skelcher, *Working across Boundaries: Collaboration in Public Services*, Macmillan International Higher Education, 2017.

38. Barbara Gray, *Collaborating: Finding Common Ground for Multiparty Problems* (San Francisco: Jossey-Bass, 1989).

39. John Kania and Mark Kramer, "Collective Impact," *Stanford Social Innovation Review*, Winter 2011, 36–41.

40. Fay Hanleybrown, John Kania, and Mark Kramer, "Channeling Change: Making Collective Impact Work," *Stanford Social Innovation Review*, January 2012, 1–8.

41. Tom Wolff, Meredith Minkler, S. Wolfe, Bill Berkowitz, Linda Bowen, Frances Dunn Butterfoss, and K. S. Lee, "Collaborating for Equity and Justice: Moving beyond Collective Impact," *Nonprofit Quarterly* 9 (2017): 42–53.

42. Barbara Gray and Jill Purdy, *Collaborating for Our Future: Multistakeholder Partnerships for Solving Complex Problems* (Oxford: Oxford University Press, 2018).

1. PROMOTING NEIGHBORHOOD SAFETY AND WELL-BEING

1. "Characteristics and Guidelines of Great Public Spaces," American Planning Association, accessed November 28, 2016, https://www.planning.org/greatplaces/spaces/characteristics.htm.

2. Austin Troy, Ashley Nunery, and J. Morgan Grove, "The Relationship between Residential Yard Management and Neighborhood Crime: An Analysis from Baltimore City and County," *Landscape and Urban Planning* 147 (March 2016): 78–87, https://doi.org/10.1016/j.landurbplan.2015.11.004.

3. Jane Jacobs, *The Death and Life of Great American Cities* (New York: Random House, 1960).

4. Ann Markusen and Anne Gadwa Nicodemus, "Creative Placemaking: How to Do It Well," *Community Development Investment Review*, no. 2 (2014): 35–42.

5. Debra Webb, "Placemaking and Social Equity: Expanding the Framework of Creative Placemaking," *Artivate: A Journal of Entrepreneurship in the Arts* 3, no. 1 (2014): 35–48. See also Ceri Davies, Nick Gant, Juliet Millican, David Wolff, Bethan Prosser, Stuart Laing, and Angie Hart, "Exploring Engaged Spaces in Community-University Partnership," *Metropolitan Universities* 27, no. 3 (November 16, 2016): 6–26.

6. John M. Levy, *Contemporary Urban Planning* (New York: Routledge, 2015).

7. US Census Bureau, "QuickFacts Brooklyn Borough (Kings County)," accessed July 11, 2016, http://www.census.gov/quickfacts/table/PST045215/36047,00.

8. Michael Bloomberg et al., *NYC2010: Results from the 2010 Census; Population Growth and Race/Hispanic Composition* (New York: NYCPlanning, Department of City Planning, 2011).

9. US Census Bureau, "QuickFacts Brooklyn Borough."

10. Ellen Shaw, "Gardening and the City Child," *Natural History* 22, no. 1 (1922): 141–51.

11. Shaw, "Gardening," 144.

12. For additional detail see "A Brief History of BBG," accessed May 31, 2017, http://www.bbg.org/about/history.

13. For additional detail see "Livability Index," accessed June 17, 2017, https://www1.nyc.gov/assets/manhattancb1/downloads/pdf/studies-and-reports/july2017-cb1-livability-index-study.pdf.

14. James Q. Wilson and George L. Kelling, "Broken Windows," *Critical Issues in Policing: Contemporary Readings* (1982): 395–407.

15. Robert J. Sampson and Stephen W. Raudenbush, "Seeing Disorder: Neighborhood Stigma and the Social Construction of 'Broken Windows,'" *Social Psychology Quarterly* 67, no. 4 (2004): 319–42.

16. Ellen Kirby (former director and founder, GreenBridge), interview by Meghan Gough, July 20, 2016.

17. "Community Greening—Brooklyn Botanic Garden," accessed May 31, 2017, https://www.bbg.org/community.

18. Nina Browne (BBG community program manager), interview by Meghan Gough, September 5, 2018.

19. Nina Browne, interview by Meghan Gough, September 29, 2015; Kirby interview, July 20, 2016.

20. Browne interview, September 5, 2018.

21. Browne interview, September 5, 2018.

22. "Office of the Brooklyn Borough President," September 10, 2018, http://www.brooklyn-usa.org/.

23. Kirby interview, July 20, 2016.

24. Robin Simmen (then director of community greening programs), interview by Meghan Gough, January 5, 2011.

25. Kirby interview, July 20, 2016.

26. Browne interview, September 29, 2015.

27. All criteria are available on Brooklyn Botanic Garden's website, http://www.bbg.org/greenbridge/greenestblock.

28. Browne interview, September 29, 2015.

29. For more information see "2014 Commercial Block Winners," accessed July 23, 2018, https://www.bbg.org/community/greenest_block_2014.

30. For more information see "The Greenest Blocks in Brooklyn Are in Prospect-Lefferts Gardens and Boerum Hill," accessed July 23, 2018, http://www.bbg.org/press/gbb2013_winners.

31. Browne interview, September 29, 2015.

32. Browne interview, September 29, 2015.

33. For more information see "Greenest Block in Brooklyn," accessed September 5, 2018, https://www.bbg.org/community/greenestblock.

34. Browne interview, September 29, 2015.

35. For more information see "Greenest Block in Brooklyn," accessed September 5, 2018, https://www.bbg.org/community/greenestblock.

36. Browne interview, September 5, 2018.

37. "2014 Commercial Block Winners."

38. "Greenest Block in Brooklyn."

39. Robert D. Putnam, *Making Democracy Work: Civic Traditions in Modern Italy* (Princeton, NJ: Princeton University Press, 1992), 165–69.

40. Kelly Main and Gerardo Francisco Sandoval, "Placemaking in a Translocal Receiving Community: The Relevance of Place to Identity and Agency," *Urban Studies*, March 5, 2014, https://doi.org/10.1177/0042098014522720.

41. Zachary P. Neal and Jennifer Watling Neal, "The (In)compatibility of Diversity and Sense of Community," *American Journal of Community Psychology* 53, no. 1–2 (November 6, 2013): 1–12, https://doi.org/10.1007/s10464-013-9608-0.

42. Queens Botanical Garden, *Queens Botanical Garden Master Plan* (Queens, NY: Queens Botanical Garden, 2002), https://queensbotanical.org/wp-content/uploads/2015/12/masterplan_complete.pdf.

43. Fred Fu (president of the Flushing Development Center), interview by Meghan Gough, March 11, 2011.

44. Queens Botanical Garden, *Queens Botanical Garden Master Plan*.

45. Susan Lacerte, interview by Meghan Gough, April 7, 2016.

46. Radhika Mohan and Uma Mysorekar, Hindu Temple Society of North America, interview by Meghan Gough, January 7, 2011.

47. American Association of Museums, Task Force on Museum Education, *Excellence and Equity: Education and the Public Dimension of Museums; A Report from the American Association of Museums, 1992* (New York: American Association of Museums, 1992).

48. Roger Schonfeld and Liam Sweeney, *Diversity in the New York City Department of Cultural Affairs Community* (New York: Ithaka S+R, January 28, 2016), https://doi.org/10.18665/sr.276381.

49. Schonfeld and Sweeney, *Diversity.*

50. James Surowiecki, *The Wisdom of Crowds* (New York: Anchor, 2005).

51. Doris Ash and Judith Lombana, "Reculturing Museums: Working toward Diversity in Informal Settings," *Journal of Museum Education* 38, no. 1 (March 1, 2013): 69–80, https://doi.org/10.1080/10598650.2013.11510757.

52. Lacerte interview, April 7, 2016.

53. Ash and Lombana, "Reculturing Museums."

54. Kimberley Hodgson and Kelly Beavers, "How the Arts and Cultural Sector Strengthen Cultural Values and Preserve Heritage and History," American Planning Association, March 1, 2011, https://www.planning.org/publications/document/9147998/.

55. Mohan and Mysorekar interview, January 7, 2011.

56. John W. Reps, "William Penn and the Planning of Philadelphia," *Town Planning Review* 27, no. 1 (1956): 27.

57. Mark Alan Hughes, "Dirt into Dollars," *Brookings Review* 18, no. 3 (2000): 36.

58. Justin B. Hollander, "Can a City Successfully Shrink? Evidence from Survey Data on Neighborhood Quality," *Urban Affairs Review* 47, no. 1 (August 27, 2010): 129–41, https://doi.org/10.1177/1078087410379099; Ann O'M. Bowman and Michael A. Pagano, "Transforming America's Cities: Policies and Conditions of Vacant Land," *Urban Affairs Review* 35, no. 4 (March 1, 2000): 559–81, https://doi.org/10.1177/10780870022184534.

59. Hughes, "Dirt into Dollars," 36.

60. "Vacant Lot Program," City of Philadelphia, accessed June 28, 2019, https://www.phila.gov/programs/vacant-lot-program/.

61. Michael A. Pagano and Ann O'M. Bowman, *Vacant Land in Cities: An Urban Resource* (Washington, DC: Brookings Institution, Center on Urban and Metropolitan Policy, 2000).

62. Bowman and Pagano, "Transforming America's Cities."

63. "Vacant and Abandoned Properties: Turning Liabilities into Assets," Winter 2014, https://www.huduser.gov/portal/periodicals/em/winter14/highlight1.html; Charles C. Branas, Rose A. Cheney, John M. MacDonald, Vicky W. Tam, Tara D. Jackson, and Thomas R. Ten Have, "A Difference-in-Differences Analysis of Health, Safety, and Greening Vacant Urban Space," *American Journal of Epidemiology* 174, no. 11 (2011): 1296–306.

64. John Accordino and Gary T. Johnson, "Addressing the Vacant and Abandoned Property Problem," *Journal of Urban Affairs* 22, no. 3 (2000): 301–15.

65. Edmund N. Bacon, "A Diagnosis and Suggested Treatment of an Urban Community's Land Problem," *Journal of Land & Public Utility Economics* 16, no. 1 (1940): 72–88; Pagano and Bowman, *Vacant Land in Cities.*

66. Megan Heckert and Jeremy Mennis, "The Economic Impact of Greening Urban Vacant Land: A Spatial Difference-in-Differences Analysis," *Environment and Planning* 44, no. 12 (2012): 3011–14.

67. Econsult Corporation and Penn Institute for Urban Research, eds., *Vacant Land Management in Philadelphia: The Costs of the Current System and the Benefits of Reform* (Philadelphia: Econsult Corp., 2010).

68. Stephen J. McGovern, "Philadelphia's Neighborhood Transformation Initiative: A Case Study of Mayoral Leadership, Bold Planning, and Conflict," *ResearchGate* 17, no. 3 (January 1, 2006): 529–70, https://doi.org/10.1080/10511482.2006.9521581; Eugenie L. Birch and Susan M. Wachter, eds., *Growing Greener Cities: Urban Sustainability in the Twenty-First Century* (Philadelphia: University of Pennsylvania Press, 2008), http://www.jstor.org/stable/j.ctt3fhps5.

69. Susan M. Wachter and Grace Wong, "What Is a Tree Worth? Green-City Strategies, Signaling and Housing Prices," *Real Estate Economics* 36, no. 2 (2008): 213–39.

70. Pennsylvania Horticultural Society, *Managing Vacant Land in Philadelphia: A Key Step toward Neighborhood Revitalization; Final Report on the Vacant Land Management Study* (Philadelphia: Pennsylvania Horticultural Society, March 2000).

71. Pennsylvania Horticultural Society, *From Vacant Land to Open Space: An Evaluation of the New Kensington Neighborhood Open Space Management Project* (Philadelphia: Pennsylvania Horticultural Society, October 1999).

72. Deborah McColloch (former DHCD director), interview by Meghan Gough and Sharon Lee, December 7, 2015.

73. Pennsylvania Horticultural Society, *An Asset Management Approach to Vacant Land: A Pilot Program for Easter North Philadelphia* (Philadelphia: Pennsylvania Horticultural Society, October 1999).

74. Pennsylvania Horticultural Society website, accessed October 27, 2016, http://phsonline.org/.

75. McColloch interview, December 7, 2015.

76. Pennsylvania Horticultural Society website.

77. McColloch interview, December 7, 2015.

78. Pennsylvania Horticultural Society website.

79. McColloch interview, December 7, 2015.

80. Megan Heckert and Michelle Kondo, "Can 'Cleaned and Greened' Lots Take on the Role of Public Greenspace?," *Journal of Planning Education and Research* 38, no. 2 (2018): 211–21.

81. Mary Emery and Cornelia Flora, "Spiraling-Up: Mapping Community Transformation with Community Capitals Framework," *Community Development* 37, no. 1 (2006): 19–35.

82. Chris Benner and Manuel Pastor, "Moving On Up? Regions, Megaregions, and the Changing Geography of Social Equity Organizing," *Urban Affairs Review* 47, no. 3 (2011): 315–48; Bruce Katz and Jeremy Nowak, *The New Localism: How Cities Can Thrive in the Age of Populism* (Washington, DC: Brookings Institution Press, 2018).

83. Meghan Z. Gough and John Accordino, "Public Gardens as Sustainable Community Development Partners," *Urban Affairs Review* 49, no. 6 (2013): 851–87; Joseph Schilling and Jonathan Logan, "Greening the Rust Belt: A Green Infrastructure Model for Right Sizing America's Shrinking Cities," *Journal of the American Planning Association* 74, no. 4 (2008): 451–66.

84. Eugenia C. Garvin, Carolyn C. Cannuscio, and Charles C. Branas, "Greening Vacant Lots to Reduce Violent Crime: A Randomised Controlled Trial," *Injury Prevention*, August 7, 2012, https://doi.org/10.1136/injuryprev-2012-040439.

85. Eugenia C. South, Bernadette C. Hohl, Michelle C. Kondo, John M. MacDonald, and Charles C. Branas, "Effect of Greening Vacant Land on Mental Health of Community-Dwelling Adults: A Cluster Randomized Trial," *JAMA Network Open* 1, no. 3 (2018).

86. Eugenia South et al., "Neighborhood Blight, Stress, and Health: A Walking Trial of Urban Greening and Ambulatory Heart Rate," *American Journal of Public Health* 105, no. 5 (2015): 909–13.

87. Susan Wachter, *The Determinants of Neighborhood Transformations in Philadelphia: Identification and Analysis; The New Kensington Pilot Study* (Philadelphia: University of Pennsylvania Press, 2005).

88. Grace Bucchianeri, Kevin C. Gillan, and Susan M. Watcher, *Valuing Conversion of Urban Greenspace* (2012), accessed November 12, 2015, http://phsonline.org/uploads/resources//Bucchianeri_Gillen_Wachter_Valuing_Conversion_Urban_Greenspace_Final_Draft_KG_changesacceptes.pdf.

89. Heckert and Mennis, "Economic Impact."

90. Charles C. Branas, interview by Meghan Gough, February 8, 2016.

91. Guillaume Marche, "What Can Urban Gardening Really Do about Gentrification? A Case-Study of Three San Francisco Community Gardens," *European Journal of American Studies* 10, no. 3 (2015).

92. Winifred Curran and Trina Hamilton, "Just Green Enough: Contesting Environmental Gentrification in Greenpoint, Brooklyn," *Local Environment* 17, no. 9 (2012): 1027–42.

93. Jennifer R. Wolch, Jason Byrne, and Joshua P. Newell, "Urban Green Space, Public Health, and Environmental Justice: The Challenge of Making Cities 'Just Green Enough,'" *Landscape and Urban Planning* 125 (2014): 234–44.

94. Wolch, Byrne, and Newell, "Urban Green Space."

2. IMPROVING THE QUALITY OF SCIENCE EDUCATION

1. Committee on Strengthening Science Education through a Teacher Learning Continuum, *Science Teachers' Learning: Enhancing Opportunities, Creating Supportive Contexts*, ed. Suzanne Wilson, Heidi Schweingruber, and Natalie Nielsen (Washington, DC: National Academies Press, 2015), 11.

2. Committee on Strengthening Science Education, *Science Teachers' Learning*, 56.

3. Committee on Strengthening Science Education, *Science Teachers' Learning*, 63.

4. Committee on Strengthening Science Education, *Science Teachers' Learning*, 55–56.

5. David E. Kanter and Spuros Konstantopoulos, "The Impact of a Project-Based Science Curriculum on Minority Student Achievement, Attitudes and Careers: The Effects of Teacher Content and Pedagogical Content Knowledge and Inquiry-Based Practices," *Science Education* 94, no. 5 (2010): 855–87, https://doi.org/DOI 10.1002/sce.20391.

6. Committee on Strengthening Science Education, *Science Teachers' Learning*, 215.

7. "Next Generation Science Standards Explained," National Science Teachers Association, accessed May 3, 2016, https://NSTA.org/why/standards-matter.aspx.

8. "Next Generation Science Standards Explained."

9. Committee on Strengthening Science Education, *Science Teachers' Learning*, 1–2.

10. *The Opportunity Equation: Transforming Mathematics and Science Education for Citizenship and the Global Economy* (Carnegie Corporation of New York; Institute for Advanced Study, 2009), 58, https://www.carnegie.org/media/filer_public/80/c8/80c8a7bc-c7ab-4f49-847d-1e2966f4dd97/ccny_report_2009_opportunityequation.pdf.

11. *Opportunity Equation*, 58.

12. Barbara A. Crawford, "Learning to Teach Science as Inquiry in the Rough and Tumble of Practice," *Journal of Research in Science Teaching* 44, no. 4 (2007): 613–42.

13. Barbara Kurland, e-mail to Sharon Lee, October 27, 2016.

14. Sonal Bhatt, e-mail to Sharon Lee, October 27, 2016.

15. Barbara Kurland and Sara Epstein, "Public Gardens and Community Revitalization," e-mail to Sharon Lee, July 19, 2018.

16. *Principal Survey: Project Green Reach Fall 2012* (Brooklyn Botanic Garden, Project Green Reach, Fall 2012).

17. Committee on Strengthening Science Education, *Science Teachers' Learning*, 148.

18. *Project Green Reach Teacher Evaluation Summary, Spring 2015* (Brooklyn Botanic Garden, Project Green Reach, April 28, 2015), 2.

19. *Project Green Reach Teacher Evaluation Summary*, 2.

20. *Project Green Reach Teacher Evaluation Summary*, 2–3.

21. Student participants in Project Green Reach summer program, conversation with Sharon Lee, October 24, 2015.

22. Parents of student participants in Project Green Reach, interview by Sharon Lee, October 24, 2015.

23. "Mission & Reports," Brooklyn Botanic Garden, 2020, https://www.bbg.org/about/mission.

24. Fairchild Challenge, *The Fairchild Challenge: Grades 6 to 12, 2015–2016; The Voyages of Plants* (Fairchild Tropical Botanic Garden, 2015), 2.

25. Amy Padolf, interview by Sharon Lee, August 19, 2016.

26. Amy Padolf, e-mail to Sharon Lee, September 24, 2018.

27. Fairchild Challenge, *The Fairchild Challenge: 2013–2014 Annual Report* (Fairchild Tropical Botanic Garden, 2014), 3.

28. Fairchild Challenge, *Fairchild Challenge: 2013–2014 Annual Report*, 3.

29. Fairchild Challenge, *Fairchild Challenge: 2013–2014 Annual Report*, 3.

30. Jennifer Schwarz Ballard, e-mail to Sharon Lee, October 2, 2018.

31. Jennifer Schwarz Ballard, e-mail to Sharon Lee, July 21, 2016.

32. Schwarz Ballard e-mail, October 2, 2018.

33. Schwarz Ballard e-mail, October 2, 2018.

34. Chicago Botanic Garden, *Science Career Continuum: Science First and College First, 2008–15 Evaluation Results* (Chicago Botanic Garden, 2015), 1.

35. Schwarz Ballard, e-mail to Sharon Lee, October 1, 2018.

36. Chicago Botanic Garden, *Science Career Continuum: Science First and College First, 2008 Evaluation Results* (Chicago Botanic Garden, 2008), 4.

37. Melissa Salazar, telephone interview by Meghan Gough, November 6, 2015.

38. Terry Moore, telephone interview by Meghan Gough, November 5, 2015.

39. Chicago Botanic Garden, *Science Career Continuum: Science First and College First, 2008–15 Evaluation Results* (Chicago Botanic Garden, 2015), 2.

40. Schwarz Ballard e-mail, October 2, 2018.

41. Associated Press, "Scientists: Plant Knowledge Lost in Botany Decline," *Baxter Bulletin*, May 25, 2015.

3. ACCESS TO HEALTHY FOOD AND PROMOTING HEALTHY LIVES

1. "What Is a Healthy Community?," HealthyFamiliesBC, accessed July 3, 2018, https://www.healthyfamiliesbc.ca/your-community/what-is-healthy-community.

2. A. V. Diez-Roux, F. J. Nieto, L. Caulfield, H. A. Tyroler, R. L. Watson, and M. Szklo, "Neighborhood Differences in Diet: The Atherosclerosis Risk in Communities (ARIC) Study," *Journal of Epidemiology and Community Health* 53, no. 1 (1999): 55–63.

3. Diez-Roux et al., "Neighborhood Differences in Diet."

4. Judith Bell, Gabriella Mora, Erin Hagan, Victor Rubin, and Allison Karpyn, *Access to Healthy Food and Why It Matters: A Review of the Research* (Policy Link; The Food Trust, 2013), 9–11, http://thefoodtrust.org/uploads/media_items/access-to-healthy-food.original.pdf.

5. Blake Angelo and Brittany Goldstein, *Denver Food System—a Baseline Report* (Denver: Denver City Government, 2016), 19.

6. Angelo and Goldstein, *Denver Food System*.

7. "USDA Defines Food Deserts," USDA Economic Research Service, accessed April 11, 2017, https://www.ers.usda.gov/webdocs/DataFiles/80591/archived_documentation.pdf?v=41332.

8. Deja Hendrickson, Chery Smith, and Nicole Eikenberry, "Fruit and Vegetable Access in Four Low-Income Communities in Minnesota," *Agriculture and Human Values* 23, no. 3 (2006): 371.

9. Hendrickson, Smith, and Eikenberry, "Fruit and Vegetable Access."

10. Julie Beaulac, Elizabeth Kristjansson, and Steven Cummins, "A Systematic Review of Food Deserts, 1966–2007," *Preventing Chronic Disease* 6, no. 3 (2009): 1–3.

11. Beaulac, Kristjansson, and Cummins, "Systematic Review."

12. Janne Boone-Heinonen, Penny Gordon-Larsen, Catarina Kiefe, James M. Shikany, Cora E. Lewis, and Barry M. Popkin, "Fast Food Restaurants and Food Stores: Longitudinal Associations with Diet in Young to Middle-Aged Adults; The CARDIA Study," *Archives of Internal Medicine* 171, no. 13 (2011): 1162–70.

13. Bell et al., *Access to Healthy Food*, 4.

14. Steven Cummins, Ellen Flint, and Stephen Matthews, "New Neighborhood Grocery Store Increased Awareness of Food Access but Did Not Alter Dietary Habits or Obesity," *Health Affairs* 33, no. 2 (2014): 283–91.

15. Steven Cummins, Anne Findlay, Cassie Higgins, Mark Petticrew, Leigh Sparks, and Hillary Thomson, "Reducing Inequalities in Health and Diet: Findings from a Study on the Impact of a Food Retail Development," *Environment and Planning* 40, no. 2 (2008): 402–22.

16. Neil Wrigley, Daniel Warm, Barrie Margetts, and Michelle Lowe, "The Leeds 'Food Deserts' Intervention Study: What the Focus Groups Reveal," *International Journal of Retail & Distribution Management* 32, no. 2 (2004): 123–36.

17. Nevin Cohen and Kristin Reynolds, "Urban Agriculture Policy Making in New York's 'New Political Spaces,'" *Journal of Planning Education and Research* 34, no. 2 (2008): 221–34.

18. Kimberley Hodgson, Marcia Caton Campbell, and Martin Bailkey, *Urban Agriculture: Growing Healthy, Sustainable Places*, APA Planning Advisory Service Reports, Report No. 563, January 2011.

19. *Garden to Table: A 5-Year Look at Food Gardening in America* (National Gardening Association Special Report, 2014), 3, https://garden.org/special/pdf/2014-NGA-Garden-to-Table.pdf.

20. Cohen and Reynolds, "Urban Agriculture Policy Making," 225.

21. Megan Horst, Nathan McClintock, and Lesli Hooey, "The Intersection of Planning, Urban Agriculture, and Food Justice," *Journal of the American Planning Association* 83, no. 3 (2017): 277–95.

22. Domenic Vitiello and Michael Nairn, *Community Gardening in Philadelphia: 2008 Harvest Report* (Penn Planning and Urban Studies, 2009), 4, https://millcreekurbanfarm.org/sites/default/files/Philadelphia%20Harvest%20(with%20images).pdf.

23. V. Been and I. Voicu, "The Effect of Community Gardens on Neighboring Property Values," *New York University Law and Economics Working Papers Paper* 46 (2006).

24. Melissa Poulsen, Kristyna Hulland, Caroline Gulas, Hieu Pham, Sarah Dalglish, Rebecca Wilkinson, and Peter J. Winch, "Growing an Urban Oasis: A Qualitative Study of the Perceived Benefits of Community Gardening in Baltimore, Maryland," *Culture, Agriculture, Food and Environment* 36, no. 2 (2014): 69–82.

25. Jill S. Litt, Mah-J. Soobader, Mark S. Turbin, James W. Hale, Micael Buchenau, and Julie Marshall, "The Influence of Social Involvement, Aesthetics, and Community Garden Participation on Fruit and Vegetable Consumption," *American Journal of Public Health* 101, no. 8 (2011): 1466–73.

26. Nancy M. Wells, Beth M. Meyers, Lauren E. Todd, Charles R. Henderson Jr., Karen Barale, Brad Gaolach, Gretchen Ferenz, et al., "The Carry-Over Effects of School Gardens on Fruit and Vegetable Availability at Home: A Randomized Controlled Trial with Low-Income Elementary Schools," *Preventative Medicine* 112 (2018): 152–59.

27. Michelle Ver Ploeg, Vince Breneman, Paula Dutko, Ryan Williams, Samantha Snyder, Chris Dicken, and Philip Kaufman, *Access to Affordable and Nutritious Food: Updated Estimates of Distance to Supermarkets Using 2010 Data*, USDA Economic Research Report 143, November 2012.

28. "America's Worst 9 Urban Food Deserts," NEWSONE for Black America, September 22, 2011, https://newsone.com/1540235/americas-worst-9-urban-food-deserts.

29. "Bronx, New York (NY) Income Map, Earnings Map, and Wages Data," City-Data.com, accessed July 3, 2019, http://www.city-data.com/city/Bronx-New-York.html.

30. *Income Inequality in New York City—2012*, New York City Comptroller's Office, May, 2012, http://comptroller.nyc.gov/wpcontent/uploads/documents/NYC_IncomeInequality_v17.pdf.

31. "The New York Botanical Garden Bronx Green-Up Program," New York Botanical Garden, accessed September 16, 2017, https://www.nybg.org/gardens/bronx-green-up/about/.

32. "New York Botanical Garden Bronx Green-Up Program."

33. "New York Botanical Garden Bronx Green-Up Program."

34. Small Axe Peppers Hot Sauce website, accessed June 11, 2017, https://smallaxepeppers.com/our-story-2/.

35. "Mission and History of the New York Botanical Garden," New York Botanical Garden, accessed November 21, 2017, https://www.nybg.org/about/mission-and-history/.

36. Ursula Chanse (director, BGU), e-mail to Donald Rakow, September 5, 2014.

37. Chanse e-mail, September 5, 2014.

38. Karen Washington, telephone conversation with Donald Rakow, August 25, 2016.

39. Ken Iwuoha, "Concrete Jungle Flourishes through Green-Up," *Plant Talk* (blog), New York Botanical Garden, August 28, 2015, http://blogs.nybg.org/plant-talk/2015/08/people/concrete-jungle-flourishes-through-green-up/.

40. "Rates of Poverty in Cleveland, Ohio," accessed February 27, 2020, http://www.city-data.com/poverty/poverty-Cleveland-Ohio.html.

41. "World Population Review," Population of Cleveland, Ohio, accessed February 27, 2020, http://worldpopulationreview.com/us-cities/cleveland-population/.

42. "History," Cleveland Botanical Garden, accessed July 11, 2017, http://www.cbgarden.org/about/history.aspx.

43. "History," Cleveland Botanical Garden.

44. "History," Cleveland Botanical Garden.

45. Cyleste Collins, Robert Fischer, and Elizabeth Miller, *Cleveland Botanical Garden Green Corps Final Evaluation Report (2009–2014)* (Cleveland: Center on Urban Poverty & Community Development, Case Western Reserve University, 2015), 7–8.

46. Collins, Fischer, and Miller, *Cleveland Botanical Garden Green Corps Final Evaluation Report*, 7–8.

47. "About Us," Franklin Park Conservatory and Botanical Gardens, last modified June 11, 2019, https://www.fpconservatory.org/about-us/.

48. *Alissa Widman Neese*, "Columbus Retains Position as 14th-Largest City, for Now," Columbus Dispatch, May 24, 2018.

49. *US Census Bureau*, "The South Is Home to 10 of the 15 Fastest-Growing Large Cities," May 25, 2017, https://www.census.gov/newsroom/press-releases/2017/cb17-81-population-estimates-subcounty.html.

50. "Columbus, Ohio Demographics," accessed February 27, 2020, City-Data.com, http://www.city-data.com/city/Columbus-Ohio.html.

51. Bill Dawson, in-person interview with Donald Rakow, May 27, 2016.

52. "Growing to Green," Franklin Park Conservatory and Botanical Gardens, accessed May 15, 2017, http://www.fpconservatory.org/The-Experience/Gardening-Programs/Growing-to-Green.

53. "Growing to Green."

54. Bill Dawson, in-person interview.

55. Katherine Alaimo, Elizabeth Packnett, Richard A. Miles, and Daniel J. Kruger, "Fruit and Vegetable Intake among Urban Community Gardeners," *Journal of Nutrition Education and Behavior* 40, no. 2 (2008), 94–101.

56. "The Value of School Gardens," GreenHeart Education, accessed June 11, 2017, http://www.greenhearted.org/school-gardens.html.

57. Dawson, in-person interview.

58. Jazmyn Benjamin, in-person interview with Donald Rakow, May 27, 2016.

59. "Growing to Green Resource Guide," Franklin Park Conservatory, accessed May 29, 2017, https://www.fpconservatory.org/growing-to-green-resource-guide/.

60. *Franklin Park Conservatory and Botanical Garden, 2018 Annual Report*, Franklin Park Conservatory and Botanical Garden, https://www.fpconservatory.org/wp-content/uploads/2020/03/2018.pdf.

61. "Our Mission and Vision," Bartram's Garden, accessed July 7, 2019, https://bartramsgarden.org/about/mission-vision/.

62. "About Our History," Bartram's Garden, accessed July 7, 2019, https://bartramsgarden.org/about/history/the-bartrams/.

63. "Connect. Learn. Be Inspired." Bartram's Garden, accessed July 7, 2019, https://bartramsgarden.org/about/mission-vision/.

64. "Southwest Philadelphia Demographics," Point2Homes, accessed July 11, 2019, https://www.point2homes.com/US/Neighborhood/PA/Philadelphia-County/Philadelphia/Southwest-Philadelphia-Demographics.html.

65. Jenn Hall, "Fresh Food for All—Building a More Inclusive Philly Farmers' Market," *Edible Philly*, Summer 2019.

66. Caroline Winschel, phone interview with Donald Rakow, July 23, 2019.

67. "Sankofa Farm," Bartram's Garden, accessed July 7, 2019, https://bartramsgarden.org/explore-bartrams/the-farm/.

4. TRAINING AND EMPLOYMENT PROGRAMS

1. Rob Grunewald, "The Connection between Poverty and the Economy," Federal Reserve Bank of Minneapolis, November 2006, https://www.minneapolisfed.org/article/2006/the-connection-between-poverty-and-the-economy.

2. David Hilfiker, *Poverty in Urban America: Its Causes and Cures* (Washington, DC: Potter's House Bookservice, 2000), 1–13.

3. Tom Philpott, "The History of Urban Agriculture Should Inspire Its Future," *Grist*, August 4, 2010, https://grist.org/article/food-the-history-of-urban-agriculture-should-inspire-its-future/.

4. "Detroit, Michigan 2016 Report," City-Data.com, accessed July 12, 2016, http://www.city-data.com/city/Detroit-Michigan.html.

5. "Detroit Residential Parcel Survey," DataDrivenDetroit, accessed March 4, 2020, http://detroitparcelsurvey.org.

6. "Detroit Residential Parcel Survey."

7. Jane C. Timm, "Urban Farming Takes Hold in Blighted Motor City," MSNBC, March 25, 2014, http://www.msnbc.com/morning-joe/urban-farming-takes-hold-blighted-motor.

8. Kimberley Hodgson, Marcia Caton Campbell, and Martin Bailkey, *Urban Agriculture: Growing Healthy, Sustainable Places*, APA Planning Advisory Service Reports, Report No. 563, January 2011.

9. Anthony Flaccavento, "Eat Locally, Ease Climate Change Globally," *Washington Post*, March 9, 2008.

10. Mathew M. Kling and Ian J. Hough, "The American Carbon Foodprint: Understanding Your Food's Impact on Climate Change," Brighter Planet Inc., 2010, 3–4, http://brighterplanet.com.

11. Nevin Cohen and Kristin Reynolds, "Urban Agriculture Policy Making in New York's 'New Political Spaces,'" *Journal of Planning Education and Research* 34, no. 2 (2008): 228.

12. "The Heartland Harvest Garden," Powell Gardens, accessed May 14, 2019, https://powellgardens.org/visit/gardens/heartland-harvest-garden.

13. Angela Mason (associate vice president for urban agriculture/Windy City Harvest), e-mail to Donald Rakow, August 31, 2016.

14. Mason e-mail, August 31, 2016.

15. Nova Biro, "What Is Social-Emotional Learning (SEL)?," Kickboard, accessed May 14, 2019, https://www.kickboardforschools.com/blog/post/what-is-social-emotional-learning-sel.

16. Mason e-mail, August 31, 2016.

17. Mason e-mail, August 31, 2016.

18. Angela Mason, e-mail to Donald Rakow, May 19, 2019.

19. Windy Harvest City graduate, interview with by Donald Rakow, September 12, 2016. The interviewee's name, and names of other unnamed quoted sources, have been withheld by mutual agreement.

20. "Year-End Appeal Video," Chicago Botanic Garden, accessed May 14, 2019, https://www.chicagobotanic.org/urbanagriculture/youthfarm.

21. Chantell Frazier, "BLS Reports Post-9/11 Vets' Unemployment Rates Increased in Sep 2015," Bureau of Labor Statistics (blog), October 5, 2015, http://iava.org/blogs/bls-reports-post-911-vets-unemployment-rates-increased-in-september-2015/.

22. "Employment Situations of Veterans—2018," US Bureau of Labor Statistics, accessed May 14, 2019, https://www.bls.gov/news.release/vet.nr0.htm.

23. Jennifer L. Humesky, Neil Jordan, Kevin T. Stroupe, and Denise M. Hynes, "How Are Iraq/Afghanistan-Era Veterans Faring in the Labor Market?," *Armed Forces & Society* 39, no. 1 (2013): 158–83.

24. "Veterans' Employment Challenges: Perceptions and Experiences of Transitioning from Military to Civilian Life," Prudential Financial, 2012, http://www.prudential.com/documents/public/VeteransEmploymentChallenges.pdf.

25. Kimberly Curry Hall, Margaret C. Harrell, Barbara Bicksler, Robert Stewart, and Michael P. Fisher, *Veteran Employment: Lessons from the 100,000 Jobs Mission*, RAND Corporation Report RR-836-JPMCF, 2014, https://www.rand.org/pubs/research_reports/RR836.html.

26. Anh-Luu Huynh-Hohnbaum, Valentine M. Villa, and Nancy Harada, *Lessons Learned from Vietnam War Veterans: Applications to the War in Iraq*, Society for Social Work and Research, 2007, https://sswr.confex.com/sswr/2007/techprogram/P5663.HTM.

27. "Organizational Mission and Values," Denver Botanic Gardens, accessed April 15, 2019, https://www.botanicgardens.org/mission-values.

28. "Our Mission and Values," Veterans to Farmers, accessed May 14, 2019, https://www.veteranstofarmers.org/who-we-are#OurMissionandValues.

29. CVF alumnus, e-mail to Donald Rakow, October 12, 2016.

30. Lucius Couloute and Daniel Kopf, "Out of Prison and Out of Work: Unemployment among Formerly Incarcerated People," Prison Policy Initiative, July 2018, https://www.prisonpolicy.org/reports/outofwork.html.

31. Chris L. Jenkins, "Report Finds Overwhelming Unemployment among Formerly Incarcerated," *Washington Post*, November 17, 2011.

32. John Nally, Susan Lockwood, Taiping Ho, and Katie Knutson, "Post-release Recidivism and Employment among Different Types of Released Offenders: A 5-Year Follow-Up

Study in the United States," *International Journal of Criminal Justice Science* 9, no. 1 (2014): 16–34.

33. Tim Majoros, e-mail toDonald Rakow, December 10, 2015.

34. R2R alumnus, e-mail toDonald Rakow, December 8, 2015.

35. Lini S. Kadaba, "Roots to Re-entry Plants a Seed," *Philadelphia Inquirer*, June 19, 2015.

36. Kadaba, *Philadelphia Inquirer*, June 19, 2015.

37. Quoted in Diane Cornman-Levy, Francis Lawn, and Elizabeth Guman, *A Case Study: Workforce to Reentry Partnership* (Philadelphia: Thomas Scattergood Behavioral Health Foundation, September 14, 2014).

38. "Rikers Island," Wikipedia, accessed March 16, 2016, https://en.wikipedia.org/wiki/Rikers_Island.

39. James Jiler, *Doing Time in the Garden* (Oakland, CA: New Village, 2006), 17.

40. Horticultural Society of New York, "Greenhouse," https://www.thehort.org/programs/greenhouse/.

41. Hilda Krus, e-mail to Donald Rakow, November 15, 2016.

42. Horticultural Society of New York, "Greenhouse."

43. Jiler, *Doing Time*, 146.

44. Krus e-mail, November 15, 2016.

45. "Education and Training: Post-9/11 GI Bill," US Department of Veterans Affairs, last updated October 29, 2019, http://www.benefits.va.gov/gibill/post911_gibill.asp.

5. INITIATIVES TO PROMOTE ECOSYSTEM AND HUMAN HEALTH

1. Joseph Schilling and Jonathan Logan, "Greening the Rust Belt: A Green Infrastructure Model for Right Sizing America's Shrinking Cities," *Journal of the American Planning Association* 74, no. 4 (2008): 451–66.

2. Florian Lederbogen, Peter Kirsch, Leila Haddad, Fabian Streit, Heike Tost, Philipp Schuch, Stefan Wüst et al., "City Living and Urban Upbringing Affect Neural Social Stress Processing in Humans," *Nature* 474, no. 7352 (2011): 498.

3. Robert D. Bullard, *Dumping in Dixie: Race, Class, and Environmental Quality* (Boulder, CO: Westview, 1990); Dorceta Taylor, *Toxic Communities: Environmental Racism, Industrial Pollution, and Residential Mobility* (New York: NYU Press, 2014).

4. Christopher Coutts and Micah Hahn, "Green Infrastructure, Ecosystem Services, and Human Health," *International Journal of Environmental Research and Public Health* 12, no. 8 (2015): 9768–98.

5. Office of Air and Radiation, US Environmental Protection Agency, "Heat Island Effect," accessed January 3, 2017, https://www.epa.gov/heat-islands.

6. Roy Sudipto, Jason Byrne, and Catherine Pickering, "A Systematic Quantitative Review of Urban Tree Benefits, Costs, and Assessment Methods across Cities in Different Climatic Zones," *Urban Forestry and Urban Greening* 11 (2012): 351–63. See also Briony A. Norton, Andrew M. Coutts, Stephen J. Livesley, Richard J. Harris, Annie M. Hunter, and Nicholas S. G. Williams, "Planning for Cooler Cities: A Framework to Prioritise Green Infrastructure to Mitigate High Temperatures in Urban Landscapes," *Landscape and Urban Planning* 134 (2015): 127–38.

7. Julia Kennedy, Peter Haas, and Bill Eyring, "Measuring the Economic Impacts of Greening: The Center for Neighborhood Technology Green Values Calculator," in *Growing Greener Cities: Urban Sustainability in the Twenty-First Century*, ed. Eugenie Birch and Susan Wachter (Philadelphia: University of Pennsylvania Press, 2008), 326–45.

8. Hashem Akbari, "Shade Trees Reduce Building Energy Use and CO2 Emissions from Power Plants," *Environmental Pollution* 116 (2002): 119–26.

9. Md Nazrul Islam, Khandkar-Siddikur Rahman, Md Mezbaul Bahar, Md Ahsan Habib, Keisuke Ando, and Nobuaki Hattori, "Pollution Attenuation by Roadside Greenbelt in and around Urban Areas," *Urban Forestry and Urban Greening* 11 (2012): 460–64

10. Mireia Gascon, Margarita Triguero-Mas, David Martínez, Payam Dadvand, Joan Forns, Antoni Plasència, and Mark Nieuwenhuijsen, "Mental Health Benefits of Long-Term Exposure to Residential Green and Blue Spaces: A Systematic Review," *International Journal of Environmental Research and Public Health* 12, no. 4 (2015): 4354–79.

11. D. Nutsford, A. L. Pearson, and S. Kingham, "An Ecological Study Investigating the Association between Access to Urban Green Space and Mental Health," *Public Health* 127, no. 11 (2013): 1005–11.

12. Louise Chawla, "Benefits of Nature Contact for Children," *Journal of Planning Literature* 30, no. 4 (November 2015): 433–52, https://doi.org/10.1177/0885412215595441.

13. Elizabeth A. Richardson et al., "Role of Physical Activity in the Relationship between Urban Green Space and Health," *Public Health* 127, no. 4 (2013): 318–24.

14. Amy J. Lynch, "Is It Good to Be Green? Assessing the Ecological Results of County Green Infrastructure Planning," *Journal of Planning Education and Research* 36, no. 1 (2015): 1–15.

15. Isabel Wilkerson, *The Warmth of Other Suns: The Epic Story of America's Great Migration* (New York: Vintage, 2011).

16. Jeannette Cooperman, "The Story of Segregation in St. Louis," *St. Louis Magazine*, October 17, 2014, https://www.stlmag.com/api/content/296b6cf0-53bb-11e4-b9fe-22000a4f82a6/.

17. John R. Logan et al., "Creating the Black Ghetto: Black Residential Patterns before and during the Great Migration," *Annals of the American Academy of Political and Social Science* 660, no. 1 (July 1, 2015): 18–35, https://doi.org/10.1177/0002716215572993.

18. Logan et al., "Creating the Black Ghetto."

19. Priscilla A. Dowden-White, *Groping toward Democracy: African American Social Welfare Reform in St. Louis, 1910–1949* (Columbia: University of Missouri Press, 2011).

20. Tim O'Neil, "March: For African-Americans in St. Louis, a Long March for Justice," *St. Louis Post-Dispatch*, August 31, 2014, https://www.stltoday.com/news/local/metro/for-african-americans-in-st-louis-a-long-march-for/article_bf3105cc-1fa3-5e07-8750-aed319193492.html.

21. Richard Rothstein, *The Color of Law: A Forgotten History of How Our Government Segregated America* (New York: Liveright, 2017). See also "The End of the Segregated Century: Racial Separation in America's Neighborhoods, 1890–2010," Manhattan Institute, August 24, 2015, https://www.manhattan-institute.org/html/end-segregated-century-racial-separation-americas-neighborhoods-1890-2010-5848.html.

22. "Crossing a St Louis Street That Divides Communities," BBC, March 14, 2012, http://www.bbc.com/news/magazine-17361995.

23. *City of St. Louis Sustainability Plan*, City of St. Louis (website), accessed January 4, 2017, https://www.stlouis-mo.gov/government/departments/mayor/documents/city-of-st-louis-sustainability-plan1.cfm.

24. *Mayor Slay Sustainability Action Agenda, 2013–2018*, City of St. Louis (website), accessed January 4, 2017, https://www.stlouis-mo.gov/government/departments/mayor/documents/mayor-slay-sustainability-action-agenda-2013-2018.cfm.

25. *FY 2014–15 Reference Paper: City of St. Louis Urban Vitality & Ecology Initiative*, August 7, 2015, 2.

26. Deborah Frank, interview by Meghan Gough, January 10, 2017.

27. Catherine Werner, e-mail to Meghan Gough, September 9, 2016.

28. "Urban Wildlife Refuge Initiative Connects Millions to Conservation," US Fish and Wildlife Service, last updated September 25, 2013, https://www.fws.gov/refuges/news/UrbanWildRefInitiativeConnectsMillions.html.

29. "OneSTL—Many Communities. One Future, accessed January 4, 2017, http://www.onestl.org/.

30. "BiodiverseCity St. Louis," accessed January 4, 2017, http://www.missouribotani calgarden.org/sustainability/sustainability/biodiversecity-st.-louis.aspx.

31. *City of St. Louis Community Health Improvement Plan*, 22, City of St. Louis (website), accessed February 18, 2017, https://www.stlouis-mo.gov/government/departments/health/city-of-st-louis-community-health-improvement-plan.cfm.

32. Jacob Barker, "MSD Proposes to Spend $13.5 Million to Demolish Vacant St. Louis Structures," *St. Louis Post-Dispatch*, December 22, 2015, http://www.stltoday.com/business/local/msd-proposes-to-spend-million-to-demolish-vacant-st-louis/article_a9ac8476-b96b-5d11-a4de-578e9a72f5a0.html.

33. Jacob Barker, "MSD Buyout of Flooding Homes Leaves Vacancies, but Baden Boosters See Opportunity," *St. Louis Post-Dispatch*, December 3, 2015, https://www.stltoday.com/business/local/msd-buyout-of-flooding-homes-leaves-vacancies-but-baden-boosters/article_0479dfec-6986-5f75-9a64-b39389b258cc.html.

34. Barker, "MSD Proposes to Spend $13.5 Million."

35. Meg Hoester, Missouri Botanic Garden, interview by Don Rakow and Sharon Lee, October 15, 2015.

36. Betsy Crites, interview by Meghan Gough, January 23, 2017.

37. Jacob Barker, "MSD Buyout of Flooding Homes Leaves Vacancies, but Baden Boosters See Opportunity," *St. Louis Post-Dispatch*, December 3, 2015, https://www.stltoday.com/business/local/msd-buyout-of-flooding-homes-leaves-vacancies-but-baden-boosters/article_0479dfec-6986-5f75-9a64-b39389b258cc.html.

38. Sheila Voss, interview by Meghan Gough, January 10, 2017.

39. Starr Butler, e-mail to Meghan Gough, February 10, 2017.

40. Ted Curran, interview by Meghan Gough, January 23, 2017.

41. Steven J. Hoffman, *Race, Class and Power in the Building of Richmond, 1870–1920* (Jefferson, NC: McFarland, 2004).

42. Christopher Silver, *Twentieth-Century Richmond: Planning, Politics, and Race* (Knoxville: University of Tennessee Press, 1984).

43. Kenneth T. Jackson, *Crabgrass Frontier: The Suburbanization of the United States* (New York: Oxford University Press, 1985).

44. "Maps Reveal Persistence of Damaging Effects of Historic Redlining Practices," *Virginia Tech Daily*, October 23, 2016, http://vtnews.vt.edu/content/vtnews_vt_edu/en/articles/2016/10/clahs-redlining.html.

45. Christopher Silver and John V. Moeser, *The Separate City: Black Communities in the Urban South, 1940–1968* (Lexington: University Press of Kentucky, 1995), x.

46. "Redlining Richmond," Digital Scholarship Lab, University of Richmond, accessed February 19, 2017, http://dsl.richmond.edu/holc/.

47. Marita Sturken, *Tangled Memories: The Vietnam War, the AIDS Epidemic, and the Politics of Remembering* (Berkeley: University of California Press, 1997).

48. Sara Zewde, "Theory, Place, and Opportunity: Black Urbanism as a Design Strategy for the Potential Removal of the Claiborne Expressway in New Orleans" (master's thesis, Massachusetts Institute of Technology, 2010), http://dspace.mit.edu/handle/1721.1/59769.

49. John Kretzmann and John P. McKnight, "Assets-Based Community Development," *National Civic Review* 85, no. 4 (1996): 23–29.

50. *RVAgreen: A Roadmap to Sustainability*, City of Richmond (website), accessed January 3, 2017, http://www.richmondgov.com/Sustainability/documents/RVAGreen_ARoadmapToSustainability.pdf.

51. "Mission and Goals," Lewis Ginter Botanical Garden, accessed February 21, 2017, http://www.lewisginter.org/visit/about/mission-goals/.

52. Catherine Komp, "Beautiful RVA Partnership Seeks to Expand Urban Green-ing," Community Idea Stations, October 2, 2014, http://ideastations.org/radio/news/beautiful-rva-partnership-seeks-expand-urban-greening.

53. "Beautiful RVA Place-Making Initiatives in Urban Beautification," Lewis Ginter Botanical Garden, accessed February 22, 2017, https://www.lewisginter.org/visit/about/mission-goals/beautiful-rva/.

54. John Kania and Mark Kramer, "Collective Impact," *Stanford Social Innovation Review*, Winter 2011, https://ssir.org/articles/entry/collective_impact.

55. Duron Chavis, "Beautiful RVA—Setting the Stage for Growth," LinkedIn Pulse, November 2, 2016, https://www.linkedin.com/pulse/beautiful-rva-setting-stage-growth-duron-chavis.

56. Fay Hanleybrown, John Kania, and John Kramer, "Channeling Change: Making Collective Impact Work," *Stanford Social Innovation Review* (website), January 26, 2012.

57. "Beautiful RVA," accessed May 31, 2017, http://www.beautifulrva.org.

58. Hanleybrown, Kania, and Kramer, "Channeling Change."

59. "Garden Hires Duron Chavis as New Community Engagement Coordinator," Lewis Ginter Botanical Garden, accessed May 31, 2017, http://www.lewisginter.org/visit/about/news/garden-hires-duron-chavis-new-position-community-engagement-coordinator/.

60. Duron Chavis, interview by Meghan Gough, November 1, 2016.

61. Zachary P. Neal and Jennifer Watling Neal, "The (In)compatibility of Diversity and Sense of Community," *American Journal of Community Psychology* 53, no. 1–2 (November 6, 2013): 1–12, https://doi.org/10.1007/s10464-013-9608-0.

62. Chavis interview, November 1, 2016.

63. Stacy Parker and A. Haven Kiers, interviews with Donald Rakow, April 3, 2017.

64. Tracy Neumann, "Reforging the Steel City: Symbolism and Space in Postindustrial Pittsburgh," *Journal of Urban History* 44, no. 4 (2018): 582–602.

65. Neumann, "Reforging the Steel City."

66. Catherine DeLoughry, interview by Meghan Gough and Sharon Lee, June 9, 2015.

67. Neumann, "Reforging the Steel City," "Allegheny Conference—History," accessed January 5, 2017, http://www.alleghenyconference.org/about/history/.

68. "What Is RAD?," RAD Works Here, accessed January 5, 2017, http://radworkshere.org/pages/what-is-rad.

69. "Who We Fund," RAD Works Here, accessed January 5, 2017, http://radworkshere.org/pages/who-we-fund.

70. "About," US Green Building Council, accessed January 5, 2017, http://www.usgbc.org/About.

71. "Green Pittsburgh: Green Buildings in Pittsburgh," City of Pittsburgh (website), accessed January 5, 2017, http://www.pittsburghpa.gov/green/buildings.htm.

72. Andre Perry, "Who Gets Left Out of the Urban Tech Boom?," *New York Times*, July 19, 2018.

73. "1893," Phipps Conservatory and Botanical Gardens, accessed January 5, 2017, https://phipps.conservatory.org/visit-and-explore/explore/phipps-history/eighteen-ninety-three.

74. Richard Piacentini, interview by Meghan Gough and Don Rakow, June 8, 2015.

75. Piancentini interview, June 8, 2015.

76. Diana Nelson Jones, "Pittsburgh Recognized as Biophilic City," *Pittsburgh Post-Gazette*, September 17, 2016, http://www.post-gazette.com/local/city/2016/09/17/Pittsburgh-s-cap-gets-another-feather-with-induction-into-Biophilic-Cities-network-an-effort-to-integrate-nature-into-daily-city-life/stories/201609170031.

77. Timothy Beatley, *Biophilic Cities: Integrating Nature into Urban Design and Planning* (Washington, DC: Island, 2011).

78. Jones, "Pittsburgh Recognized."

79. Richard Piacentini, interview by Meghan Gough, February 24, 2017.

6. STRATEGIES FOR THE DEVELOPMENT OF SUCCESSFUL PARTNERSHIPS

1. "Chatfield Farm Veterans Program," Denver Botanic Gardens, accessed June 9, 2018, https://www.botanicgardens.org/chatfield-farms-veteran-program.

2. "Chatfield Farm Veterans Program."

3. "Growing to Green Program," Franklin Park Conservatory and Botanical Garden, accessed November 12, 2018, https://www.fpconservatory.org/education-programs/out reach-programs/growing-to-green/. See also Highland Youth Garden, accessed September 9, 2018, https://www.highlandyouthgarden.org/.

"New York Compost Project," New York Botanical Garden, accessed November 12, 2018, https://www.nybg.org/gardens/bronx-green-up/nyc-compost-project/.

4. "New York Compost Project."

5. "Growing beyond Earth," Fairchild Tropical Botanical Garden and the National Aeronautics and Space Administration, accessed July 10, 2019, https://sites.google.com/site/growingbeyondearth/.

6. "Incorporating Soil Health into Plant Community Restoration," Chicago Botanic Garden, accessed March 10, 2017, https://www.chicagobotanic.org/research/conservation_and_restoration/incorporating_soil_health_plant_community_restoration.

7. "Meet Beautiful RVA," Lewis Ginter Botanical Garden, accessed February 6, 2018, https://www.lewisginter.org/meet-beautiful-rva/.

8. "Ginter Urban Gardeners," Lewis Ginter Botanical Garden, accessed February 6, 2018, https://www.lewisginter.org/ginter-urban-gardeners/.

9. Brian Vogt, e-mail to Don Rakow, June 12, 2018.

10. Jana Kasperkevic, "A Tale of Two Brooklyns: There's More to My Borough Than Hipsters and Coffee," *US Money* (blog), *Guardian* (US edition), August 27, 2014, https://www.theguardian.com/money/us-money-blog/2014/aug/27/two-brooklyns-economy-hipsters-coffee.

11. Alan Ehrenhalt, "What, Exactly, Is Gentrification?," *Governing*, February 2015, http://www.governing.com/topics/urban/gov-gentrification-definition-series.html.

12. Derek Hyra, "The Back-to-the-City Movement: Neighbourhood Redevelopment and Processes of Political and Cultural Displacement," *Urban Studies* 52, no. 10 (August 1, 2015): 1753–73, https://doi.org/10.1177/0042098014539403.

13. Kenneth A. Gould and Tammy L. Lewis, "The Environmental Injustice of Green Gentrification," in *The World in Brooklyn: Gentrification, Immigration, and Ethnic Politics in a Global City*, ed. J. N. Desena and T. Shortell (Plymouth, MA: Lexington Books, 2012), 113–46. Melissa Checker, "Wiped Out by the 'Greenwave': Environmental Gentrification and the Paradoxical Politics of Urban Sustainability," *City & Society* 23, no. 2 (2011): 210–29.

14. Personal communication between Sonal Bhatt and Casey Morgan, March 18, 2019.

15. Quentin Brummet and Davin Reed, *The Effects of Gentrification on the Well-Being and Opportunities of Original Resident Adults and Children*, Federal Reserve Bank of Philadelphia, July 2019.

16. Personal communication between Nancy Cartes and Casey Morgan, April 20, 2019.

17. "Mayor's Sustainability Initiatives," City of St. Louis (website), accessed January 25, 2016, https://www.stlouis-mo.gov/government/departments/mayor/initiatives/sustainability/urban-vitality-ecology/.

18. "Community Resilience," RAND Corporation, accessed July 9, 2019, https://www.rand.org/topics/community-resilience.html.

19. M. Patrick Griffith, Gregory Barber, Joanna Tucker Lima, Michelle Barros, Claudia Calonje, Larry Noblick, Michael Calonje, et al., "Plant Collection 'Half-Life': Can Botanic Gardens Weather the Climate?," *Museum Journal* 60, no. 4 (October 2017).

20. "Worcester Tree Initiative," Tower Hill Botanical Garden, accessed July 9, 2019, https://www.towerhillbg.org/worcester-tree-initiative/.

21. Jana Dilley, personal communication with Donald Rakow, November 5, 2015.

EPILOGUE

1. "Vision Statement," American Public Gardens Association, accessed March 10, 2020, https://www.publicgardens.org/about-us.

2. University of Leicester, "The Anthropocene: Hard Evidence for a Human-Driven Earth," ScienceDaily, January 7, 2016, www.sciencedaily.com/releases/2016/01/160107 151738.htm; https://www.britannica.com/science/Anthropocene-Epoch.

3. "Nature's Dangerous Decline 'Unprecedented'; Species Extinction Rates 'Accelerating,'" Intergovernmental Science-Policy Platform on Biodiversity and Ecosystem Services (IPBES), accessed March 10, 2020, https://www.ipbes.net/news/Media-Release-Global-Assessment.

4. "What Is a Public Garden?," American Public Gardens Association, accessed March 10, 2020, https://www.publicgardens.org/about-public-gardens/what-public-garden.

5. "NYBG: Saving the Plants of the World," New York Botanical Garden Science Book (2017), 8–9, https://www.nybg.org/content/uploads/2017/05/ScienceBook_2017.pdf.

6. World Intellectual Property Organization, "Intergovernmental Committee on Intellectual Property and Genetic Resources, Traditional Knowledge and Folklore," Twenty-Eighth Session, Geneva, July 7–9, 2014, https://www.cbd.int/doc/meetings/tk/wg8j-09/other/wg8j-09-wipo-grtlf-iwg2-inf2-en.pdf.

7. "Global Strategy for Plant Conservation—Targets," Convention on Biological Diversity, accessed March 10, 2020, https://www.cbd.int/gspc/targets.shtml.

8. "The Daniel F. and Ada L. Rice Plant Conservation Science Center," Chicago Botanic Garden, accessed March 10, 2020 https://www.chicagobotanic.org/research/building.

9. "Pounder Vegetable Garden and Climate Change Garden," Cornell Botanic Gardens, accessed March 10, 2020, https://cornellbotanicgardens.org/location/vegetable-garden/.

10. Allan Frei and William Solecki, "Responding to Climate Change in New York City," Brooklyn Botanic Garden, accessed March 20, 2020, https://www.bbg.org/gardening/article/cultivating_resilience_responding_to_climate_change_in_new_york_city.

11. "Center for Sustainable Landscapes," Phipps Conservatory and Botanical Garden, accessed March 20, 2020, https://www.phipps.conservatory.org/green-innovation/at-phipps/center-for-sustainable-landscapes-greenest-building-museum-garden-in-the-world/.

12. Global World Health Observatory (GHO) data, World Health Organization, accessed March 10, 2002, https://www.who.int/gho/urban_health/situation_trends/urban_population_growth_text/en/.

13. "Sustainable Development Goals," United Nations, accessed March 20, 2020, https://www.un.org/sustainabledevelopment/sustainable-development-goals/.

14. Rutherford H. Platt, ed., *The Humane Metropolis: People and Nature in the 21st-Century City* (Amherst: University of Massachusetts Press, 2006).

15. Alyce Sadongeiand, Marie Long, Victor Hugo "Tonatiuh" Ochoa, Shannon Martin, and David C. Michener, "Partnering with Our Nations' First Peoples," *Public Garden* 34, no. 2 (2019): 6–9.

16. "A Brief History of Horticultural Therapy," Tucson Botanical Garden, accessed March 20, 2002 https://tucsonbotanical.org/hort-therapy/; https://www.chicagobotanic.org/education/certificate_programs/horticultural_therapy.

17. Melanie Morgan, William B. Collins, Glenn G. Sparks, and Jessica R. Welch, "Identifying Relevant Anti-science Perceptions to Improve Science-Based Communication: The Negative Perceptions of Science Scale," *Social Science* 7, no. 4, https://doi.org/10.3390/socsci7040064.

18. "Fiddleheads Forest School," University of Washington Botanic Gardens, accessed March 20, 2020, https://botanicgardens.uw.edu/education/youth-family/fiddleheads-forest-school/.

19. Laura Fernanda Barrera-Hernández, Mirsha Alicia Sotelo-Castillo, Sonia Betriz Echeverria-Castro, and César Octavio Tapia-Fonllem, "Connectedness to Nature: Its Impact on Sustainable Behaviors and Happiness in Children," *Frontiers in Psychology* 11, https://doi.org/10.3389/fpsyg.2020.00276.

Index

Note: Page numbers in *italics* indicate figures; those with a *t* indicate tables.

CPSIA information can be obtained
at www.ICGtesting.com
Printed in the USA
LVHW092121131120
671654LV00004B/260

9 781501 702594